The
EVERYTHING.
Conversational Japanese Book

Dear Reader:

Writing this book has been a personally enriching experience. My appreciation for Japanese people and culture has deepened. My understanding of the language has been clarified. Learning another language has made me a better listener and communicator in many ways.

My family's daily life is a strange hybrid of Japanese and American cultures. Experiencing, firsthand, an interracial, bicultural marriage has challenged not only my linguistic abilities, but has pushed me to better understand my own culture. It took leaving the Midwest to realize the unique advantages of small-town life; and, likewise, living in Japan has romanticized for me the amazing diversity of people, culture, language, and life in the United States.

Balancing the many roles of my life to create time for this project was a character-building experience. Many nights I typed with one hand while nursing my daughter to sleep. My husband did more than his share of the cooking and cleaning throughout my affair with the laptop without batting an eye. What we have gained from this experience is the satisfaction that an essential blend of language, culture, colloquialisms, and idioms are being passed on to someone who will make good use of them.

Molly Hakes

The EVERYTHING® Series

Editorial

Publishing Director	Gary M. Krebs
Managing Editor	Kate McBride
Copy Chief	Laura MacLaughlin
Acquisitions Editor	Eric M. Hall
Development Editor	Julie Gutin
Production Editor	Jamie Wielgus
Technical Reviewer	Keizo Takao

Production

Production Director	Susan Beale
Production Manager	Michelle Roy Kelly
Series Designers	Daria Perreault
	Colleen Cunningham
	John Paulhus
Cover Design	Paul Beatrice
	Matt LeBlanc
Layout and Graphics	Colleen Cunningham
	Rachael Eiben
	Michelle Roy Kelly
	John Paulhus
	Daria Perreault
	Erin Ring
Series Cover Artist	Barry Littmann

THE
EVERYTHING®
CONVERSATIONAL JAPANESE BOOK

Basic instructions for speaking this
fascinating language in any setting

Molly Hakes

Adams Media
Avon, Massachusetts

To my family, whose unwavering support is my shushoku.

An Everything® Series Book.
Everything® and everything.com® are registered trademarks of F+W Publications, Inc.

Published by Adams Media, an F+W Publications Company
57 Littlefield Street, Avon, MA 02322 U.S.A.
www.adamsmedia.com

ISBN: 1-59337-147-0
Printed in the United States of America.

J I H G F E D C B A

Library of Congress Cataloging-in-Publication Data
Hakes, Molly.
The everything conversational Japanese book / Molly Hakes.
    p.   cm. -- (Everything series book)
ISBN 1-59337-147-0
1. Japanese language--Conversation and phrase books--English. I. Title. II. Series: Everything series

PL539.H25 2004
495.6'83421--dc22

2004013357

Master audio recording produced by Radio Garage Productions, West Des Moines, IA.

This book is available at quantity discounts for bulk purchases.
For information, call 1-800-872-5627.

Contents

Acknowledgments

My gratitude goes to Barb Doyen, of Doyen Literary Services, for always watching my back. Thanks are due to all the people who let me quote their stories and pick their brains: Sara Snyder, Maki Ueda, Shoo Kamei, Sooei Kodama, and the countless others who have both directly and indirectly influenced this book. I need to thank my first editor, Eric Hall, for his positive attitude. Julie Gutin's flexibility and humble nature made for smooth editing. Jay Weiss, too, made recording the audio CD a joy. My husband, Nobuhiro Watanabe, deserves "props" for his perserverence in late-night editing sessions and for his patience during practices for the recording of the audio CD. My parents, too, deserve thanks for their love, support, and flexibility as holiday festivities and production deadlines butted heads.

Top Ten Reasons
to Learn Japanese

1. While traveling, hidden treasures are discovered by those who know how to ask for them.

2. With some rudimentary Japanese, you'll know where you're going and how to get there!

3. Sushi, sushi, and more sushi! Do you want to be able to order what you want to eat, or would you rather be stuck with delicacies like sea urchin gonads?

4. You can make special requests, from asking for an extra pillow to ordering vegetarian entrées.

5. You can gain the immediate respect of residents, wherever you go.

6. You will not go into shock at the cash register.

7. You'll have the skills to be able to decipher the ultrapolite lingo of a business lunch!

8. You can discover the world of Japanimation, especially the work of Hayao Miyazaki, Japan's top animator, political commentator, and conservationist.

9. You never know when Japanese may come in handy, even after you leave Japan.

10. Gaining a deeper understanding of Japanese may just help you with your English!

Introduction

▶ The great samurai warrior Katsumoto would have his work cut out for him today. He is best remembered for his heroic efforts to protect Japanese culture from Western influences, an issue that is prevalent even in the twenty-first century. Increased globalization is threatening many cultures and languages around the world, and Japan is no exception.

By learning to speak another language, you are doing the world a favor. For all its amazing advances in technology, travel, and communications, globalization has also paved the way for unbridled importing and exporting of culture. Residents of the countries being threatened are becoming increasingly aware of how quickly language and culture can be lost. By learning another language, you make your own contribution to keeping it alive and in use.

Japanese, too, is changing to accommodate the homogenization of popular culture. Words from other languages are now part of everyday conversations. Some would call this progress. Others might say it is a necessary evil. Still others will insist that language reflects culture and vice versa. Moreover, some Japanese fear that westernization is making the Japanese language bland or even corrupted. The polite phrases and manners that were once standard Japanese are absent from many young people's speech today.

Here is where you can help: By learning Japanese the way it is spoken now, you will be perpetuating the beauty of this ancient tongue. Not only that, but by speaking Japanese in Japan to Japanese people, you may inspire the natives to start protecting their endangered culture.

Hearing a foreigner use the proper words for presenting a gift, give an eloquent self-introduction, or enunciate a beautifully indirect "no" with ease makes native speakers proud of their language. Seeing a Westerner bow appropriately, hold chopsticks correctly, or relish dancing the local folk-dance at a festival reminds Japanese people of the importance of their history. Who knows, you may inspire a revival of some of the "old ways."

If you are traveling, it's important to remember that the more you know of the country, people, culture, and language, the more you get out of your trip. Being able to order the best sushi or the house specialty can make all the difference. You may not be able to decipher your friends' tattoos, but you will be able to identify them as *kanji*, and impress them with your knowledge of its prevalence and history. Knowing a little about the language, too, will surely increase your appreciation for Eastern-influenced movies, books, and music.

Adopting some aspects of this intricate, amazing culture into your own life can't hurt, either. Who would object to a little more modesty, politeness, and consideration in their daily life? This book is an exercise in the preservation of some of those phrases that make life a little more pleasant. You may be surprised how much learning and speaking Japanese can influence your thoughts, behavior, and communication style. So what are you waiting for? *Douzo.*

Chapter 1

Japanese Through the Centuries

Language is such a mystery. Spoken word grows out of the desire to communicate, but what sparks the need to write things down? Poets and great composers have the ability to move people centuries after their deaths. Schools attempt to prepare the population with the writing skills necessary for personal expression while societies regulate the cultural nuances of communication. Japanese too, continues to grow with the times, often engulfing that which seems worthy of inclusion into its ever-evolving format.

Japanese in Writing

Bequeathed our writing system, we are easily able to describe what we see, hear, feel, smell, taste, and think. In the West, our alphabet's phonetic design allows individual sounds to be represented and combined in countless possible ways. The Roman alphabet is also helpful when pronouncing words in other languages.

Japanese writing is often cited as one of the most complicated in the world. Comprised of a combination of three different types of characters—*kanji*, *hiragana*, and *katakana*—it overwhelms Western visitors. Even phone numbers are sometimes written in unrecognizable form.

Travelers in Japan will surely get a sense of what it is like to be illiterate. Although most major cities now have public signs written in Roman letters, there are still many others that are written exclusively in *kanji* or *kana*. This is especially true in small, rural towns and villages.

FACT

Restaurant menus are often entirely in Japanese with no Roman lettering. Luckily, most eating establishments have plastic replicas of their specialties in a glass case outside the restaurant. Simply point at what looks most appetizing and hope for the best.

Use of Chinese Characters

The earliest writing system employed by Japanese was *kanji* (Chinese characters). There's some controversy about the origin of Chinese characters. Some believe they were invented by Tsang-Hsich in 2,500 B.C. There's evidence of about 3,000 characters found in central China that can be linked to artifacts dating to nearly 2000 B.C. A dictionary from between 221–206 B.C. has 3,300 entries. By about the 6th century, when Chinese and Koreans began immigrating to Japan, 16,917 characters had been recorded. Modern dictionaries encompassing characters from all over China, including some no longer in use, list more than 56,000 characters.

A Language of Its Own

Somewhere between A.D. 250 and A.D. 350, Chinese characters were adopted to create a written language for spoken Japanese. Consequently, many Chinese words also became integrated into Japanese. Some characters ended up with two or more pronunciations: the original Chinese pronunciation and the Japanese one. In Japanese, different ways of reading a given *kanji* are referred to as *onyomi* (the Chinese reading) and *kunyomi* (the Japanese reading). This is why the character for water can be read *sui* (Chinese reading) or *mizu* (Japanese reading), depending upon the context in which it is used.

Not all *kanji* currently used in Japan came from China. Over the past 1,500 years, the Japanese have created more than 400 characters specifically for Japanese words. Some of these include the ones for "work," "kite," "woodworker," and "hemlock."

Each *kanji* character represents something and can stand on its own or be combined with others to create new words. Many of the simpler ones like "fire" and "car" actually resemble the objects they represent, making it easy to see how *kanji* were developed from pictographs. Even the more complicated characters are usually made up of combinations of simpler ones.

Travelers from Japan to China and Korea can also utilize their knowledge of *kanji* to navigate unknown territory. A Japanese woman traveling with her family in China found her experience with *kanji* to be both helpful and a hindrance at times. At a guesthouse, she was able to clear up some confusion by having a written conversation in *kanji*. But, at a restaurant, what she read as the *kanji* for "vegetables" ended up being the character for "a lot."

High Expectations

In 1946, the Japanese Ministry of Education decided to make some order out of all these characters and did a study of the most commonly used *kanji*.

Their research resulted in a list of 1,850 basic characters that were necessary to read most Japanese literature and publications. From 1981 on, that number was changed to 1,945 characters. Of these 1,945 *joyo kanji*, as they are called, 881 must be memorized by children before graduating from elementary school. Later, in 1992, that number was upped to 1,006. Currently, all Japanese high school graduates are required to read and write the 1,945 *joyo kanji*, as well as recognize an additional 1,500 plus characters.

The Importance of Hiragana

Hiragana stands out in Japanese text because it is written with far fewer strokes than *kanji* and yet more curving than *katakana*. Each symbol represents either a pure vowel sound or a vowel combined with a consonant (with the exception of *n*, the only single consonant sound in the Japanese language). There are 46 *hiragana* symbols, all derived from *kanji*. Two short lines or a circle added to some of the symbols either harden or soften the sound it makes.

Hiragana was first developed during the eighth century to provide a phonetic way of reading Chinese characters. Buddhist scholars initially scorned it, convinced that *kanji* was the language of the elite. Women, however, were excluded from the study of *kanji*, so they jumped at the chance to learn *hiragana*. With this simple phonetic writing system, Lady Murasaki Shikibu was able to record the famous story *The Tale of Genji* during the Heian Era (795–1192).

Hiragana is also valuable because it provides a way to write down verb endings and modify many other parts of speech—adjectives, adverbs, and nouns. All prepositions and particles, including the subject identifier *wa* are written in *hiragana*. Without *hiragana*, written Japanese would not make any sense.

FACT

Japan boasts a literacy rate of nearly 99 percent. Some who have investigated this claim believe it is due, in part, to the presence of *hiragana*. Without it, people would be forced to memorize and remember the thousands of *kanji* characters used in newspapers and other publications.

Katakana: *A Necessary Evil*

Katakana was developed alongside *hiragana*, but got the short end of the fancy stick. Both are taken from simplified *kanji*, but *katakana* is like printing and *hiragana* looks more like cursive writing. *Katakana* also contains 46 symbols with diacritical markings (marks above the symbol). These markings consist of either two short lines or a small circle. They indicate whether the consonant in the syllable is hard or soft.

Katakana was initially created for the interpretation of Buddhist scriptures, but was quickly applied to all foreign words—"loan words"—used in the Japanese language. Loan words make up a substantial part of everyday Japanese conversation. Many Japanese people assume that most loan words are of Chinese or English origin, but in fact they come from many different languages around the world. The Japanese word for bread, *pan,* comes from the Portuguese; *piero* is the word used for "clown" in both Japanese and French.

Katakana can be extremely convenient in teaching the pronunciation of non-Japanese words to Japanese speakers. Of course, not all sounds in other languages are represented within *katakana*, making it difficult to achieve proper pronunciation in some situations. Foreign names, for example, are often butchered by *katakana* (e.g., Larry becomes *Rah-ree,* Vicky turns into *Bikki,* and so on).

Roundabout Dialogue

Due to its geographic location and, during some periods, self-imposed antisocial foreign policy, Japan has been isolated from the rest of the world for extended periods of time. This situation has allowed the culture to develop extremely strong roots. Strictly observed rules for interaction and communication govern conversations in a variety of settings and situations.

Indirectly Speaking

One nice thing about Japanese is that it is difficult to speak in a directly rude manner. Often, subtle gestures are used in place of actual confrontation. Instead of asking someone to extinguish his cigarette, it is recommended to cough gently into your hand. Rather than ask someone to be quiet, a quick patting of the ears is supposed to convey the message.

Circumventive language helps to keep the peace. Japanese cities are extremely crowded and sparks flying constantly could be a dangerous thing. In the countryside, some families have lived on the same land for up to 500 years. People are thoughtful about the potential effects of their words on the relations between neighbors for the next generation and beyond.

If a Japanese person fails to meet your gaze when you speak, he or she is not trying to be rude. In fact, the intention is exactly the opposite. The idea that direct eye contact is rude remains deeply rooted in local culture. Lately, increased contact with foreigners is changing this tradition, but it seems to remain an almost instinctive response.

Opening Lines

As a general rule, most conversations in Japan begin with a reference to the weather or changing seasons. This is considered poetic as well as polite. Once the uniqueness of the season has been acknowledged, other "safe" and popular topics like top news stories or television programs are broached.

After all of this, the true point of the conversation may be addressed, or it may have to wait until next time. A request that is padded with niceties is more likely to be agreed to or at least given some thought. On the other hand, some discussions may seem to get off track easily, with everyone very politely circling the main objective.

Silences in conversation are viewed as a natural occurrence in Japan. Unlike Westerners, who often rush to fill any lull in dialogue, Japanese people tend to utilize a pause for purposes of changing the subject or as an opportunity to elicit responses from quieter participants.

Japanified English or "Engrish"

A Christmas card sent from a family in Japan to their daughter-in-law's relatives in the United States proclaimed, "We are enjoying Christmas in a small cake." Students wear shirts with phrases like "I want to get naked and dance on the moon with poetry." Small children grab their heads in mock horror and shout, "Oh, my Goddo!" On bags, pencils, cups, beer cans, the sides of vehicles—everywhere in Japan—you'll see English written with ghastly spelling and grammar.

Why don't these advertisers and designers hire better editors, you may wonder? Perhaps they are relying on the many computer software programs in Japan that will conveniently translate text from Japanese to English. Machines are hardly sensitive to nuance, however, which is why the results of directly translated slogans are so amusing to native English speakers.

QUESTION?

Is Japanese written vertically from right to left?
People often assume that Japanese is always written in the opposite direction of English. In the past, Japanese was written from right to left, when writing either vertically or horizontally. Nowadays, it is usually written from right to left only when vertical, and from left to right when horizontal.

What is Japan's fascination with English and where does it stem from? The presence of English on high school and college entrance examinations has made it mandatory curriculum from junior high school on. The average Japanese has studied English formally for between three and ten years. Adult English conversation classes and proficiency tests are found in even the most remote mountain villages.

Thanks to afterschool television shows such as "Eigo de Asobou" (Let's Play in English), many kids are familiar with basic self-introduction phrases, number and color words, and terms for different foods. NHK, the Japanese Broadcasting Corporation, also runs a daily radio show for adults who want to improve their English. The *Reader's Digest*–type monthly textbooks that accompany these radio broadcasts are often sold out by midmonth.

Several words in everyday Japanese conversation sound like English, but seem way out of context. This is because the Japanese have taken many English words and appropriated them in ways that Westerners may not immediately recognize. Take the word "service," for example; in Japanese, it is pronounced *saabisu* and means "something for free."

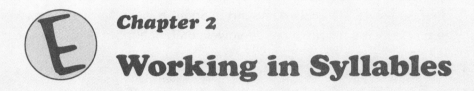

Chapter 2

Working in Syllables

English speakers are often quick to pick up Japanese because all the sounds present are familiar to them. The actual number of sounds in Japanese is considerably less than in English, but nuances in the form of elongated vowels and double consonants require some getting used to. Unique aspects of both English and Japanese present challenges to learners on either side, sometimes with hilarious results. Your name will, hopefully, remain unscathed.

The Sounds

Once you become familiar with the pronunciation of Japanese syllables, reading Japanese words spelled in Roman letters will be a snap. Japanese vowels always make the same sound. If you have any experience with speaking or studying Spanish, you will find Japanese vowels to be identical to Spanish vowels. The rolled *r* sound in Spanish can also be used as a guide in pronouncing the Japanese *r* + vowel combinations.

FACT

You may often hear Japanese people referring to Roman letters as *room-aji*. This word is a combination of the English word "Roman" and the Japanese word for "character," *ji. Roomaji* has enjoyed more frequent use in mainstream Japanese publications and periodicals due to the fairly recent acceptance of writing characters horizontally from left to right.

The Hepburn method of writing Japanese in Roman letters was developed with Westerners in mind. It is written so that English speakers can easily pronounce Japanese sounds properly. The following table presents a list of basic sounds in the Japanese language. Vowel sounds are accompanied by English equivalents to clarify pronunciation. Consonants are pronounced as in English, with the exception of *r*. When reading *ra, ri, ru, re, ro*, try touching the roof of your mouth with your tongue at the beginning of the sound. The result should be similar to a *d* sound (e.g., *da*), or to the rolled *r* sound in Spanish. Also, *ga, gi, gu, ge, go* are pronounced with a hard *g* as in "good."

01

Guide to Pronunciation of Japanese Sounds	
Japanese Vowels	**English Equivalents**
a	as in "aquarium"
i	as in "eat"
u	as in "school"

Japanese Vowels			English Equivalents	
e			as in "apron"	
o			as in "open"	

Consonant-Vowel Combinations

ka	*ki*	*ku*	*ke*	*ko*
ga	*gi*	*gu*	*ge*	*go*
sa	*shi*	*su*	*se*	*so*
za	*ji*	*zu*	*ze*	*zo*
ta	*chi*	*tsu*	*te*	*to*
da	*ji*	*zu*	*de*	*do*
na	*ni*	*nu*	*ne*	*no*
ha	*hi*	*fu*	*he*	*ho*
ba	*bi*	*bu*	*be*	*bo*
pa	*pi*	*pu*	*pe*	*po*
ma	*mi*	*mu*	*me*	*mo*
ya	–	*yu*	–	*yo*
ra	*ri*	*ru*	*re*	*ro*
wa	–	–	–	*wo*

Single Consonant Sound	English Equivalent
n	as in "born"

Consonant-Vowel Variations

Syllable Combinations

kya	*kyu*	*kyo*
gya	*gyu*	*gyo*
sha	*shu*	*sho*
ja	*ju*	*jo*
nya	*nyu*	*nyo*

Consonant-Vowel Variations (continued)		
Syllable Combinations		
hya	hyu	hyo
bya	byu	byo
pya	pyu	pyo
mya	myu	myo
rya	ryu	ryo
Variations Used for Foreign Words		
kya	fi	fo

It should be noted that *ga, gi, gu, ge, go* are considered the "hard cousins" of *ka, ki, ku, ke, ko*. When writing in hiragana, *ga, gi, gu, ge, go* are written with the same characters for *ka, ki, ku, ke, ko* with the addition of two short dashes on the upper-right-hand side of each character. The same is true for *sa, shi, su, se, so* and *za, ji, zu, ze, zo*; as well as, *ta, chi, tsu, te, to* and *da, ji, zu, de, do*. *Ha, he, fu, he, ho* has two sets of variations in *ba, bi, bu, be, bo* and *pa, pi, pu, pe, po*. The "b" sounds are indicated by two short dashes to the upper-right side of the appropriate "h" character, while "p" versions can be identified by a small circle in the upper-right-hand corner.

Elongated Vowels

Japanese words and their meanings are easily altered by extending vowel sounds. When using Roman letters, these elongated vowel sounds are written as double vowels. For example, *iie* ("no") is differentiated from *ie* ("house") by writing the "i" twice.

When you come across these elongated vowels, it is not necessary to repeat the vowel sound twice. Instead, elongate the sound for an extra second or two. This will alleviate confusion as to whether you are referring to a math exercise (*tasu*) or the majority political party (*tasuu*).

In some situations, what may sound elongated is actually two different vowels. For example, the word *keito* ("knitting wool") is made up of two different words *ke* ("wool") and *ito* ("thread"). When spoken, the vowels of this compound word seem to run together. This differentiation is really only evident when reading written Japanese.

ALERT!

An elongated *o* sound can be written various ways in *roomaji*. In this book, an elongated *o* sound will be represented by a double vowel. If an *o* is followed by another *o*, the word should be pronounced with an extended sound. When you say the word *shoogakkoo,* for example, you should elongate the *o* sound in both the first syllable and the last syllable.

Double Consonants

Another way in which Japanese words are subtly varied is through double consonants. When spoken, double consonants include an audible space or pause between them.

Written in *roomaji,* these audible pauses are identified by repeating the letter at the desired point of emphasis. In this way, the word for person, *hito,* is differentiated from the word for "hit," *hitto,* by doubling the consonant. Unlike in English, both "t" sounds in the Japanese word *hitto* are audibly spoken.

Hidden Tricksters

Foreigners who have lived in Japan for a long time often end up grateful for having grown up speaking English—it's just not easy to learn as a second language. English pronunciation, spelling, and grammar are considerably more complicated than Japanese. Irregular verbs and plurals, silent letters, long and short vowel sounds, as well as other inexplicables become more apparent when attempting to teach English, or when compared with studying Japanese. Having said that, there are some doozies in Japanese, as well.

Contemplating **Wa**

Probably one of the most common sounds in the Japanese language, the tiny syllable *wa* carries some lofty responsibilities. Not only is it used as a prefix for anything that is characteristically Japanese, its presence is virtually demanded in every properly uttered sentence. (To make matters even more complicated, it can be written with any number of different characters.)

Attach *wa* to *fuu* and you have a word that encompasses anything resembling traditional Japanese style: *wafuu no ie* (Japanese housing), *wafuu-ryoori* (Japanese cooking). Written with different *kanji*, it also refers to a circle or loop; change the *kanji* again and you have "unity" or "harmony." Combined with *hei*, it becomes *heiwa*, the word for "peace." Left alone, it is an expression of pure emotion or admiration, *Wa!*

Now comes the tricky part. *Wa* may be used as a subject identifier. For example, if you want to say something about your dog, you have to say *wa* after referring to your pet. Your listeners will then know that the main subject of your sentence is your dog.

FACT

Dropping the "w" from *watashi* leaves you with an ultrafeminine version of saying "I": *atashi*. This word is used primarily by women and often in romantic or erotic situations. It is considered to be very soft.

Once your ears become adjusted to Japanese, you may notice that *wa* is not uttered in every sentence. This is because in conversational Japanese, the subject is often not articulated, only implied or assumed. In some situations, therefore, *wa* is not audible, but its invisible presence is acknowledged.

Where Are You Going?

Three different direction or place identifiers exist in Japanese. Similar to the English "to" and "at," these words communicate where someone or something is going (*ni* or *e*), or they can indicate the location at which an event or situation is taking place (*ni* or *de*). Having three to choose from, however, makes things a little complicated.

Ni alone has over eighteen different uses listed in Merriam Webster's *Japanese-English Learner's Dictionary*. These include:

- Existence at a certain point
- Final location of something that has been moved
- Moving toward something or somewhere
- Giving and receiving
- The changing of seasons
- Making a decision or comparison

However short and innocent it may appear, the syllable *ni* wears many hats in the Japanese language.

Coming in a close second to *ni, de* is another indicator of where the action is. It also helps you describe how you found the action when it is tacked on after the means of transportation:

Baiku de kita.
I came by bike.

Other uses of *de* include setting limits of time or space and giving a reason or identifying a cause:

Juppun de dekita.
I did it in ten minutes.

Sore de kimemashita.
That's how we decided.

E is another direction indicator. Often interchangeable with *ni, e* is most noticeably used in welcoming or directing someone:

Yookoso, Kanai Shoogakkoo e.
Welcome to Kanai Elementary School.

Soko e haite kudasai.
Please, go in.

All on Its Own

Another trickster in Japanese is the particle *o*. The particle *o* usually follows a noun and helps to identify the direct object. In romanized transliteration, a hyphen separates the direct object from the particle:

> *Banana o tabetai.*
> I want to eat a banana.

Sometimes acting like a place-identifier, *o* can also be used to indicate movement or location as well as the action of leaving a place or institution. For example:

> *Watashi wa mai asa hachi-ji ni uchi o demasu.*
> I leave home every morning at eight.

Common Errors

When learning to speak a new language, it is important to be fearless about making mistakes. Native residents of most countries in the world applaud even bare-minimum efforts of visitors who attempt to communicate in a foreign tongue. Sooei Kodama, a locally famous folktale guru and retired junior high school teacher, says foreigners in Japan can do no wrong: "Japanese people do not expect foreigners to know how to speak Japanese, or to know anything about our culture," he humbly admits. Any attempt at something that resembles Japanese will be met with gratitude. With that in mind, there are a few areas that deserve a word of caution.

As with all languages, certain words in Japanese sound alike but have different meanings. Mixing up words is a common mistake for beginners. How many foreigners in Japan have stared into a baby bassinet and exclaimed *Kowai!* ("scary") when what they really wanted to say was *Kawaii!* ("cute")? And by the way, please do not ask someone to carry your *omutsu* ("diapers") when what you are really looking for is help with your *nimotsu* ("luggage").

At a recent art exhibit, a young English teacher assured a group of Japanese men and women that her baby would not be frightened of the men's beards because her own breasts had beards. Having made the very innocent mistake of putting *watashi no* in front of the word *chichi* changed the intended meaning from "my father" to "my breasts."

At a welcome party for new teachers, someone brought homemade rice cakes with various toppings. These happened to be a particular favorite of some Australian visitors. Sitting next to the vice principal, who happened to have a severely receding hairline, the visitors went on and on, while stuffing their mouths full of the sweet treats, about their love of *o-hage* ("baldness"); but what they were really consuming were *o-hagi*.

Your Japanese Name

If you're traveling to Japan, it'll be convenient to know what the Japanese version of your name might be. Sure, Japanese study English in school, but they might have difficulty understanding the pronunciation of your name and being able to repeat it. That's because some English sounds aren't represented in the Japanese language. In Japanese, the sounds for "f," "l," and "v" simply do not exist. The consonant blend "th" is also absent. Vowel-consonant blends such as the "ci" in "circle," "di" in "did," and "ddy" in "daddy" are also difficult for Japanese to pronounce. Recognizing the difference between a soft *g* and *z* can also pose problems for Japanese when trying to understand spoken English.

To compensate for the difficulty in correctly pronouncing certain sounds in the English language, the Japanese opt for convenience over precision. "F" becomes a whispery *h* sound, making the word "foot" into *hoot*. Likewise, "th" is substituted with the sound of *s* or *z* so that "the" becomes *za*. As the English language is introduced to Japanese children at younger and younger ages, the ability to pronounce sounds outside of their mother tongue will most likely increase. Until that time, though, the Japanese must make due with their *katakana* versions of challenging English sounds.

A Useful Technique

Now that you are becoming familiar with the availability of sounds in Japanese, you can begin to determine how to translate your name into something people can pronounce. First, write your name on a piece of paper. Now, say it out loud to yourself, and see if you can break it up into syllables.

Then, see which of the syllables don't exist in Japanese (you can use the tables in this chapter to check yourself). For each foreign syllable, substitute a Japanese syllable that is closest in sound. Note that if your name ends in a consonant, an "o" sound is usually added to the end. For example, "David" would be *Dabido*.

Chapter 3

Japan at a Glance

Eastern traditions and western influences often exist side by side. Japan
is a land where school principals in three-
piece suits think nothing of passing out *sake*
to demon dancers who visit the schools
during festivals. Knowing even a little of its
history and mythology will give you added
insight into both the language and people
of modern Japan.

Divine Origins

According to Japanese mythology, the eight main islands that make up Japan were created by two gods dripping water from a sacred stick. Consequently, all things are believed to have come directly from the gods and goddesses. This belief lends insight into the Shinto shrines that are dedicated to the worship of just about anything (even cigarettes!). One of the major deities is *Amaterasu Oomikami* (the Sun Goddess). It may be said that her story illustrates the character of Japanese history and culture.

When the Sun Goddess was young, she was deceived by her younger brother and retreated into a cave in despair, thus thrusting both heaven and earth into darkness. The other gods and goddesses gathered outside her hiding place, armed with prayer beads and chants, determined to lure her out.

Another young goddess decided to dress up in a crazy costume to give the situation some humor. Her antics caused the deities gathered there to laugh with such merriment that the Sun Goddess poked her head out to see what was going on. When she did, a young god grabbed her and slung her back up into the sky. A rope was hung across the cave's entrance to prevent her from going into hiding ever again.

These ropes can still be seen in many places in Japan. They are usually found at the entrances to Shinto shrines, but sometimes you'll see them hanging between two big boulders in the mountains or at sea. If you see one, you can be sure some deity is being honored there.

Emperor Jinmu

Early Chinese documents describe encounters with scattered tribes on the islands of Japan. Eventually, these tribes adopted agriculture and settled down, but they could never get along with each other. For centuries, these fierce clans waged battles against each other.

To bring order to the Japanese, it is said that the Sun Goddess sent her grandson to make an attempt at governing the people, but it didn't work. Then, in about A.D. 300, the young Emperor of Yamato vowed to organize the battling tribes into a nation. He gathered together an army, prepared his campaign, and set off to defeat the warring groups. According to legend, a golden bird flew over the battlefield and rested on the Emperor's bow. Light emanating from the bird dazzled the enemies, and they soon surrendered.

Later, the Emperor became known as Emperor Jinmu; the name *Jinmu* means "divine and valiant." This is how the Japanese came to believe that their emperors are divine.

Behind Closed Doors

Fast forward several centuries to the early seventeenth century, when Japan was ruled by a farmer-turned-emperor, Emperor Hideyoshi Toyotomi. This was a time when Christian missionaries went out into the world in hopes of converting people to Christianity. The Emperor felt threatened by the Christians— if Japan were to accept Christianity, he would lose his status as a divine figure.

The Tokugawa family of shoguns (top samurai appointed by the emperor) who ruled expertly throughout the Edo Period also feared Christians. A group of 30,000 peasants, who happened to be predominately Christian, had successfully organized themselves and overthrown a crooked feudal lord. This small revolution was all the Tokugawas needed to convince the Japanese people that Christians were dangerous and that Japan was better off without them.

FACT

In something akin to a reverse Inquisition, Christians were forced to convert to Buddhism; if they didn't, they were crucified, boiled, or burned. In order to test their faith, suspects were asked to step on a painting of the Virgin Mary. Those who refused were arrested and sentenced to death.

This marked the beginning of the Edo Period (A.D. 1603–1867). For more than 250 years, Japan refused entry to most foreigners. Exceptions to this rule were the Dutch and the Chinese due to the absence of missionaries in these countries. Keeping Christians out was Japan's main reason for slamming the door in the world's face.

Knock, Knock

Following an important battle in 1615, the Tokugawa shogunate reigned supreme, and a period of peace began. Martial arts, literature, tea ceremony, kabuki theater, and other art forms were developed and enjoyed by many townspeople. Domestic trade and agriculture thrived.

But Tokugawa's heavy-handed governing had some drawbacks as well. In 1633, travel abroad was forbidden and by 1639 foreign trade was limited to China and the Netherlands. Foreign books were also banned.

Eventually, outside pressures from Russia, England, and the United States, as well as internal unrest, caused Japan to reconsider its official isolation. Commodore Perry of the U.S. Navy eventually forced open Japan's ports in 1853, and again in 1854. By 1868, Emperor Mutsuhito's power was restored, the Meiji Era began, and the world poured in.

In a Perilous Position

It is common knowledge that the islands of Japan occupy a perilous position on the oceanic and continental plates. Natural disasters in the form of earthquakes, tidal waves, volcanic eruptions, and typhoons are frequent visitors.

Fortunately, most cities now have extensive response systems in place, should an emergency occur. Japanese school children practice escape routes and other emergency procedure routines on a monthly basis.

Earthquakes and Tidal Waves

The Japanese rank an earthquake according to the *shindo* scale, which measures how strongly it is felt by people at a certain moment in a given area. A grade one earthquake is probably only felt by people who are standing still. At four, you cannot help but notice, as things begin to fall. Five and above are cause for alarm.

In the past, the *shindo* levels were determined by phone calls. People who had experienced an earthquake in a certain area reported their "feelings" by phone to a localized center. For the past twenty years or so, however, a machine has been used to estimate the *shindo* measurement. A running joke among Japanese science teachers is that a strong earthquake could cause the machine to topple and break. So much for modern technology.

Those living in coastal regions run the risk of having to deal with tidal waves that may follow an earthquake. In 1964, a *tsunami* off the coast of Niigata Prefecture in northwest Japan emptied Ryootsu Bay near Sado Island. People are reported to have run out into the bay to capture flailing fish with their bare hands as those who escaped into the mountains looked on.

ALERT!

If you happen to experience an earthquake while in Japan and are living in an apartment or house, make sure you turn off the main gas valve to avoid potential fires and explosions. It is also a good idea to have an emergency kit packed with water, canned food, and other essentials.

Typhoons and Volcanic Eruptions

September is officially marked as typhoon season, but the typhoons do not always abide by the rule. Strong winds send villagers hurrying to tack boards across their windows. Farmers' wrinkles grow noticeably deeper as pelting rains shower rice stalks. Landslides and flooding rivers send students and teachers on long detours to get to school.

Volcanic eruptions are another threat in many regions of Japan. The view of the world's most famous volcano, Mt. Fujii, is visible from Tookyoo (Tokyo) on a clear day. The volcano last erupted in 1707. Twenty-six different volcanoes remain volatile around Japan. The University of Tookyoo has a Web site that monitors their activity, including the submarine volcano Fukutoku Okanoba.

Worthy of Your Visit

People come to Japan for many different reasons. Some are here to put to use the language skills they acquired in school. Others have studied Japanese art or literature and are interested in seeing "the real thing." Still others have no clue what they are getting into, but are game to try anything. No matter your purpose, there are some things that should not go unexplored.

Shinto Shrines

Look for a red gate and the requisite dog statues to identify a *jinja*, a Shinto shrine. Shrines vary in size and splendor depending on their caretakers. Their weather-beaten wood walls may appear plain at first glance, but you will find them cleverly constructed upon further inspection.

At the entrance dangles a thick rope of twisted cloth. Grab it and swing it to jostle the bell hanging at the top. This will awaken the resident deity. Two claps and a bow, followed by another clap will make you look like a pro. Inside the shrine, at the back, you will find a steep staircase with extremely narrow steps. This is what Shinto priests, in their tall black hats and fancy robes, climb to place offerings of rice, fish, vegetables, salt, and *sake* for the god of that particular shrine.

Sushi Bars

Take a seat at the counter, preferably right in front of the sushi chef. Order *namazake* (raw Japanese rice liquor) and, if you are brave, tell the chef you trust his judgment.

Note the chef's technique. Watch how his hands shape the rice into a perfect platform especially suited to the type of fish he is about to lay on it. Pick the sushi up with your hands when it is placed on the counter in front of you, dip it in soy sauce if you like and put the whole thing in your mouth at one time. Chew thoughtfully, paying attention to the balance of flavors and textures in your mouth. This is slow-food, Japanese style.

QUESTION?

How can I let the chef know what fish to serve me?
The phrase *o-makase shimasu* (I leave it up to you) is one used by veteran sushi goers. Obviously, you can let the chef know of anything you absolutely cannot eat. Most sushi bars also have an eight-, ten-, or twelve-piece course option with corresponding prices.

Public Baths

Public bathhouses, *sento,* have enjoyed a steady stream of popularity since the mid 1500s. Before Western standards infiltrated Japan, baths were unisex. Now, there are almost always separate baths for men and women.

Various types of *sento* are located all over Japan. The number peaked in 1987 at 17,000 but is currently on the decline. Some spots are fed by volcanic hot springs, others by pristine rivers. Outdoor baths with scenic views are not uncommon. Weary travelers can take an opportunity to immerse themselves in something very Japanese while refreshing body and spirit.

Tea Houses and Ceremonies

Expertly crafted from wood and bamboo, yet maintaining an utterly simple design, the Japanese tea-room, or *suki-ya,* offers a welcome respite from hectic city streets. Ideally limited to holding about five people at a time, the *suki-ya* sets the stage for intimacy and conversation. If you are lucky enough to stumble upon a Japanese tea-room and are able to witness the tea ceremony performed by a tea master or apprentice, please take advantage of the experience.

You will need to duck as you enter through a small door, a reminder that all are equal in the *suki-ya.* Try to observe with patience the precise and efficient movements of the performance: how the *kimono* sleeve is lifted out of the way, the care with which the tea towel is folded. When the cup is handed to you, turn it three times to the right before bringing it to your lips. The bitterness of the tea will be countered by a sweet, resulting in a harmony of taste in your mouth.

The philosophy of the Japanese tea ceremony is *ichi go ichi-e,* meaning that each cup of tea should be prepared, served, and drunk with the attitude that this is a once-in-a-lifetime experience.

Major Festivals

In a normally subdued culture with strict rules for social interaction and behavior, festivals are an absolute necessity. Garish clothing, extreme tests of physical endurance, ancient dances, role-reversals, demons, dragons, and excessive eating allow the Japanese to let their hair down several times a year. Most festivals are derived from the Shinto religion and take place in the spring and fall, centering around the planting and harvesting of rice. However, it is possible to find a festival somewhere in Japan at almost any given time. The two major festivals are the New Year Festival and the Demon Dancing and Drumming Festival.

Celebrate the New Year

O-shoogatsu, the New Year Festival, is a time when Japanese families get together. Children, especially, look forward to receiving *o-toshidama,* a gift of money from grandparents and other relatives. Traditionally, the Japanese eat long strands of buckwheat noodles to ensure a long life. Sticky rice cakes with sweet, red bean jam inside are also popular.

FACT

Just before the New Year, Japanese greet friends and relatives with *Yoi o-toshi o o-mukae kudasai!* or just *yoi o-toshi o.* It is a wish for good luck in the upcoming year—it's a formulaic expression without a direct translation in English. When meeting friends and relatives for the first time after the New Year has passed, people say, *Akemashite, omedetoo gozaimasu!* ("Happy New Year!")

Dancing and Drumming

Oni-daiko, the Demon Dancing and Drumming Festival, is unique to Sado Island in the Sea of Japan. The folktale accompanying the festival tells of a time when demons occupied the mountains, villagers farmed the valley, and both respected each others' domain. A spat between a local shrine's deity and the head of the demons was the catalyst for the demons to crash the villagers' annual spring planting festival. Frightened villagers offered *sake, mochi* (rice cakes), and various other festival delicacies in appeasement and the demons responded positively, promising to return every year.

Even in these modern times, come February you can hear the drums of different neighborhoods practicing for the festival. On the day of the festival in April, these groups traverse their respective neighborhoods, sometimes visiting more than 120 houses from morning till midnight. The demons, wearing wooden masks with horse-mane hair that often weigh several pounds, dance at each home to chase out evil spirits: a kind of spring cleaning of the soul. Grandmothers wait patiently on their front stoops, heads bowed in the hopes of being bitten by the lion-esque *shi-shi* (for good luck), but small children flee the frightening dragons maneuvered by two or sometimes ten people.

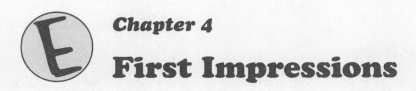

Chapter 4

First Impressions

Dazed after a lengthy flight, all you want is a hot bath and a cozy bed. Immigration, baggage claims, and customs may try your patience. To make the best of things, pack light and be patient. Once you're out of the airport, all that's left is getting to your first night's resting spot.

Meeting the Immigration Officers

Your first destination after arriving is immigration. Follow the signs, written in a variety of languages, directing you to the baggage claim area, customs, and immigration. Immigration lines usually move fairly quickly, so it is important to have your passport ready and your disembarkation card, if applicable, filled out with the necessary information.

Two Questions

Immigration officers are usually interested in two things: what you are doing in Japan and how long you plan to stay.

> *Nihon de wa nani o suru tsumori desu ka.*
> What do you plan to do in Japan?

> *Dore gurai imasu ka.*
> How long will you be staying?

FACT

The *ka* at the end of each sentence is a verbal question mark. English questions have a rise in tone at the end. In Japanese, inquiries can be identified by the tacked-on *ka*.

Appropriate responses vary according to different reasons for being in Japan. The following list encompasses the majority of reasons people visit.

1. *Ryokoo shimasu.* (I will travel.)
2. *Eigo o oshiemasu.* (I will teach English.)
3. *Shigoto desu.* (I am here on business.)

Answers also vary depending on the length of time you will be in Japan.

1. *Tooka kan gurai.* (About ten days.)
2. *San shuu kan.* (Three weeks.)

3. *Rokka getsu kan.* (Six months.)
4. *Ichi nen kan.* (One year.)

One Day, Two Days, Red Days, Blue Days

English has a few terms for counting certain classes of objects. We count grapes in bunches, for example, and paper in reams. Japanese, on the other hand, has a special way of counting everything! Items to be counted are usually grouped by shape, but even days and nights have their own counting words. The following table presents the unique terms for counting days two to ten.

Numbers and Day Counters		
Japanese Number	Number of Days	English Definitions
ichi	*ichi-nichi*	one; one day
ni	*futsuka kan*	two; two days
san	*mikka kan*	three; three days
yon, shi	*yokka kan*	four; four days
go	*itsuka kan*	five; five days
roku	*muika kan*	six; six days
shichi, nana	*nanoka kan*	seven; seven days
hachi	*yooka kan*	eight; eight days
kyuu	*kokonoka kan*	nine; nine days
juu	*tooka kan*	ten; ten days
juu-ichi	*juu-ichi-nichi kan*	eleven; eleven days
ni-juu	*hatsuka kan*	twenty; twenty days
ni-juu yon	*ni-juu yokka kan*	twenty-four; twenty-four days

From eleven on, with the exception of the twentieth and days that end in four, the number word plus *nichi* ("day") and *kan* ("while") will usually suffice. When referring to travel, anything past two weeks is usually communicated in average weeks, so it may be rare to hear people say twenty-four days.

With the exception of *ichi-nichi,* note that days from two on are followed by the term *kan.* Without *kan,* the number terms refer to a calendar date. For example, *sangatsu mikka* means "March 3." *Kan* is also tacked on when referring to hours, weeks, months, and years, as in *ni-shuu kan* or *ichi-nen kan.*

Words for Getting Through Immigration	
Nihon	Japan
nani	what
suru, shimasu	do
desu	to be, is
iru, imasu	to be, refers to live animals (including humans)
kan	while (refers to a period of time)
shuu	week
getsu	month
nen	year

Note the verbs "to do" and "to be" are written two different ways. Polite forms of regular, non-past Japanese verbs most often end in *–masu,* while the plain, non-past forms end in *ru, ku, bu, mu,* and so on. Immigration officers may use either version.

Japanese verbs almost always come at the end of a sentence, or at the end of a phrase if the sentence is compound. The two questions asked by immigration, translated into English with Japanese grammar rules, would look like this: "Japan in what do intention is?" and "How long about stay?"

When Your Bag Has Exploded

No one wants to start a trip with baggage problems, but sometimes it happens. If your baggage is missing, or if there is anything wrong with your luggage, please proceed directly to a baggage assistant.

The baggage assistant will most likely ask your name (*o-namae wa . . . ?*) and lead you to bags that have already been taken from the turnstile. If you do not see your bag among them, please say:

Sumimasen, watashi no nimotsu ga arimasen.

If you do see your suitcase but there is damage, they will take your name and the address of where you are staying in Japan, and repack your things in a box to be shipped to your hotel or temporary residence.

02 Sample Baggage Claims Area Conversation and Highlights

Visitor: *Sumimasen, watashi no nimotsu ga kowaremashita.*
Excuse me, my luggage is broken.

Baggage Assistant: *Gomennasai! Sumimasen, doko ni tomatte-imasu ka.*
I'm sorry! Excuse me, but where are you staying?

Visitor: *Koko desu.*
Here.

Baggage Assistant: *Hai, wakarimashita. O-nimotsu wa naoshite kara sugu okurimasu. Mooshiwake arimasen deshita.*
I see. As soon as we fix your luggage, we will send it to you. I'm sorry for the inconvenience.

Expect a lot of bowing and apologizing. Japanese people, in general, are very accommodating of visitors to their country and want to make a good impression. The baggage assistant will most likely take it personally that your bags were either lost or damaged.

Broken Baggage Talk	
sumimasen	excuse me
watashi no	my

Broken Baggage Talk (continued)	
nimotsu	baggage
arimasen	is not
kowaremashita	is broken
koko	here
hai	yes; no; I see; okay; that is right

Please note the *–sen* in *arimasen* is a common suffix for negative verbs. *Arimasen* is reserved for missing objects:

> *Watashi no saifu ga arimasen.*
> My wallet is not here.

Imasen refers to a person or animal being absent:

> *Watashi no inu ga imasen.*
> My dog is not here.

The *–mashita* ending on *kowaremashita* is the past-tense form of the verb. Remember, many verbs end in *–masu*, and that ending becomes *–mashita* when referring to something that has already happened:

> *Ringo o tabemashita.*
> I ate an apple.

QUESTION?

Why does *hai* have so many different and seemingly contradictory definitions?
In order to answer this question, please think about all the different ways the word "yes" is used in English. We say "yeees" when we are waiting to hear the end of a strange story. Sometimes "yes" is used as "what?" when responding to someone calling your name. *Hai*, too, has a plethora of uses, so don't assume it always means the affirmative "yes."

Talking with Customs Officials

Once you have collected your baggage, proceed to the customs checkout counter with your customs card and passport ready. Customs officials will want to know whether you have any food, seeds, plants, or other living things that may harm the local environment. Gifts of packaged goods such as chocolates are usually not a problem, but there are limits on some items. You may be asked to open your bag for inspection.

Customs Vocabulary	
naka	inside
haitte imasu, hairimasu	be in (inside)
o-miyage	gifts, souvenirs
mite, mimasu	see, look
doozo	please, go ahead

03

Here's the kind of conversation you may have with the customs official:

Customs Official: *O-nimotsu no naka ni wa, nani ga haitteimasu ka.*
What do you have in your bags?

Visitor: *O-miyage ya fuku, kamera nado ga haitte imasu.*
There are gifts, clothing, a camera, etc., inside.

Customs Official: *Naka o mite mo ii desu ka.*
Do you mind if I look inside?

Visitor: *Doozo.*
Please, go ahead.

Customs officials may look menacing, but once you are through this last checkpoint your trip really starts!

The Japanese Version of "-ing"

Two new verbs with different endings are included in the customs sample dialogue: *haitte-imasu* and *mite*. The first verb modification is similar to English verbs with the suffix "–ing" (e.g., "running" and "speaking"). The regular form of the verb is *hairu* ("enter," "contain," "include"). To make it into its present perfect form, the *–ru* ending must be dropped. After that, first a *–te* and then an *–imasu* are added to create a verb conjugation that indicates the action is going on right now. In romanized spellings, the main verb is often separated from *–imasu* by a hyphen. In less formal situations, *–imasu* may be replaced with *–iru*.

Verbs whose plain forms end in *bu, mu,* or *nu* need *–nde* instead of *–te* followed by *–imasu,* or *–iru.* Following this rule, *yobu* ("to call") becomes *yonde-iru* ("calling") and *nomu* ("to drink") becomes *nonde-iru* ("drinking").

04

Nani o tabete imasu ka.
What are you eating?

Nani o kiite-iru ka.
What are you asking?

Bideo o mite imasu.
I'm watching a video.

Nani o nonde-iru ka.
What are you drinking?

Dare o yonde imasu ka.
Who are you calling?

In the previous examples, notice that the *–te* of *mite* becomes *–de* in verbs such as *nonde* and *yonde. –te* and *–de* are related and so can be used interchangeably in order to make the conjugation roll off the tongue more easily.

Do You Mind?

Requesting permission to smoke, eat, drink, or take a look is relatively easy as far as verb conjugations go. In the phrase *mite mo ii desu ka,* the verb *miru* ("to see") is changed by dropping the plain *–ru* ending and simply adding *–te.* This modified verb followed by the phrase *mo ii desu ka,* is a polite way to ask permission to do anything:

> *Tabete mo ii desu ka.*
> May I eat?

> *Koko de matte mo ii desu ka.*
> Is it alright if I wait here?

If you would like to have something, you have to say:

> *Bananas o moratte mo ii desu ka.*

A Catchall Word

Doozo is a word you will hear thousands of times from the beginning to the end of your visit to Japan. It is used in countless situations and is a great fallback word when you do not know what else to say. *Doozo* usually accompanies an offer to sit down, eat, drink, receive, or enter:

> *Moo ikko, doozo.*
> Please have another.

It can also be used to mean "sure, of course," therefore making it an easy reply to requests for permission to do something:

> *Tabete mo ii desu ka. Doozo.*
> May I eat? Of course, go ahead.

Lightening Your Load

People utilize various delivery service companies in Japan to make travel light and easy. By sending bags ahead to the airport, hotel, or temporary residence, train and bus travel become less overwhelming. It is also an act of consideration for other passengers as Japanese public transportation is often crowded.

Several delivery service companies have counters near the customs exit at the airport. Depending on where you are headed, the price of sending a bag may vary slightly from company to company, but not by much. Delivery service personnel will label things "fragile" if necessary, box smaller parcels together, and generally do their best to make your load lighter.

05   Here's a sample dialogue at the delivery service counter:

Traveler: *Kono nimotsu o Fukushima made okuritai-n desu ga, ryookin wa o-ikura desu ka.*
How much would it cost to send this bag to Fukushima?

Clerk: *Hai, juusho o oshiete kudasai.*
I see. Please tell me the address.

Traveler: *Koko desu.*
This is it.

Clerk: *Hai, chotto misete kudasai.*
Please let me take a look at this.

Traveler: *Doozo.*
Certainly.

Clerk: *Sumimasen, o-nimotsu wa, kono hitotsu dake de yoroshii desu ka.*
Excuse me, is it just this one bag you would like to send?

Traveler: *Hai.*
Yes.

Clerk: *Jaa, Fukushima made wa, sen roppyaku en ni narimasu.*
Alright then, the cost to send it to Fukushima is 1,600 yen.

Traveler: *Onegai shimasu.*
Please take care of it for me.

Making a Request

If you have not already noticed, Japanese verbs carry a lot of responsibility. Most communication relies heavily on the verb and its various endings. Some sentences consist of a solitary verb.

The above dialogue contains two verbs with the ending *–te* followed by *kudasai*, the Japanese word for "please." Whenever you see this combination, you will know a request is being made:

> *Misete kudasai. Oshiete kudasai.*
> Please show me. Please teach/tell me.

This rule also goes for the *bu* and *mu* verbs with their *–nde* endings. The verb *yobu* becomes *yonde kudasai*, "please read," and *nomu* becomes *nonde kudasai*, "please drink."

Softening the Request

In the first sentence of the delivery service dialogue is a verb with the ending *–tai*. This is how verbs are modified to indicate a desire to do something. The *–n* that follows is a way of softening the request:

> *Watashi wa tabetai-n desu.*
> I want to eat.

Remember, Japanese communication strives to keep the peace, so even basic desires need to be muted in a public setting, or with people you do not know well. Among friends and family, the *–n* modification is unnecessary:

> *Nemutai.*
> I want to sleep.

> *Juusu o nomitai.*
> I want to drink some juice.

Phoning in Reservations

Whether you plan to look for a place to stay upon your arrival or have made arrangements beforehand, it is always reassuring to phone ahead. Speaking on the phone in a foreign language can be a little overwhelming. This is where the following two phrases will come in very handy:

> *Moo ichido onegaishimasu.*
> Could you repeat that please?

> *Moo chotto yukkuri hanashite kudasai.*
> Could you please speak more slowly?

Take Your Pick

Modern hotels, or "business hotels" as they are often referred to, are common in any Japanese city. Rooms tend to be smaller than what Westerners are used to, and it is rare to find anything bigger than a twin-sized bed. Bathrooms are similar to Western-style hotels (albeit in miniature) with a shower and sit-down toilet. Breakfast at the hotel restaurant may be offered as an option for an additional fee.

FACT

Other hotel options are *ryokan* (Japanese-style hotels) and *minshuku,* which are more traditional bed-and-breakfast establishments and are usually family-run. It is customary to be served both an evening meal and breakfast at a *minshuku.* Japanese-style rooms with *tatami* (rice) mats, paper doors, and *futons* will quickly immerse you in the Japanese experience.

06

Sample Dialogue for Making Phone Reservations at a Business Hotel

Traveler: *Konya, ni-haku tomaritai-n desu ga, akishitsu wa arimasu ka.*
I would like to reserve a room for two nights. Do you have any available?

Hotel Clerk: *Hai arimasu. Nan mei sama desu ka.*
Yes, we do. How many people are in your party?

Traveler: *Futari desu. O-ikura desu ka.*
Just two of us. How much will that be?

Hotel Clerk: *Sudomari desu ka. Sore tomo chooshoku o torimasu ka.*
Just the room, or would you like to include meals?

Traveler: *Sumimasen, moo ichido onegai shimasu.*
I'm sorry, could you repeat that please?

Hotel Clerk: *Sudomari desu ka. Sore tomo chooshoku, eto asagohan, wa irimasu ka.*
Just the room, or do you need a meal, a breakfast?

Traveler: *Sudomari desu.*
Just the room.

Hotel Clerk: *Wakarimashita. O-namae wa . . .*
I understand. What is your name?

Traveler: *Jonson to mooshimasu.*
My name is Johnson.

Hotel Clerk: *Jonson san desu ne. Ni-man nana-sen en ni narimasu.*
I see, Mr. Johnson. The total comes to 27,000 yen.

Traveler: *Sumimasen, moo chotto yukkuri hanashite kudasai.*
Excuse me, could you please speak more slowly?

Hotel Clerk: *Gomennasai. Ni-man nana-sen en ni narimasu.*
I'm sorry. The total comes to 27,000 yen.

Traveler: *Sore de onegai shimasu.*
We'll take it.

Hotel Clerk: *Arigatoo gozaimasu. Sore de wa o-machi shite orimasu.*
Thank you! We look forward to seeing you.

You Can Say That Again!

When conversing in a foreign language, one of the most important skills is knowing how to ask the speaker to repeat something. The phrase *onegai shimasu* is respectful and polite, communicating the fact that something is not clicking and challenging the speaker to rephrase. Say it as many times as it takes for you to understand what the person is trying to convey.

Onegai shimasu is right up there with *doozo* in terms of frequency and utility. It has been poetically described as the lubricant of Japanese society, allowing massive numbers of people in a crowded space to move smoothly among each other. There is not a one-word equivalent in English, but "please take care of this favor, or request, for me," comes close. When someone says *onegai shimasu*, it is very hard to refuse whatever is being asked of you.

Counting People and Nights

Night counters have a pattern, but it may be difficult to catch on to right away. "One," "three," "six," "eight," and "ten" stand out with *paku* or *ppaku*. With people counters, only the first few are irregular.

Counters for Nights	
ippaku	one night
ni-haku	two nights
san-paku	three nights
yon-haku	four nights
go-haku	five nights
roppaku	six nights
nana-haku	seven nights
happaku	eight nights
kyu-haku	nine nights
juppaku	ten nights

Counters for People	
hitori	one person
futari	two people
san-nin	three people
yon-nin	four people
go-nin	five people

Double-Checking Your Destination

It has happened to every traveler at least once. You board a train and sit down, confident that it will take you where you need to go. Then, as the doors close you get a sickening feeling that something is not right. Groping your way towards the map of lines, you notice the next stop is exactly the opposite of where you intended to go.

In a country where deciphering the map requires extensive schooling, it is important to have the conversational know-how to ask the people around you for assistance.

Kono tsugi no eki wa nan desu ka.
What is the next station?

Kono densha wa Shibuya ni ikimasu ka.
Does this train go to Shibuya?

Kono basu wa Narita de tomarimasu ka.
Does this bus make a stop at Narita?

ALERT!

Notice the use of *ni* and *de* in these examples. The second question asks where the train is going, indicating motion, so *ni* is used. The third question wonders about a specific stop. The focus is on where something is happening, so *de* is used.

Quizzes and Exercises

1. What will be your responses to the two questions posed by the immigration officer?

   _____

   _____

2. What short little word is necessary when referring to the length of your stay? _____

3. Which of the following two sentences is a question?

   Ringo o tabemasu ka.
   Ringo o tabemashita.

4. Draw a line to match the numbers on the left with their English equivalent on the right.

mikka kan   two people

shichi   the 4th

ippaku   three days

yekka   five nights

futari   one night

go-haku   seven

5. Reorganize the following words into a sentence: *misete sumimasen juusho o kudasai*

_____

6. Fill in the appropriate verb endings for the following sentences.

Sumimasen, banana o tabe_____ mo ii desu ka.
Nani o yonde_____ ka.
Shibuya ni iki_____ desu ga, oshie_____ kudasai.

Chapter 5

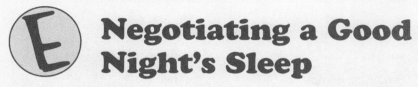

Negotiating a Good Night's Sleep

Many of the same services available at any U.S. hotel are offered at hotels in major Japanese cities as well. Eager managers and clerks will bend over backwards in an effort to make you comfortable. Other options exist in the form of Japanese-style hotels, similar to a bed-and-breakfast. You can expect professional performances by hotel staff regarding everything from wake-up calls to receipts. Enjoy your stay.

Checking In and Out

The front desk is conveniently referred to as *furonto* in Japanese. Pleasant clerks in spotless uniforms will assist you in the check-in procedure. If you have already made a reservation, simply supplying your name will get the ball rolling.

Essential Check-in Vocabulary	
yoyaku	reservation
o-namae, namae	name
go-juusho, juusho	(honorable) address and address
soo (desu)	like that, or that's right
kaite, kaku, kakimasu	to write
eigo de	in English
kekko	fine
narimasu, naru	to become
doomo arigatoo gozaimasu	thank you very much

08

Here's a check-in dialogue you might overhear at a Western-style hotel.

Hotel Clerk: *Irasshaimase, konbanwa!*
Welcome, good evening!

Guest: *Konbanwa. Denwa de yoyaku o torimashita.*
Good evening. I called in a reservation.

Hotel Clerk: *Kashikomarimashita. O-namae wa . . .*
I see (polite). Your name . . .

Guest: *Jonson desu.*
It's Johnson.

Hotel Clerk: *Shoo-shoo machi kudasai. Hai, Jonson-sama arimashita. Ni-haku de o-futari sama desu ne.*

Just a moment, please. Here it is. Two people for two nights, is that correct?

Guest: *Hai, soo desu.*

That's right.

Hotel Clerk: *Koko ni o-namae to go-juusho o kaite kudasai.*

Please write your name and (honorable) address here.

Guest: *Eigo de kaite mo ii desu ka.*

Is it okay to write it in English?

Hotel Clerk: *Hai, kekko desu. Sore de, ni-man nana-sen en ni narimasu.*

That is fine. Alright then, the total is 27,000 yen.

Guest: *Hai.*

Okay.

Hotel Clerk: *Doomo arigatoo gozaimasu. Hyaku ni-juu go-shitsu ni narimasu. Doozo, go-yukkuri shite kudasai.*

Thank you very much. Your room number is 120. Please relax and enjoy your stay.

Guest: *Sumimasen, chekku-auto wa nan-ji ni narimasu ka.*

Excuse me, what time is check-out?

Hotel Clerk: *Chekku-auto jikan wa juu-ichi ji ni narimasu. Yoroshiku onegaitashimasu.*

Check-out time is 11:00. Please do us the favor of observing this policy.

Breaking It Down

In the check-in dialogue, you may recognize a few phrases or verb endings. The verb *kakimasu*, "to write," appears in the *–te* form twice, with two different intentions. The first appearance is as a request to the customer:

O-namae to go-juusho o kaite kudasai. The second time is to ask permission to write in English: *Eigo de kaite mo ii desu ka.*

When conjugating verbs with a plain ending of *ku* or *gu* the final syllable is dropped before adding the conjugated form of the verb to the stem. In the case of the verb *kaku* the verb is first stripped down to *ka*, then *ite* is added.

This also goes for the verb *oyogu*, to swim. Made into a participial, which is the form used in a request, *oyogu* becomes *oyoide*. Do you notice a pattern? The *–ku* at the end of *kaku* becomes *–ite*, and the *–gu* at the end of *oyogu* becomes *–ide*. From this you can deduce that other verbs ending in *–ku* and *–gu* will follow similar patterns.

Irregularities in verb conjugations do exist; most notably in the verb *iki-masu*, or *iku*, "to go." Even though it ends with *–ku*, its *–te* form is written in *roomaji* as a double consonant: *itte*. As you'll soon notice, *iku* is one of the most troublesome verbs in the Japanese language.

What Will You Naru?

Another verb used frequently in the check-in dialogue is *narimasu*, or *naru*, "to become." The plain form of *naru* ends in *–ru*. When changing *naru* to the *–te* form, the ending is pronounced with an audible pause: *natte*. This form can be used with commands or requests.

Motto otona ni natte kudasai.
Please be more adult!

Massugu ni natte kudasai.
Please straighten up.

Most often prefaced by the particle *ni, narimasu* is used with prices, seasons, descriptions, times, and changes.

09

Haru ni narimashita.
It has become spring.

Kimono o kitara, kirei ni naru.
If you put on a kimono, you will become beautiful.

San-man en ni narimasu.
The total is 30,000 yen.

Moo sorosoro hachi-ji ni narimasu.
It is going on eight o'clock.

For extremely polite expressions, the honorific *o* is placed in front of the verb (minus its *–masu* ending), then *ni narimasu* is added.

09

O-kaeri ni narimasu ka.
Are you going home now?

O-yasumi ni narimasu ka.
Are you going to bed now?

Honing In on Honorifics

Note the honorific forms of "name" and "address" are indicated with the prefixes *o* and *go*. The front desk clerk's response to whether it is okay to write in English, *kekko desu,* is a polite version of *ii desu,* "it's okay."

The longest, possibly most intimidating word in the dialogue, *kashiko-marimashita,* is just the polite way of saying, "I understand." The less formal version of *kashikomarimashita* is *wakarimashita.*

The hotel clerk's final comment, *yoroshiku onegai itashimasu,* is also the polite form of the phrase *onegai shimasu,* another one used repeatedly in a variety of situations in Japan.

Requesting a Wake-up Call

Many modern hotel rooms come equipped with a clock radio, making wake-up calls obsolete. Just in case the procedure for setting the alarm is confusing, it is good to have a backup plan. Conveniently, "wake-up call" in Japanese is *mooningu kooru* ("morning call").

The Japanese word for "o'clock" is *ji*. Similar to references to time in English, *ji* is tacked on to a number word to indicate a certain time. Minutes are referred to as *fun* (but, remember the Japanese "f" sounds more like a breathy "h") or *pun*, depending on the final sound of the number word.

Numbers in Reference to Minutes		
Japanese Numbers	**Minutes**	**English**
juu-go	*juu-go-hun*	fifteen (minutes)
ni-juu yon	*ni-juu yon-hun*	twenty-four (minutes)
san-juu	*san-juppun*	thirty (minutes)
yon-juu roku	*yon-juu-roppun*	forty-six (minutes)
go-juu hachi	*go-juu happun*	fifty-eight (minutes)

Minutes that end in "one," "three," "six," "eight," or "zero" are cited as *pun*. Numbers that end in two, four, five, seven, and nine become *hun*. Similar to the English "half-past," the half-hour time reference in Japanese is *han*.

10

Ima wa roku-ji desu.
It is now six o'clock.

Gakkoo wa hachi-ji kara hajimarimasu.
School starts at 8:00.

Ima wa san-ji ni-fun desu.
It is now 3:02.

Shichi-ji juppun ni okimashita.
I woke up at 7:10.

Tsugi no densha wa juu-ji ni-juu san-pun ni kimasu.
The next train will come at 10:23.

Kono basu wa yo-ji-han ni eki ni tsukimasu.
This bus arrives at the train station at 4:30.

A Sample Request

Requests for wake-up calls can be made by phone or, if you feel more comfortable speaking face-to-face, by going to the front desk in person.

11

Guest:	*Mooningu kooru o onegai shimasu.* I would like to request a wake-up call.
Hotel Clerk:	*Nan-ji ga yoroshii desu ka.* What time would you like the call ?
Guest:	*Asa no go-ji-han ni onegai shimasu.* I would like it for 5:30 A.M.
Hotel Clerk:	*Hai, asa no go-ji-han desu ne. Kashikomarimashita.* Right, 5:30 A.M. I will take care of it.

Room Service and Midnight Snacks

Room service is usually only available in the more expensive, executive-style hotels. As Japan grows more and more Westernized, familiar items such as *hanbaagaa* ("hamburgers") and *aisu kuriimu* ("ice cream") may be included on the menu. *Onigiri* (white rice shaped into a triangle and wrapped in dried seaweed, sometimes with a surprise in the middle) or *karee raisu* (the Japanese version of curry with rice) are often available.

Then, of course, there is sushi. Fancy hotels may even have their own sushi bar. When it comes time to order, first name the menu item followed by the number of orders you would like to request. Use the counters table as a reference. Then, simply tack on the word *kudasai* ("please").

Counters for Most Menu Items	
hitotsu	one
futatsu	two
mittsu	three
yottsu	four
itsutsu	five

Counters for Individual Pieces of Sushi	
ikkan	one piece
ni-kan	two pieces
san-kan	three pieces
yon-kan	four pieces

Counters for Rolled Sushi	
ippon	one roll
ni-hon	two rolls
san-bon	three rolls

Note that the pattern for counting rolled sushi resembles that for minutes, with the exception of "three." When referring to "an order" of something (like French fries), it is acceptable to use the first set of counters:

> *Furaido poteto o futatsu kudasai.*
> Two orders of French fries, please.

FACT

Thanks to counters, plural forms of nouns are virtually nonexistent in Japanese. Words like "we," and "kids" have plural forms, but the number of objects, amount of food, and how many cars are all determined by the counter word that comes in front.

Venturing Outdoors

Vending machines are another option for late-night snacking. They can be found nearly anywhere in Japan. Most hotels have cigarette, snack, drink, and maybe even beer vending machines. If there are no vending machines in the hotel, there is probably one nearby on a local street.

If food from vending machines does not appeal to you, take a walk around the block and you will most surely bump into a *raamen* shop with massive, steaming bowls of noodles, a convenience store, or a fast-food restaurant.

Making Sure You Are Comfortable

Remembering to pack everything, especially when you are traveling abroad, can be stressful. Basic everyday items are easily forgotten. Luckily, hotels realize this and are stocked with the essentials.

Comforts of Home Vocabulary	
haburashi	toothbrush
hamigakiko	toothpaste
kamisori	razor
kushi	comb
makura	pillow
moofu	blanket
wasuremashita	forgot
hoshii	want
yobun	extra

Sumimasen, haburashi o wasuremashita. Yobun no wa arimasu ka.
Excuse me, I forgot my toothbrush. Do you have an extra one?

Simply substitute another desired item for *haburashi*. You can also combine these two sentences into a one-phrase request:

Sumimasen, yobun no makura wa arimasu ka.
Excuse me, do you have an extra pillow?

Twin beds are the standard in most business hotels—tall westerners may find their feet dangling over the edges. Pillows tend to be filled with tiny plastic pellets. Blankets often appear to be a hybrid of towels and sheets.

Confusing Contraptions

Directions for things like the television, heater/cooler, and toilet may be written in *kanji* characters that make it challenging to even find the "on" switch. Summoning a staff member to assist you may prove to be essential.

Contraption Traps Vocabulary	
heya	room
hiitaa	heater
kuuraa	cooler
terebi	television
eigo no jimaku	English subtitles
toire	toilet
rimokon	remote control
tsukaikata	way of using
tsukekata	way of turning on
samui	cold, chilly

atsui	hot
zenzen	not at all
wakarimasen	to not understand
oshiete	teach me

12

Sumimasen, heya ga chotto samui no de, hiitaa no tsukaikata o oshiete kudasai.

Excuse me, my room is a little chilly; please show me how to work the heater.

Sumimasen, heya ga chotto atsui no de, kuuraa no tsukaikata o oshiete kudasai.

Excuse me, my room is a little hot; please show me how to work the cooler.

Sumimasen, bideo no tsukekata o oshiete kudasai.

Excuse me, please show me how to turn on the VCR.

Sumimasen, kono terebi ni wa, eigo no jimaku o dasu botan ga arimasu ka.

Excuse me, is there a button for English subtitles on the television?

Sumimasen, toire no rimokon no tsukaikata ga zenzen wakarimasen.

Excuse me, I have no clue how to use the toilet remote control.

FACT

The Japanese are known for taking the inventions of other countries and making them ten times better. Nowhere is this more obvious than in the electric toilet seat with remote control. With the touch of a button, you can wash, dry, heat, and spray yourself, and even listen to music. Now, if you could just find the flusher.

At the Japanese-Style Hotel

Travelers who opt for a *ryokan* or a bed and breakfast–type *minshuku* rather than a Western-style hotel can expect an interesting experience. Your bathroom and toilet (the Japanese almost always separate the two) will most likely be Japanese-style and communal. Meals, too, are often served in a common room although times are usually flexible.

Minshuku **Vocabulary**	
doo	How about? What?
itadakimasu	I humbly receive.
taberu, tabemasu	to eat
taberarenai	unable to eat
tabetai	would like to eat
yuhan	dinner, the evening meal
asagohan	breakfast
itsu	when
o-furo	bath (honorific)
hairitai-n, hairimasu	would like to get in, get in
junbi	preparation

When's Dinner?

Check-in procedures at a *minshuku* are similar to a business hotel. You will be asked to register your name and address. Prices may be somewhat cheaper, even with meals included. Dinner and breakfast are still optional, though, and you should discuss the inclusion of meals with the manager.

13 **Manager:** *Chooshoku wa doo shimasu ka.*
What would you like to do about meals?

Guest: *Itadakimasu.*
I humbly receive.

Manager: *Arigatoo gozaimasu. Nani ka taberarenai mono wa arimasu ka.*
Thank you! Is there anything you cannot eat?

Guest: *Iie. Nan demo kekko desu.*
No, I eat anything.

Manager: *Yokatta. Yuhan wa nan-ji ni tabemasu ka.*
What time would you like to eat dinner?

Guest: *Shichi-ji gurai ni tabetai-n desu.*
I would like to eat at seven.

Manager: *Wakarimashita. Asagohan wa hachi-ji goro de doo desu ka.*
I see. How about breakfast at 8:00 A.M.?

Guest: *Onegai shimasu.*
Yes, please.

Family-run establishments are, by nature, usually more relaxed and casual than big hotels. That homey feeling is reflected in the less formal language of this dialogue. Phrases like *doo shimasu ka* and *yokatta* are common in everyday exchanges. *Doo shimasu ka* is a way of asking people what they would like to do in a particular situation:

> *Yuhan wa doo shimasu ka.*
> What should we do for dinner?

It can also be used in the form of *doo desu ka* to gauge opinion or desire:

> *Raamen wa doo desu ka.*
> How would you like some ramen?

Yokatta is another great catch-all phrase that simply means "I'm glad," or "Isn't that nice?" It can be used in a variety of situations to express pleasure and approval.

A Nighttime Bath

It is customary for Japanese people to bathe every evening before going to bed. Your *minshuku* manager will gladly prepare a hot bath for you, but remember to wash thoroughly before getting in, as other guests will also be using the same water. You may be asked when you plan on bathing so that the bath will be ready when you are, or so that times can be coordinated with other people staying at the establishment.

14

Manager:	*O-furo wa itsu hairimasu ka.*	
	When would you like to take a bath?	
Guest:	*Sugu hairitai-n desu.*	
	I'd like to get in as soon as possible.	
Manager:	*Jaa, junbi o shite okimasu. Go yukkuri doozo.*	
	Then, I'll get it ready. Please take your time.	
Guest:	*Onegai shimasu.*	
	Please take care of it for me.	

Sleeping Arrangements

In a *minshuku*, everything is Japanese-style, which means you will be sleeping on a *futon* on the floor. Depending on the place, the proprietor may lay out your *futon* for you, or you may be expected to do it yourself. All the necessary supplies will be stacked in a closet in the room. The harder, thinner futon goes down first, followed by a slightly thicker, softer version. A flat sheet goes next, followed by a towel-type blanket and the fluffy comforter on top.

Traditional Japanese toilets are flush with the floor and require the user to squat. Face the plumbing and place your feet on either side of the latrine. Until you get the hang of it and to avoid "spills," it is recommended that you remove any clothing below the waist. *Kanji* characters for "big" and "small" are written on the flusher (big to the left and small to the right), and determine how much water is used. Please use your best judgment.

Getting a Stamped Receipt

Western influences in Japan's tourist industry are evident from the many signs and labels that have English origins: *hoteru, mooningu kooru, saabisu, suutsukeesu,* and so on. Likewise, the Japanese word for "receipt" sounds much like its English counterpart: *reshiito*. This term usually refers to a till receipt. If no one offers, you may need to request one yourself:

> *Reshiito onegai shimasu.*
> I would like a receipt, please.

If you need something a little more formal—for business reimbursement purposes, for example—it is better to use the word *ryooshuusho* in place of *reshiito*.

When checking your receipt, please look for a bright red, circular stamp. This is the Japanese equivalent of a formal signature, called an *inkan*. All *ryooshuusho* require an *inkan* and red ink is the standard.

Quizzes and Exercises

1. Match the dictionary form with its *–te* conjugation.

   oyogu   *natte*

   oshieru   *kaite*

   kaku   *oyoide*

   naru   *mite*

   mieru   *oshiete*

2. Underline the honorific prefixes in the following sentence: *O-namae o go-hon ni kaite kudasai.*

3. Write the following times in Japanese:

   3:30   _____
   10:45 _____
   12:23 _____

4. What is being requested in the following sentence: *Sumimasen, hamigakiko o onegai shimasu.* _____

5. Translate: *Yuhan wa nan-ji desu ka.*

   _____

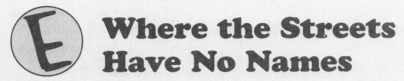

Chapter 6

Where the Streets Have No Names

Streets in Japan—in the city and countryside alike—rarely have signs with their names written on them. Buildings and houses might have numbers, but they are often written in curious places or not marked at all. Landmarks and expansive city maps serve as the main means of deciphering the layout. Luckily, Japan's extensive subway, train, and bus routes are well labeled and organized.

In the Subway

The subway, *chikatetsu*, is the fastest way to get around the city. Japan's subways are clean and comfortable—as long as it's not rush hour. Each station has several signs in both Japanese and *roomaji* stating the name of the stop. Maps within the train may or may not have Roman lettering.

Walking is another great way to explore, but knowing where you are can be a challenge. Possibly the most essential phrase when asking directions is "[destination] *wa doko desu ka.*" Master it and your mobility in Japan will increase tenfold.

15

Kuukoo wa doko desu ka.
Where is the airport?

Basutei wa doko desu ka.
Where is the bus stop?

Takushii noriba wa doko desu ka.
Where is the taxi stand?

Directions Vocabulary	
massugu	straight
hidari	left
migi	right
magatte, magaru, magarimasu	to turn
kado	(street) corner
koko	here
soko	there
asoko	over there
chikai	close
chikatetsu no eki	subway station
doko	where

gawa	side
michi	street
eki	train station

16 Here's a sample conversation for asking directions to a subway station:

Traveler: *Sumimasen, koko kara ichiban chikai chikatetsu no eki wa doko desu ka.*
Excuse me, where is the nearest subway station from here?

Passerby: *Sou desu ne. Kono michi wo massugu ni itte, asoko no kado de, hidari ni magarimasu. Soshite, mata massugu ni itte, tsugi no kado de migi ni magatte, soko ga eki desu.*
Hmmm. Go straight on this road and turn left at that street corner. Then, continue going straight and at the next corner turn right. There is the station.

Traveler: *Michi no dochira gawa ni arimasu ka.*
Which side of the street?

Passerby: *Migi gawa ni arimasu.*
It is on the right side.

Traveler: *Wakarimashita. Doomo arigatoo gozaimashita.*
I see. Thank you very much.

Directions can be challenging to follow even in your own language. Remembering the basics like "left," "right," and "straight ahead" will keep you on track.

ALERT!

You may sometimes hear the word for hand, *te*, substituted for *gawa*, when receiving directions. For example, *migi te ni* means "on your right hand side"; *hidari te ni* means "on your left."

Revisiting the Tricksters

How many times did you see the prepositions *de* and *ni* in the previous dialogue? Now you can see why people get confused about which one to use where. Notice that *ni* indicates direction while *de* shows the scene of some action.

17

Massugu ni itte.
Go straight.

Hidari ni magaru.
Turn left.

Asoko no kado de.
At that corner.

Notice, also, the double consonant plus *–te* endings on *itte* and *magatte*. These are the imperative (command) forms of the verbs, "to go" and "to turn." A *–te* ending can also be used when the sentence is compound (when there is more than one verb in the sentence).

17

Massugu ni itte, hidari ni magarimasu.
Go straight, turn left.

Hidari ni magatte, soko ga eki desu.
Turn left, and there is the train station.

Migi ni magatte, massugu ni ikimasu.
Turn right, go straight.

Notice the first verb, *itte*, has a *–te* ending whereas the second verb is the regular polite form with *–masu*. In this case, the *–te* is doing double duty; it is giving a command, but also identifying itself as the first in a series of verbs. Whether there are two verbs, or five verbs in the same sentence, the –*te* suffix is used for all the verbs except the last one. The final verb in the list is conjugated with the tense-appropriate ending, depending on the context of the sentence.

Localities

Soko and *asoko* also need some clarification. Both terms are used to discuss something at a distance. Which one to use is determined by the visibility of the topic of conversation.

Soko can be used in reference to something either in-sight of or unseen by the speaker. In the previous dialogue, the Japanese person says, *Soko ga eki desu,* but the station cannot be seen by the speaker. *Asoko* is only used when the subject of the conversation is in plain view. The speaker refers to the street corner visible from where the pair are conversing: *Asoko no kado de . . .* When wondering which term to use, check for visibility first.

Train travel, though expensive, is an efficient way to get around Japan. A vast network of lines span out in all directions from most major cities. Local trains are also useful for exploring the vicinity around large cities like Kyooto (Kyoto) and Tookyoo.

Ticket Counters and Turnstiles

Depending on where you are, the map above the ticket machines may or may not have the station stops written in *roomaji*. Several lines may be displayed at once, but do not be deceived by their colors. Like Shibuya fashion, maps and platforms are not necessarily color-coordinated.

In order to determine your ticket fare, it is essential to know where you are going. The cost of your trip will be written underneath the destination on the guide-map above the ticket machines. Fellow travelers can probably help you figure out the cost of your trip:

> *Sumimasen, shibuya made wa o-ikura desu ka.*
> Excuse me, how much does it cost to go to Shibuya?

If you know the name of the subway line or station stop but the map is all in *kanji*, you can ask someone nearby for assistance:

>*Sumimasen, ano chizu de, Shibuya wa doko desu ka.*
>Excuse me, where is Shibuya on that map?

Kono, sono, and *ano* parallel *koko, soko,* and *asoko* in terms of perspective and visibility. Like *asoko, ano* refers to something that both parties can see. Sono can be in reference to something previously discussed, or towards something closer to the listener.

Taking the Bullet Train

Shinkansen trains depart for destinations all over Japan nearly every half-hour or so from central cities like Tookyoo. Japan functions on military time, so train departure times will be written that way. The destination cities are almost always written in *kanji*, so be sure to underline your departure point and final destination for later reference.

18

>*Sumimasen, Niigata iki no Shinkansen wa, nan-ji ni shuppatsu shi-masu ka.*
>Excuse me, at what times does the Niigata-bound bullet train depart?

>*Sumimasen, doko ni Niigata to kaite arimasu ka.*
>Excuse me, where does it say "Niigata"?

>*Sumimasen, dore ga Tookyoo desu ka.*
>Which one is Tookyoo?

There are two options for seating: reserved and nonreserved. Obviously, reserved seating ensures you a spot; your seat number will be printed on the ticket. Nonreserved seats are usually in cars one through four (most likely, two of those cars will be smoking!), but it is usually not difficult to obtain a seat unless you are traveling during a national holiday.

Purchasing Shinkansen Tickets: A Dialogue

19

Traveler: *Sumimasen, Nagano made no Shinkansen no kippu o ni-mai kudasai.*
Excuse me, I would like two tickets for the bullet train to Nagano, please.

Employee: *Shiteiseki ni shimasu ka. Jiyuuseki ni shimasu ka.*
Would you like a reserved seat or a nonreserved seat?

Traveler: *Jiyuuseki ni shimasu.*
I will take the nonreserved seat ticket.

Employee: *Hai, wakarimashita. Ni-man ni-sen en ni narimasu.*
Okay. That's 22,000 yen.

The counter for tickets is *mai*. Luckily, this is a simple counter and the same word can be used for any number of tickets. Just place the number word in front of *mai*.

Departure Decks

Now that you have your tickets and schedule, it is a good idea to figure out which platform your train will be leaving from. The platform number will be written above the departure time on your schedule, but it is often reassuring to double-check.

20

Sumimasen, juu-san-ji ni-juppun no Niigata iki Shinkansen wa nan-ban sen desu ka.
Excuse me, from which platform does the 1:20 P.M. bullet train for Niigata depart?

Sumimasen, ku-ji-han no Niigata iki Shinkansen wa, yon-ban sen desu ka?

Excuse me, does the 9:30 bullet train for Niigata depart from platform four?

Shinkansen trains have their own separate platform. Once inside the *Shinkansen* area, large announcement boards will flash arrival and departure information in both Japanese and *roomaji*. Here you can triple-check your platform and departure time as well as the name of your train.

If you have trouble deciphering which seat is yours, please show your ticket to someone who looks like she is able to read Japanese.

20

Sumimasen, watashi no seki wa nan-ban ka wakarimasu ka.

Excuse me, can you tell me which seat I'm supposed to be in?

Sumimasen, dore ga watashi no seki ka yoku wakarimasen.

Excuse me, I have no idea where my seat is.

Local Trains and Buses

Local train schedules are printed on billboards at each platform. Likewise, bus stop signs have schedules posted on them. Weekday and weekend routes may differ. The times will most likely be written in military form.

21

Tsugi no basu wa nan-ji ni kimasu ka.

What times does the next bus come?

Kyoo no jikokuhyou wa dore desu ka.

Which one is today's schedule?

In Japan, you board the bus in the back and take a ticket from a little machine. Match the number on your ticket to the screen above the driver's seat. This screen lets you know your fare when it is time to get off.

Before boarding the bus or train, ask someone around you whether it stops at your desired point of interest. If you ask upon boarding, bus drivers will usually agree to let you know when you have arrived at your stop.

21

Sumimasen, kono basu wa, Asakusa de tomarimasu ka.
Excuse me, does this bus stop at Asakusa?

Sumimasen, kono densha wa, Shinjuku de tomarimasu ka.
Excuse me, does this train stop at Shinjuku?

Sumimasen, Asakusa-no basutei ni tsuitara, oshiete kudasai.
Please let me know when we have reached the bus stop for Asakusa.

Transportation Terms	
tomaru, tomarimasu	stop
basu	bus
basutei	bus stop
tsuitara, tsuku, tsukimasu	when it has reached, arrived
seki	seat
nan-ban	which platform
wakarimasen	do not understand

So Much Potential: "If," "After," and "When"

Note a new verb ending in the previous examples: *–tara*. This suffix is used to identify a potential or future situation, the English equivalent of "after" or "when":

Gohan o tabetara, ikimasu.
When I have eaten, I will go.

Eiga o mitara, tabemasu.
After I have seen the movie, I will eat.

With verbs like *yomu* ("to read"), and *nomu* ("to drink"), verbs whose regular form ends in *–mu*, this *–tara* ending becomes *–dara*:

Hon o yondara, ikimasu.
When I have read this book, I will go.

Although "when" and "if" are sometimes used interchangeably in English, they signify two totally different tenses in Japanese. Here is a quick list comparing the two tenses. Focus on the endings in each column:

Regular	Potential (if)	Potential (when)	English
taberu	*tabereba*	*tabetara*	to eat
noru	*noreba*	*nottara*	to board
miru	*mireba*	*mitara*	to see
neru	*nereba*	*netara*	to sleep
tsuku	*tsukeba*	*tsuitara*	to arrive
kuru	*kureba*	*kitara*	to come
yomu	*yomeba*	*yondara*	to read
nomu	*nomeba*	*nondara*	to drink
iku	*ikeba*	*ittara*	to go

With the exception of *kuru*, verbs that end in *–ru* are all conjugated the same way. *Iku* ends in *–ku*, but is sometimes conjugated like the verbs that end in *–ru* with a double consonant (*itte*, "go" and *itta*, "went"). Keep an eye out for those irregularites.

Securing a Rental Car

Public transportation in Japan is safe, clean, economical, fast, and convenient. Outside of major cities, however, options are more limited. If you want the freedom to explore the countryside on your own, rental cars are the way to go.

Japan is filled with interesting cars, many as petite as the alleyways of Tookyoo. You will need to determine what type of car is best for you, depending on the number of passengers, your luggage, and where you plan to go.

Rental Car Vocabulary	
rentakaa	rental car
dai	counter for cars and other large objects
ookisa	size
chiisai	small
chuukurai	medium
ookii	big, large
nin	person, people

22

Here's the kind of conversation you might have at a rental agency.

Traveler: *Konnichiwa. Rentakaa o ichi-dai onegai shimasu.*
Hello, I'd like to rent a car, please.

Rental Agent: *Arigatoo gozaimasu. Ookisa wa dore gurai ga yoroshii desu ka.*
Thank you. What size would you like?

Traveler: *Soo, desu ne. San-nin iru shi, nimotsu mo aru shi, chuu gurai no ga ii desu.*
Hmm, there are three of us, and we have luggage, a medium-sized car should be fine.

Rental Agent: *Hai, wakarimashita. Nan-nichi o-tsukai ni narimasu ka.*
I see. How many days will you be using the car?

Traveler: *Mikka kan de ii desu.*
We will need it for three days.

| Rental Agent: | *Wakarimashita. Sumimasen, menkyoshoo o misete kudasai.* |
| | May I see your license, please? |

| Traveler: | *Kokusai menkyo desu ga yoroshii desu ka.* |
| | It's an international driving permit, is that okay? |

| Rental Agent: | *Hai, kekko desu.* |
| | That's fine. |

In the third line of the dialogue, notice the use of the particle *no*. The particle *no* is a kind of pronoun, because it takes the place of the name of the object being talked about. In this case, it takes the place of "car," although the English translation does not use a pronoun in its place. *No* is often translated as "one," and it can be used in connection with size, color, shape, or any other characteristic. Study these examples:

> *Ookii no ga ii desu ka.*
> Would you like the big one?

> *Akai no ga yoroshii desu ka.*
> Do you prefer the red one?

FACT

As with the dialogue concerning the price of the hotel room, a similar pattern of the verb *narimasu* can be found in the phrase *otsukai ni narimasu ka*. This is just a polite way of asking how long they plan to use the vehicle.

Joining a Tour

Giant buses with bright logos and dapper drivers are a common sight on even the most precarious routes around Japan. Cheerfully smocked hostesses stand dutifully (and dangerously) next to the driver clutching microphones and index cards with little-known facts. Once off the bus, they hoist flags high so members know which direction to follow.

If you are a traveler who prefers having everything prearranged, where all you have to do is show up, then Japanese bus tours are for you. Efficient and economical, they are a great opportunity to immerse yourself in Japanese culture. Your language skills will get a workout, too. Expect to be joined by twenty-five to thirty other people looking for a good time.

Ask at your hotel or any tourist information center for *tsuaa* options. There are a few different types of tours you may be interested in.

> *Kono hen de taiken tsuaa wa arimasu ka.*
> Are there any experience-type tours in this area?

> *Nihon no otera ni kyoumi ga aru no desu ga, donna tsuaa ni mooshi-komeba ii desu ka.*
> I'm interested in Japanese temples, so can you recommend a tour for me?

> *Dono ryokoogaisha ga ii desu ka.*
> What tour companies can you recommend?

Two variations on the word "which" are used when referring to options: *donna* and *dono*. *Donna* refers to the range of choices available. *Dono* is more specific; it asks: "which one?"

Go Hitchhiking

Even in this day and age, Japan is a relatively safe place to hitchhike, but it should be done with a friend, if possible. Most Japanese people are extremely kind to foreigners, especially those who are interested in Japanese culture. This attitude, along with a fear that foreigners cannot function in Japan, will cause some people to bend over backward to ensure that you get where you are trying to go. Nevertheless, be sure you exercise common sense, as even seemingly harmless situations can quickly go bad.

The following dialogue is an example of an exchange between a driver and a potential hitchhiker.

THE EVERYTHING CONVERSATIONAL JAPANESE BOOK

23

| **Driver:** | *Konnichiwa. Doko ni ikitai-n desu ka.* |
| | Hello. Where do you want to go? |

| **Hitchhiker:** | *Sapporo ni ikitai-n desu kedo . . .* |
| | I would like to go to Sapporo but . . . |

| **Driver:** | *Watashi wa Sapporo no chikaku ni sundeiru kara okutte age-masu. Doozo.* |
| | I live near Sapporo so I'll give you a ride. Get in. |

| **Hitchhiker:** | *Hontoo ni daijoobu desu ka. Doomo arigatoo gozaimasu. Sumimasen, onegai shimasu.* |
| | Are you sure it's okay? Thank you very much. Excuse me (for putting you out). Please take care of me. |

In this dialogue, there's yet another combination of the verb with a *–te* ending followed by a regular or polite verb. The verb *ageru*, in particular, is special in Japanese. When *ageru* follows a *–te* form verb, it indicates that the action is being done for the benefit of another person:

Mite ageru.
I'll take a look at it for you.

Kashite ageru.
I'll let you borrow it.

Yonde ageru.
I'll read it to you.

Quizzes and Exercises

1. Translate the following sentences into English:

   Migi ni magarimasu. _____

   Massugu ni itte, asoko no kado de hidari ni magarimasu.

   _____

   Hidari te ni arimasu. _____

2. Fill in *de* or *ni* to complete the sentence: *Asoko* _____ *migi*
   _____ *magarimasu.*

3. Conjugate the verbs in parentheses to complete the following sentence:
   Kono michi o massugu ni _____ *(iku), hidari ni* _____
   (magaru), migi te ni _____ *(aru).*

4. How would you ask for three *Shinkansen* train tickets?

   _____

5. Read the following sentence, then answer the question: *Niigata iki no
   Shinkansen wa, yon-ji juppun ni, go-ban sen de shuppatsu shimasu.* At
   what time and from which platform does the train depart?

   _____

6. Match the verbs on the left with their potential (when) form on the right.

   neru   *yondara*

   nomu   *tabetara*

   yomu   *mitara*

   miru   *netara*

   taberu   *nondara*

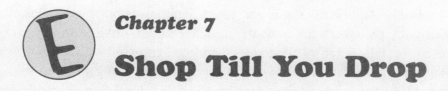

Chapter 7

Shop Till You Drop

Many visitors find shopping in Japan a pleasant experience. The staff at most stores is very polite and helpful, and there's much to catch your eye, from beautiful *sake* sets to dozens of different kinds of *tsukemono* (pickled treats).

Packing Your Wallet with Yen

Japanese money may seem a little like monopoly cash at first. Thinking in hundreds, thousands, and ten thousands takes some adjustment. Japan is notoriously expensive. Visitors to Japan may find their mouths gaping at the cash register or sheepishly scouring their wallets if not adequately forewarned.

Unlike American dollars and cents, Japan uses only yen to describe its currency. One yen is a tiny, nearly weightless coin. Ten-thousand yen comes in a crisp bill. Yen from one to ninety-nine is expressed with simply the number and the word for yen, *en*. The number words are similar to the terms used for hours and minutes introduced in Chapter 5. Something that is ten yen would be described like this: *Kore wa juu-en desu*. Something that costs thirty-five yen would be described like this: *Kore wa san-juu go en desu*.

Terms for Yen from 100 to 900	
hyaku en	one hundred yen
ni-hyaku en	two hundred yen
san-byaku en	three hundred yen
yon-hyaku en	four hundred yen
go-hyaku en	five hundred yen
roppyaku en	six hundred yen
nana-hyaku en	seven hundred yen
happyaku en	eight hundred yen
kyuu-hyaku en	nine hundred yen

Note that *hyaku* (not *ichi-hyaku*) is used for one hundred yen and that three, six, and eight hundred are irregular. For six and eight hundred, the number word is slightly altered so that when combined with *pyaku*, a double consonant sound is created.

The smallest bill in Japan is for one thousand yen, or *sen en* (not *ichi-sen*). A 2,000-yen bill was introduced in the year 2001 with a scene from Kyooto painted on it. There is also a 5,000-yen bill and a 10,000-yen bill. When discussing thousands of yen, only three (*san-zen en*) and eight (*hassen en*) are irregular, but *yon, nana,* and *kyu* are still the proper forms for four, seven, and nine.

ALERT!

When referring to 900 yen, the word *kyuu* (as opposed to *ku*) is preferred. Likewise, no one says *shi-hyaku en* or *shichi-hyaku en* for four and seven hundred, respectively.

Man is the term used for the 10,000-yen denomination in Japanese. When packing your wallet to go out in Japan, it is preferable to have a *man* or two with you. Converted into American money, it may seem ridiculous to be carrying around two hundred dollars in your wallet. In Japan, however, a *man* goes quickly.

It may seem cumbersome to be speaking in such large denominations, but using regular number words plus the term *man* makes it simple:

> *Kore wa ichi-man en desu.*
> This is 10,000 yen.

This pattern can be used for a variety of things that cost anywhere between 10,000 and 99,999 yen:

> *Sore wa nana-man en desu.*
> That is 70,000 yen.

> *Are wa kyu-man, ni-sen en desu.*
> That over there is 92,000 yen.

To continue this counting pattern, 100,000 yen becomes *juu-man,* 500,000 yen is *go-juu-man,* and so on. 1,000,000 yen is referred to as *hyaku-man.* 10,000,000 (hopefully you'll never have to use it!) is *issen-man.*

Metric Measurements

So you've found the perfect dress, but cannot figure out the size? Will a five-kilogram bag of rice feed your family for a week? Those grapes look delicious, but how many grams is a bunch? If you come from a country that does not use the metric system, it is time to dig out your old math book and start practicing conversions.

Height and Weight

If you think you are of average height in the United States, you may be surprised at how tall you feel in some places in Japan. The Japanese use centimeters to measure height, so don't be surprised to hear the following:

Se wa nan-senchi desu ka.
How many centimeters tall are you?

Whether discussing your own weight, ordering a bag of rice, or buying fruit, familiarity with grams and kilograms will also come in handy.

24

Taijuu wa nan-kiro desu ka.
How many kilograms do you weigh?

Taijuu wa dore gurai arimasu ka.
About how much do you weigh?

O-kome jukkiro onegai shimasu.
I would like ten kilograms of rice, please.

Budoo wa yon-hyaku guramu kudasai.
I'll take four hundred grams of grapes, please.

Sizing for Women

If you are a woman interested in buying *yofuku* (Western-style clothing) while in Japan, it is important to know three body measurements in centimeters: *basuto* ("bust"), *uesuto* ("waist"), and *hippu* ("hips"). As far as dress sizes go, Japanese clothing stores use S for small, M for medium, and L for large. Pronunciations must be in *katakana*-style English so that "s" comes out like *esu*, "m" is *emu* and "l" is *eru*. Average bust, waist, and hip measurements for each size are as follows:

- **Small:** bust: 78cm; waist: 60cm; hips: 80cm
- **Medium:** bust: 82cm; waist: 63cm; hips: 90cm
- **Large:** bust: 85cm; waist: 66cm; hips: 92cm

When buying pants (*zubon*), waist, hips, and inseam measurements are taken into consideration.

- **Small:** inseam: 64 cm; waist: 58-64cm; hips: 82–90cm
- **Medium:** inseam: 67cm; waist: 64–70cm; hips: 87–95cm
- **Large:** inseam: 71cm; waist: 69–77cm; hips: 92–100cm
- **Extra-large:** inseam: 75cm; waist: 77–85cm; hips: 97–105cm

Socks (*kutsushita* or *sokkusu*) for women usually come in two sizes with ranges from 22 to 24 centimeters, and 24 to 26 centimeters. Shoes (*kutsu* or *shuuzu*) usually start at 22.5 and go up to 24.5 centimeters (about a women's size 7½).

Sizing for Men

Men's fashion follows a similar pattern with the focus being on waist and inseam measurements. Typical sizes are as follows:

- **Small:** inseam: 81cm; waist: 68–76cm
- **Medium:** inseam: 84cm; waist: 76–84cm
- **Large:** inseam: 87cm; waist: 84–94cm
- **Extra-large:** inseam: 90cm; waist: 94–104cm

Shoes and socks for men also come in limited sizes. They range from about 25.5 centimeters to 27.5 centimeters. A size 27 shoe is considered large. A size 28 may be described as "really big."

FACT

Socks and shoes have their very own counter: *soku*. Two pairs of socks would be *ni-soku*. Three pairs of shoes are counted as *san-soku*, and so on. Be careful, though, the words for each half of a pair are different. If you lost one sock, you are left with *kataho*, but you are looking for *mo kataippo*.

How Much Does It Cost?

At farmers' markets, flea markets, and quaint little mom-and-pop stores, merchandise may not have price labels. With the advantage of asking in Japanese, you may even get a foreigner's discount!

25

Kore wa o-ikura desu ka.
How much is this?

Sore wa o-ikura desu ka.
How much is that?

Zenbu de o-ikura ni narimasu ka.
How much is everything all together?

Kore o kaitai-n desu ga, o-ikura de urimasu ka.
I'd like to buy this, how much are you selling it for?

With someone you do not know, it is polite to place the honorific *o* in front of the term *ikura* when asking the cost of something. Please do not confuse the honorific *o* with the *o* that identifies a direct object.

Things You Might Want to Buy

Travelers in Japan obviously have different tastes and interests. Here is just a quick list of some common souvenirs that are popular among visitors.

Popular Souvenirs	
zori	sandal worn with *kimono*
yukata	summer *kimono*
obi	belt for *kimono*
tabi	socks with a separate place for the big toe, worn with *zori*
o-sara	plate or dish
o-chawan	tea cup or rice bowl
o-choko	cup for *sake*
tokkuri	pitcher for *sake*
mimikaki	ear pick
o-tedama	fabric balls for juggling
nihon-ningyoo	Japanese doll or puppet
o-sake	Japanese rice liquor

The *o* in front of the words for "dish," "cup," "bowl," "balls for juggling," and "liquor" is also honorific but is so commonly used that it seems to have become part of the word. You leave the *o* there when inquiring about the price:

> *Sono o-sara wa o-ikura desu ka.*
> How much for the plate?

Cheap and Expensive

Finding the stores with the best buys may involve a little "shopping around":

> *Yasui yukata wa doko de kaemasu ka.*
> Where can I buy a cheap yukata?

Local townspeople may clue you in on the places with low prices:

> Asoko *no mise de wa yasui sakana o uttimasu.*
> That store over there sells cheap fish.

Shopping Vocabulary	
kau, kaimasu, kaemasu	to buy, able to buy
uru, urimasu	to sell
yasui	cheap
takai	expensive
futsuu	normal, regular
o-mise	store
-ya	shop (a suffix)
kaimono o suru	to go shopping, to shop
kaimono	shopping
o-kane	money

If you're looking for a specific item and its potential location, not a definite place, use the phrase *doko ni arimasu ka. Sumimasen, renkon wa doko ni arimasu ka.* (Excuse me, where is the lotus root?)

Try It on for Size

As with most professional staff in Japan, the salesperson will be glad to assist you with finding what you need, as long as he or she recognizes what it is you are looking for. You already know what the average sizes for different types of shoes and clothing are, but there may be exceptions, depending on where you shop. In that case, you may need to get some help:

26

Sumimasen, mo chotto ookii no wa arimasen ka.
Excuse me, don't you have a slightly bigger one?

Sumimasen, mo chotto chiisai no wa arimasu ka.
Excuse me, do you have a slightly smaller one?

Watashi-no ashi wa ni-juu-kyu senchi desu. Sono saizu wa arimasen ka.

My feet are twenty-nine centimeters. You wouldn't have that size, would you?

In English, the first and third examples may seem rather complicated and silly, but in Japanese, using the negative form of the verb is considered polite. Especially in situations where you are requesting a favor or suggesting an activity, it is wise to use the negative form of the verb accompanied by the question indicator *ka*.

26

Issho ni benkyoo shimasen ka.
Wouldn't you like to study together?

Issho ni tabemasen ka.
Wouldn't you like to eat together?

O-sooji o issho ni yarimasen ka.
Wouldn't you like to clean together?

Using the negative form of the verb is actually an expression of humbleness. The speaker must not assume that the listener will agree to the activity. With acquaintances or people you are meeting for the first time, it is best to take the humble approach and forego assumptions.

Any Color of the Rainbow

If you need to ask for a product in a particular color, you'll need to know the words for different colors. Actually, using a color word as an adjective, in most cases, requires the addition of the suffix *i*. Remember, adjectives are often modified with an extra *i* or *na* when used in front of a noun.

Color	Adjective	English
kiiro	*kiiroi*	yellow
aka	*akai*	red

Color	Adjective	English
ao	*aoi*	blue
midori	*midori iro no*	green
kuro	*kuroi*	black
shiro	*shiroi*	white
murasaki	*murasaki iro no*	purple
chairo	*chairoi*	brown

FACT

Many things that westerners would describe as green are seen as blue (*aoi*) in Japan: soybeans, the "go" color of traffic signals, the shoots of plants, and even things in an immature state.

For example: *akai booshi* ("red hat"), *kuroi neko* ("black cat"), *kirei-na kimono* ("beautiful kimono"). With some color words, like *murasaki*, it is necessary to add the word for "color," *iro*, and then the possessive *–no* before the noun:

> *Sono murasaki iro no hana wa kirei desu ne.*
> That purple flower is so beautiful.

Often, just *no* will suffice, too:

> Asoko *no orenji no kuruma ga ii desu.*
> I like that orange car over there.

Other color terms include the names of things that are naturally that color. Gray is described as *hai-iro* ("the color of ashes") or sometimes *nezumi-iro* ("the color of rats"). Brown is simply *cha-iro* ("the color of tea"). Orange is sometimes a reference to skin color, *hada-iro,* or *orenji*, in *katakana*-style English.

Can I Get That Wrapped?

Gift giving is a long-practiced custom in Japan and one that has been commercialized for optimum convenience. Souvenir shops may already have wrapped versions of their merchandise on the shelves. With food souvenirs, a plastic cross-sectioned replica of the item is often displayed. With cake shops or other stores where prewrapped is not a policy, it may be necessary to express your gift-giving intentions with either of the following phrases.

27

Kore wa o-miyage desu.
This is a gift.

Kore wa purezento desu kara, tsutsunde kudasai.
This is a present so please wrap it.

Notice the *—nde* ending on *tsutsunde*. The dictionary form of this verb is *tsutsumu;* to conjugate verbs that end in *—mu* into request form, add *—nde* (as opposed to *—te*) to the verb stem, and follow up with *kudasai*. The same goes for *nomu* ("to drink"), *kamu* ("to bite"), *yomu* ("to read"), and so on.

27

Sumimasen, kore o yonde kudasai.
Excuse me, could you please read this for me?

Gohan o yoku kande kudasai.
Please chew your food thoroughly.

Ato de biiru o ippai nonde kudasai.
Please have a beer when you are finished.

No, I Don't Need a Bag

In an age when Americans are attempting to reduce the amount of waste they generate, you may be shocked at the amount of material that is used to package products in Japan. Buy a box of cookies, and you may find not only that the plastic tray holding the cookies is encased in a foil wrap, but that each individual cookie is also wrapped. Cashiers are quick to double-bag things, too, often using their free time to prepare smaller bags to make them easily accessible for drippy things like fish and *toofu*. Please let the cashier know right away if you have brought your own bag.

28

Jibun no fukuro o motte kimashita.
I brought my own bag.

Fukuro wa arimasu.
I have a bag.

Still, you may have to stop the convenience store clerk from slipping that tiny pack of gum you bought into a plastic bag.

28

Fukuro wa irimasen.
I don't need a bag.

Fukuro wa ii desu.
I don't need a bag.

The first sentence is very straightforward, the second one, subtler. *Ii desu,* in this situation, is more like "no thank you." The English translations in both sample sentences are identical, but there is a difference in the tone of voice—the second sample sentence has a gentler, indirect tone to it.

If you choose to not bag your purchase, the cashier may want to put a sticker on the item, indicating that it has been purchased.

28

Shiiru o hatte mo ii desu ka.
Do you mind if I put on a sticker?

Shiiru o koko de harimasu ne.
I'm going to put a sticker here, okay?

Remember, if you hear a verb with a *–te* ending followed by *mo ii desu ka,* permission to do something is being asked. In this case, putting a sticker on the item purchased is the subject. In this case, *haru* becomes *hatte.* In the second sample sentence, the speaker ends with *ne.* This is a conversational technique that softens the sound of a request. *Ne,* among other things, signifies a need for confirmation from the listener.

If you plan on attending a festival in Japan, it is worth the expense to splurge on a colorful cotton summer *kimono* called a *yukata.* Luckily, *kimono* come in just one size and one size really does fit all. The desired uniform body shape (squarish) is achieved through much padding (towels and cotton are popular stuffings), folding, and wrapping. The *kimono sensei* will be on call at any store that sells *yukata*, ready to swoop in and wrap you up like a birthday present at a moment's notice.

Quizzes and Exercises

1. Translate the following prices into Japanese:

   forty-five yen   _____
   sixty-nine yen   _____
   128 yen   _____
   370 yen   _____
   500 yen   _____

2. To what is the following sentence referring? *Se ga takai ne.*

   _____

3. How do you pronounce S, M, and L in *katakana*-style English?

   _____

4. Unscramble the following sentence: *Wa kutsu o-ikura ka desu.*

_____

5. Match the Japanese adjective on the left with its English definition on the right.

ookii	small
hade	big
jimi	yellow
chiisai	flashy
kiiro	subtle

6. Make the following into a more polite question: *Issho-ni tabemasu ka.*

_____

Chapter 8
Tummy Talk

Japanese food has been popularized around the world; conversely, foreign influences have been integrated into many Japanese dishes. Most people think of sushi when they think of Japanese food, but you will find a considerable variety of things to choose from. If you have rigid eating standards, you may need to loosen them up a little or your options will quickly dwindle.

Crash Course in Menu Reading

There is something akin to a generic eatery, almost like a diner, in the Japanese *resutoran*. Menus at these establishments are nearly identical in the items they offer. You can usually find something to appease everyone's appetite if the word "restaurant" appears in the name. Even if the menu is written entirely in Japanese, you can ask if the restaurant serves a particular item.

Common Menu Items	
Noodles and Their Variations	
soba	buckwheat noodles
yakisoba	stir-fried buckwheat noodles
udon	wheat noodles
raamen	Chinese-style noodles in soup
tarako supagetei	spaghetti in a cream sauce with spicy cod eggs
tempura	deep fried vegetables and fish, often served on top of *soba* or *udon*
Rice Dishes	
karee	curry
ebi furai	fried shrimp (the long kind)
kaki furai	fried oysters
katsu-don	fried pork cutlet with onions and egg, served over rice
chaahan	fried rice, usually with some vegetables and some sort of meat
omuraisu	an omelet with rice inside, usually topped with ketchup
maabo doofu	spicy *toofu* with minced meat sauce
Sandwiches and Toast	
hamu sando	ham sandwich
tamago sando	egg salad sandwich

Sandwiches and Toast (continued)

toosuto	toast
chiizu toosuto	cheese toast

Desserts

keeki setto	cake and either coffee or tea
aisu kuriimu	ice cream
furuutsu pafe	fruit parfait

Drink Options

You may be served a complimentary cup of green tea (*o-cha*) or barley tea (*mugicha*) upon being seated. Many establishments offer alcohol, *o-sake,* as a beverage option regardless of the time of day. Both draught and bottled beer are commonly available, but the smaller 12-oz bottles are seldom available.

FACT

Sake, a rice liquor, is a drink that enjoyed a popular stint in the States during the 1970s, but its varieties and subtleties, along with its deep roots in Japanese tradition, have yet to be thoroughly explored. Hot or chilled, it is usually sold in and served from a gigantic bottle. If you would like to drink *sake*, specify that you want *Nihon-shu,* as the term *o-sake* can mean any alcoholic drink.

Counters for drinks vary according to the shape of their containers, so requesting another cup of coffee is phrased differently than when ordering small bottles of hot *sake*:

Koohii o moo ippai onegai shimasu.
One more coffee, please.

Atsukan o san-bon kudasai.
Three bottles of hot rice wine, please.

With draught beer, the basic counting words are appropriate:

Nama biiru o futatsu kudasai.
Two draught beers, please.

Beverages	
nama biiru	draught beer
bin biiru	bottled beer, but the bottles are big
kan biiru	beer in a can
gurasu wain, aka	glass of red wine
gurasu wain, shiro	glass of white wine
Nihon-shu	Japanese rice liquor
hiyazake	chilled *sake* served in an overflowing cup
atsukan	hot *sake* served in a small pitcher with tiny cups
koocha	black tea (often made from Lipton tea bags)
hotto koohii	hot coffee
aisu koohii	ice-coffee
orenji juusu	orange juice
ringo juusu	apple juice
yasai juusu	vegetable juice

For the Vegetarian

Vegetarians in Japan have it rough. Not only has meat come to be considered a status symbol, fish is a very common ingredient in soup broths. To make matters worse, you can ask if there is meat in the soup and get a negative reply, but then choke on a chunk of pork halfway through your meal.

There seems to be some discrepancy between Japanese and American definitions of what constitutes meat. The word *niku,* for example, is translated as the generic "meat," but in Japan, it is most often associated with beef. For example, *yaki-niku* ("grilled meat") shops are common throughout Japan, but they serve grilled beef almost exclusively. If you ask a server whether there is meat in the soup, he or she may say that there isn't, even if there is bacon floating around in it. To the server, bacon isn't meat because it isn't beef. If you are a strict vegetarian, it may be necessary to get very specific about what exactly you do and do not eat.

gyuu-niku	beef
tori-niku	chicken
buta-niku	pork
beekon	bacon
hamu	ham
sakana	fish

Two words for a vegetarian diet exist in the Japanese language. The first exposes Japan's Buddhist monk-style vegetarian roots: *saishokushugisha*. Lately, however, a *katakana* version of the English word has enjoyed wide circulation: *bejitarian*. Consider the following phrases as a sort of self-defense for vegetarians.

29

Watashi wa bejitarian desu.
I'm a vegetarian.

Niku o tabemasen.
I don't eat meat.

Chaahan o niku nashi ni dekimasen ka.
Can you make it without meat?

O-tsuyu no dashi wa nan desu ka.
What is the soup broth made of?

Niku ga haittenai no wa dochira desu ka.
Which items are meatless?

Some vegetarians declare a brief hiatus from their regimented diet upon arriving in Japan. In restaurants, you have some options, but what are the advantages of insulting someone who has invited you over for a feast by declaring that you cannot eat the main course? After all, how can you come to Japan and not try sushi?

Ordering with Flair

In Japan, it is up to the customer to let the server know when he or she is ready to order. Once you have deciphered the menu, or at least made an educated guess about what options may be available, you can signal your server by raising a finger. Here's a good example of what placing an order might be like:

30

Server:	*Moo o-kimari desu ka.*	
	Have you decided?	

Customer:	*Sumimasen menyu ga yomemasen. Omuraisu wa arimasu ka.*
	Excuse me, I cannot read the menu. Do you have rice omelets?

Server:	*Hai, arimasu. Sumimasen ne eigo no menyu ga arimasen.*
	Yes, we do. I'm sorry we do not have an English menu.

Customer:	*Ii desu yo. Jaa, omuraisu o hitotsu kudasai. Moo hitotsu kikitain desu ga karee raisu wa arimasu ka.*
	That's okay. We'll take one rice omelet. I have something else I'd like to ask, though. Do you have curry rice?

Server:	*Hai, arimasu.*
	Yes, we do.

Customer:	*Sono karee wa karai desu ka, sore to mo amai desu ka.* Is the curry spicy or sweet?
Server:	*Uchi no karee wa kekko karai desu. Daijoobu desu ka.* Our curry is pretty spicy. Is that okay?
Customer:	*Hai, karai hoo ga ii desu.* I'm glad it is spicy.
Server:	*Jaa, omuraisu o hitotsu to karakuchi karee raisu o hitotsu.* *Nomimono wa doo shimasu ka.* Alright, so that's one rice omelet and one spicy curry. What about drinks?
Customer:	*Nomimono wa tsukimasu ka.* Are drinks included?
Server:	*Hai, ocha ka koohii ga tsukimasu.* Yes, you can get coffee or tea with your order.
Customer:	*Jaa, hitotsu zutsu onegai shimasu.* Alright, one of each, please.

I Cannot

Look at the second line of the dialogue. The verb *yomemasen* is an example of a verb tense that is peculiar to Japanese. You already know that the formal negative form of verbs is conveyed with the *–masen* ending. Can you find the difference in spelling between *yomimasen* ("I do not read") and *yomemasen* ("I cannot read")? To pinpoint the difference, let's start by looking at the plain form of the verb: *yomu*.

The verb ending, in this case *–mu*, must be changed to its simple *–masu* form: *yomimasu*. The vowel in the middle is changed to *–e*: *yomemasu*. This means "I can read." In English, the helping verb "can" is used to convey ability, but in Japanese, ability is a verb tense unto itself. The simple form of *yomemasu* is *yomeru*. The negative forms are *yomemasen* and *yomenai*, respectively.

Verbs that end in *–ku, –gu, –ru* and so on can be conjugated in the same way. *Oyogu,* "to swim," becomes *oyogeru, oyogenai, oyogemasu, oyogemasen.* Note that the basic stem is *oyog–,* and that the various endings are tacked on to this stem. In the previous list, can you identify which conjugation means "I can swim," and which means "I cannot swim"?

Even the linguistically delinquint *iku* adheres to this rule. The *ku* is changed to *ke* to form the potential positive *ikeru,* "I can go," or the potential negative *ikenai,* "I cannot go."

Feeling Possessive

The term *uchi* has both literal and figurative meanings. Teachers often use the term *uchi no ko* when referring to their students, implying that they feel the responsibility of a parent. It can also be used in reference to one's real home and family; for example:

> *Uchi no inu wa urusai desu.*
> The dog we have at home is noisy.

FACT

The *no* following *uchi* in these examples is a possessive adjective. It changes nouns and pronouns such as *watashi, kare, kanojo, uchi,* etc., into their possessive forms (her, his, their, our, and so on).

31

> *Kanojo no kaminoke wa nagai desu.*
> Her hair is long.

> *Watashi-tachi no kome wa oishii desu.*
> Our rice is delicious.

In other situations, when following someone's name, for instance, *no* has the same function as a possessive apostrophe in written English.

31

Watanabe-san no uchi wa hiroi desu.
The Watanabe's house is spacious.

Noguchi-san no kuruma wa akai desu.
Mr. Noguchi's car is red.

Identifying Direction, Giving Advice

Using the word *hoo* in Japanese helps to identify a characteristic aspect of the subject of conversation. Used with an adjective in its regular form, *hoo* indicates a certain style, or way: "sweet," for example, or "bright." In this form, it can be used to express a preference for something:

Amai hoo ga oishii desu.
The sweeter the better.

When the phrase . . . *hoo ga ii desu* follows a verb with a past-tense ending like *–ta* or *–da*, it serves as a suggestion or recommendation:

Tabeta hoo ga ii desu.
I recommend you eat it.

Yonda hoo ga ii desu.
It would be best to read it.

What's Included

When you go to a restaurant, you can choose virtually any of the main dishes and turn it into a complete meal by saying *Teishoku onegai shimasu.* The side dishes will probably include a bowl of rice (say *oomori, kudasai* if you want a big helping), *tsukemono* (Japanese-style pickles), and *miso shiru* (soybean paste soup) or a clear soup. Salads often come with orders of spaghetti or curry. Coffee or tea is sometimes included, or can be tacked on for an extra *hyaku en* or so.

You will want to know what is included with your meal, so please ask:

Ebi furai ni wa nani ga tsukimasu ka.
What is included with the fried shrimp?

Or, if you want to know if a specific item comes with your meal, you can say, for example:

Karee ni wa sarada ga tsukimasu ka.
Does the curry come with a salad?

Some circumstances may move you to make special requests:

Koohii o tsukereba, o-ikura ni narimasu ka.
How much would it cost to add a coffee?

These examples are filled with particles, so let's review a little. The very definition of the verb *tsuku* requires the presence of *ni*, because it is referring to something being included or added. The "job" of *ni* is to identify that which is being attached.

QUESTION?

When is it appropriate to replace *wa* with *ga*?
Good question. The two are often interchangeable, but there are some instances where one is preferred over the other. For example, if you request an item that is not on the menu, the reply will be: *Sore wa arimasen.* If you request an item that is on the menu, but isn't available, the reply will be: *Sore ga arimasen.*

In the first example, the fried shrimp is followed by two different particles: *ni* and *wa*. *Ni* pinpoints the object to which something will be attached, while *wa* isolates the sentence subject (in both cases, "fried shrimp"). The same goes for *karee* in the second example: *ni* labels what is being attached and *wa* points out the subject.

The particle *ga* also wears many different hats. Notice how it follows *nani* ("what") in the first sentence and *sarada* ("salad") in the second. The role being played in these two examples is to identify the indirect object: that which is being attached, or in this case, what comes with the meal.

Ga can also take the place of *wa* in situations where the subject is being scrutinized. Its role, in that case, becomes that of the subject identifier:

> *Omuraisu ga oishisoo desu.*
> The rice omelet looks delicious.

Before and After the Meal

First introduced in Chapter 5, the phrase *itadakimasu* is used when receiving anything in Japan. "I humbly receive" is the literal translation, but it has connotations of various underlying feelings. Used sincerely, it is a sign of respect towards the gift-giver, reflects a reverence for the food, and also shows an appreciation for the work that went into preparing it.

Most often uttered before consuming a meal or snack, it is also used before accepting even a tiny piece of chocolate. At school lunches, once the servers have dished out everyone's portions, students (as well as teachers and staff) say *itadakimasu* before digging in.

FACT

You are not expected to tip your server or cab driver. Most Japanese people are aware of the custom and there is even a *katakana*-style English word for it, *chippu*. However, the practice of tipping is rare to nonexistent in Japan.

On the flipside we've got *gochisoo sama deshita*. When the meal is over, belts loosened and plates scraped, *gochisoo sama deshita* is a way of saying "thanks for running around and working so hard to prepare this meal." Put more simply it translates to, "It was a feast." Even if it was just tea and crackers, it is polite to use this phrase at the end of the meal.

Gochisoo sama desu, the present-tense version, is sometimes used in place of *itadakimasu.* This variation can be heard most often in situations where what was received will not be consumed in the presence of the gift-giver. For example, if someone brings back cookies as a souvenir from a trip, it is fine to use *gochisoo sama desu* when accepting the treat. If you plan to pop it into your mouth right away, throw in an *itadakimasu* before it touches your tongue, at least.

A Mouthful of Words

Let's end the chapter with a few other words related to eating.

oishii	delicious
oishikunai	not delicious
attakai uchi	while it is hot/warm
sameru, sametara	to cool, if it cools
kuchi	mouth
otosu, otosanai	to drop, don't drop
motte kuru, motte kite	to bring

Note that two of these words contain the suffix –*nai*; one is an adjective, *oishikunai,* and one is a verb, *otosanai. Nai* can be likened to the English words "not" and "don't." It is an indicator of the negative form and can be used with both adjectives and verbs, with slight alterations.

Performing Negative Surgery on Adjectives

Getting from *oishii* to *oishikunai* involves a little verbal surgery: Drop the last vowel and add –*kunai.* In Japanese, adjectives are like verbs in the sense that they are conjugated according to tense and case. Color words become adjectives by adding the vowel *i.* Other adjectives, such as *kirei* ("beautiful"), are followed by *na.* When changing the adjective to its negative form, it is necessary to sometimes first add –*ku* before tacking on the –*nai.* Occasionally, the –*nai* is already built into the adjective as in the word *tondemonai,* "terrible!"

The *ku* + *nai* ending rule can be applied to all adjectives that end in *i* (which is most of them) like *omoshiroi* ("interesting"). Look at these sentences:

> *Kono eiga wa omoshirokunai desu.*
> This movie is not interesting.

Okashii ("funny," "entertaining") is conjugated in the same way:

> *Sono koto wa okashikunai desu.*
> That matter is not funny.

Adjectives that do not end in *i*, such as *tokubetsu* ("special"), are conjugated in different ways. Sometimes, a –*na* is tacked on before placing the describing word in front of a noun:

> *Kare wa tokubetsuna hito desu.*
> He is a special person.

In other cases, like the adjective *nise* ("fake"), no modification is necessary at all:

> *Kore wa nise satsu desu.*
> This is a fake bill.

To change either of the above adjectives to the negative, however, the suffix –*janai* can be used. *Janai* is an informal version of the polite negative *ja arimasen*:

> *Watashi no koe wa tokubetsu janai desu.*
> My voice is nothing special.

Since *nise* has no other modifications, however, the word *mono* ("thing") must be inserted before the negative suffix:

> *Kono o-kane wa nise mono janai desu.*
> This money is not fake.

Making Verbs Negative

To change a verb into the negative form, you must first be familiar with its plain form. The verb *otosu* ("to drop"), ends in *–su*. This *–su* must first be changed to it's "a" version, *–sa*, before adding the negative *–nai*. The result is *otosanai*. This goes for most verbs with the endings *ku, ru, su, mu*, etc. *Kaku* becomes *kakanai*, *naru* becomes *naranai*, *tobu* becomes *tobanai*, and so on.

32

Otosanai de kudasai.
Please don't drop it.

Koko de wa hashiranai de kudasai.
Please don't run here.

Kutsu o hakanai de kudasai.
Please don't put your shoes on.

Kare to hanasanai de kudasai.
Please don't talk to him.

When in command form, it is rare to find a negative verb without *de* following it. Tacking on *kudasai* at the end keeps everyone happy and polite. Without the *de* and *kudasai*, the verb + *nai* conjugation becomes very direct and somewhat negative.

ALERT!

One exception is for verbs like *iu* ("to say"). In this case it is necessary to change the *u* to *–wa* before adding *–nai*. If you want someone to refrain from speaking, say *Iwanai de kudasai*.

32

Watashi wa ikanai.
I won't go.

Watashi wa shinbun o yomanai.
I don't read the newspaper.

Phrasal Verbs

Verbs in Japanese are often combined to make a new verb. In the case of *motte kite*, the verbs *motsu* ("to carry") and *kuru* ("to come") are combined to make the verb *motte kuru* ("to bring"). *Motsu*, as the first verb in the phrase, automatically gets changed to the present "–ing" form while *kuru* can stay in its plain present form, or be conjugated into any other tense: *motte kite, motte kita, motte kimasu, motte kimasen,* and so on.

Kuru and *iku* are two verbs that are regularly combined with other verbs, and even with each other. You may hear this combination most often in the saying *Itte kimasu!* which means "I will go and come back." When Japanese people take leave of their families in the morning, this is the standard parting phrase.

Quizzes and Exercises

1. Rearrange the following words to make a sentence: *kudasai juusu futatsu ringo o*

   _____

2. Imagine you are a vegetarian. Fill in the missing word: _____ *o tabemasen.*

3. Change the following verbs into their "I cannot" and "I can" versions:

   yomu _____
   suru _____
   iku _____

4. Which particle must accompany the verb *tsukimasu?*

5. When do you use the following phrases? *itadakimasu, gochisoo sama deshita*

Chapter 9

Making Introductions

Japanese culture is full of gestures, such as bowing, that reflect humility and respect. Incorporating the bow successfully into your self-introduction will take some practice. Of course, some introductions are easier than others. Many visitors to Japan discover that they have trouble keeping the names of all their acquaintances straight, but don't get discouraged. With practice, you can get everyone's name right, the first time.

Bowing Customs

From their cars, in shops and restaurants, on the street, in schools, and at their workplaces, Japanese people use bows to communicate status and express appreciation. Bows are a way to say "I'm sorry," "Thank you," "Nice to meet you," and "Excuse me." People bow as a way to start conversations, acknowledge someone's presence, and as a parting gesture. You may even see people bowing while they are talking on the phone.

QUESTION?

When should I bow?
It depends on the situation of course. If someone bows to you, return the gesture, making your own slightly deeper and longer, just in case. Bows vary from a slight nod of the head to the person letting you make a right turn in traffic to little old ladies in full prostration, heads touching the rice mats in front of them.

How to Bow

Anytime you are meeting someone for the first time, it is polite (and also culturally sensitive) to start with a bow. The angles for bowing vary from a shallow fifteen degrees (usually only made by the president of a company, school principal, or the prime minister) to a full forty-five-degree bow. Make your bows low and slightly long, and you will offend no one.

Men bow with their hands at their sides, heels together. Women touch their hands together in front. Your back should be straight and your eyes downcast.

The Do-It-All Verb

"To bow" in Japanese, is *ojigi suru*. *Suru*, "to do," is an all-encompassing verb that is often combined with other words: *kaimono suru* ("to go shopping"), *ai suru* ("to love"), *kenka suru* ("to fight"). It can often be found following *katakana*-style English verbs in an effort to make them more Japanese.

33

Kono gakkoo no seito wa yoku kanningu suru.
The students at this school cheat often.

Koko ni sain suru.
Here is where you sign.

Suru is the regular form; *shimasu* is the more formal word. Conjugations of this verb mostly start with the formal root *shi*. To make a negative, use the formal root *shi* and add *–nai*: *shinai*.

33

Kono gakkoo no seito wa kanningu shinai.
The students at this school do not cheat.

Uchi no danna to kenka shinai.
My husband and I do not fight.

To make the command form, add *–te*: *shite*. For the past tense, use *–ta*.

33

Koko ni sain shite kudasai.
Please sign here.

Koko ni sain shita.
She signed here.

Please note that the first word (in most cases, the noun) is not modified; only the second word, the verb *suru*, is conjugated.

Introducing Yourself

Here it is, the all-important moment your palms have been sweating about. Everyone wants to make a good first impression and a winning self-introduction is a good way to start.

Sample Self-Introductions

The first sample self-introduction is formal and appropriate in a work situation, at school, in an office or business establishment, or with someone who is older than you.

34

Hajimemashite.
It is nice to meet you.

Watashi wa Arekkusu Sumisu to mooshimasu.
My name is Alex Smith.

Amerika no Ohaio shuu kara kimashita.
I am from Ohio, in the United States of America.

Doozo yoroshiku onegaita shimasu.
Please regard me in your favor from now on.

Make a bow at the end of your introduction. You can time your bow so that it comes just after the final word, or you can start the bow at *doozo* and come back up around *onegai shimasu.*

The next sample self-introduction is more casual, but still polite, and would be appropriate when meeting people about the same age or younger than you.

34

Hajimemashite.
Nice to meet you.

Watashi wa Arekkusu Sumisu desu.
My name is Alex Smith.

Amerika no shussin desu.
I'm from the States.

Yoroshiku onegai shimasu.
It's a pleasure. (Literally, "Please look out for me.")

When making your self-introduction in a formal setting, it is polite to stand, bow first, and then begin your speech. Among friends, it is not necessary to stand if everyone is sitting.

ALERT!

Hajimemashite is only used when you introduce yourself. In English, upon leaving someone you may have just met, it is common to say, "It was nice to have met you." But, in Japan, you only say *hajimemashite* once, during your introduction.

Points of Consideration

During your self-introduction, it is not necessary to say *watashi* ("I") more than once. There are several words for referring to oneself in Japanese, but due to the high value placed on humility in the culture, the reference to oneself is often only alluded to. In the example self-introduction, Alex Smith gives her name in the second sentence. In the third, she states where she is from, but does not repeat *watashi wa*.

There are many ways to give your background information. The phrase *kara kimashita* follows your place of origin, or hometown and literally means "came from."

The final sentence in the two examples is a way of establishing ties with the people you are meeting. There is really no equivalent for *doozo yoroshiku onegai shimasu* in English. It is an extremely polite and formal way of saying, "please take care of me, look out for me, and remember me favorably from now on." The closest analogy in English is the phrase "It was nice to meet you," although this should not be confused with *hajimemashite*, which is used at the beginning of an introduction. The less formal, but still polite, phrase *yoroshiku* is common even among old friends and neighbors. It often accompanies a request for a favor.

A Little Background

Hajimemashite comes from the verb *hajimaru*, to start or begin. The *–te* ending suggests the present perfect tense, an attitude suitable for a first meeting. Perhaps this is why it is only used once with each person you meet.

It is also common to find a variation of this verb, *–hajimeru*, as the second half of many compound verbs. For example: *aruki hajimeru* ("to start walking"), *oshie hajimeru* ("to start teaching"), and so on. The noun form, literally "the start" or "beginning," is *hajimari* or *hajime*.

F A C T

If can't remember whether you have already met somebody or not, you can gently ask: *Hajimete desu ka.* ("Is this our first meeting?") Another way to save face is with the following: *Kao o oboete imasu da kedo o-namae wa wakarimasen.* ("You look familiar but I can't remember your name.")

Introducing Someone Else

Since you are the one studying this book, you may want to act as the spokesperson for your fellow travelers. Or, if you are alone, you may have pictures of family members or other special people that you want to share with your newfound friends. The following introduction samples are appropriate in either situation.

Family Members

In Japanese, the words for older and younger siblings are different. In addition, when talking about your own family, you use words that are different than when referring to someone else's family members. Also, the humbleness ingrained in Japanese culture requires that you refer to anything related to yourself as less than equal to the person with whom you are talking. This goes for family members, especially.

Words for Family Members and Relatives

In Reference to Your Own Family

haha-oya	mother, mommy, mama
chichi-oya	father, dad, papa
kanai, tsuma	wife
otto	husband
musume	daughter
musuko	son
ani	older brother
ane	older sister
otooto	younger brother
imooto	younger sister
oba	aunt
oji	uncle
sobo	grandmother
sofu	grandfather
mago	grandchild
oi	nephew
mei	niece

In Reference to Someone Else's Family

o-kaa-san	mother
o-too-san	father
oku-san	wife
go-shujin, danna-san	husband
musume-san	daughter
musuko-san	son
o-ko-san	child
o-nii-san	older brother

In Reference to Someone Else's Family (continued)

o-nee-san	older sister
otooto-san	younger brother
imooto-san	younger sister
oba-san	aunt
oji-san	uncle
o-baa-san	grandmother
o-jii-san	grandfather
omago-san	grandchild
oi-go-san	nephew
mei-go-san	niece

35

Kore ga kanai/otto desu.
This is my wife/husband.

Kore ga musume/musuko desu.
This is my daughter/son.

Kore ga haha-oya desu.
This is my mother.

Kore ga chichi-oya desu.
This is my father.

Kore ga uchi de katteiru inu desu.
This is my pet dog.

Kore ga otooto/ani desu.
This is my younger/older brother.

Kore ga imooto/ane desu.
This is my younger/older sister.

One Big Happy Family

The names for different family members can also be used as terms of endearment. When talking with someone who is slightly older than you, it is perfectly acceptable to refer to her as *oba-san*. Similarly, you can call an elderly woman *o-baa-san*.

Mistakes can be the source of both amusement and embarrassment. The elderly woman across the street would probably be flattered if you called her *oba-san*, but your friend's older sister probably wouldn't appreciate being called *o-baa-san*. You can use other family terms to refer to people of approximately the same age as your own family members. *O-nee-san*, for example, is used to refer to young women in general. This policy is a lifesaver when you accidentally forget someone's name.

Friends and Other Special People

Here are a few more examples for describing friendships and romantic relationships.

36

Kochira wa watashi no tomodachi desu.
This is my friend.

Kono hito wa watashi no booifurendo desu.
This is my boyfriend

Soko ni watashi no kareshi ga imasu.
My boyfriend is right there.

Kono hito wa boku no gaarufurendo desu.
This is my girlfriend.

Koko ni boku no kanojo ga imasu.
My girlfriend is here.

Note that the second and fourth examples use *katakana* English versions of the words "boyfriend" and "girlfriend." The third and fifth examples use the traditional Japanese words for "he" and "she," which can also be construed as a romantic relationship.

Boku is another way of referring to yourself. Until recently, this word was mostly used by males. Lately, elementary school girls have adopted it in reference to themselves as well. It is definitely more casual than *watashi*.

Honorific Adjustments

As can be seen in the various examples in this chapter, respect is shown with the use of three different prefixes and suffixes: *o*, *go*, and *san*. The honorific prefixes *o* and *go* are combined with certain nouns to create a more formal statement or question.

> *O-namae wa nan desu ka.*
> What is your name?

> *Go-shusshin wa doko desu ka.*
> Where are you from?

> *O-umare wa doko desu ka.*
> Where were you born?

Some things are nearly always referred to in their honorific form: *o-sake* ("rice liquor"), *o-furo* ("bath"), *o-kome* ("rice"), and *o-tomodachi* ("friend"), among others. People who speak an almost aristocratic Japanese will often put *o* in front of everything: *o-isu* ("chair"), *o-shokuji* ("meal"), and *o-hana* ("nose"), for example.

O is also used to refer to another person's family members. You would call your friend's mother *o-kaasan*, for example, and to her children as *o-oko-san*. These references to other people's relatives often have honorifics on either end: *o* in front and *san* bringing up the rear.

San is an honorific suffix that is routinely tacked on to people's names. Rarely are people addressed by their first names only. Even school teachers address their students with the suffix *san*, attached to their family name. Friends also use *san*, or sometimes the more intimate *chan*. *Chan* is also used for babies and little girls, whereas *kun* is tacked on to the names of boys, and is sometimes used when addressing men who are younger than the speaker.

Figuring Out the Names

Upon first hearing people introduce themselves in Japanese, you may be confused about what to call them. To be polite, it is best to refer to people by their last names, followed by the suffix *–san*. Now, if you could only figure out which is the surname.

Family Names and First Names

In Japanese, the last name is always given first. "Surname," in Japanese, is *myooji*. First names are referred to as *shita no namae,* literally, "the bottom name." This is perhaps due to the way in which Japanese is traditionally written—vertically, with the surname first, and the given name written below it.

> *Kanai no Watanabe Keisuke desu.*
> I'm Keisuke Watanabe from Kanai.

> *Kaizuka no Nogata Yumiko desu.*
> I'm Yumiko Nogata from Kaizuka.

Depending on the situation, it may or may not be appropriate to refer to someone by his or her first name. Even if you are on a first-name basis, it is still customary to attach *–san*, *–chan*, or *–kun* to the end: *Maki-chan, Nobu-kun,* etc.

Western Names

Japanese are familiar with the western practice of giving surnames last, but may still be confused about what to call you. When you are meeting a business associate or striking up an acquaintance for the first time, it may be best to add, after your self-introduction, "Please call me . . . ," to clear up any confusion.

> *Watashi wa Eerikku Furan to mooshimasu. Eerikku to yonde kudasai.*
> My name is Eric Flan. Please call me Eric.

FACT

Since Japanese people almost always attach some suffix (*–san, –chan, –kun, –sama*) to personal names, whether it be your given name or surname, they will most likely want to address you with some honorific or official title. If you are teaching, *sensei* ("teacher") will most likely be attached to your name, even if it's just your first name, like "Mr. Eric" or "Mrs. Alex."

Common Last Names

The ten most common surnames in Japan are:

- *Satoo*
- *Suzuki*
- *Takahashi*
- *Tanaka*
- *Watanabe*
- *Itoo*
- *Yamamoto*
- *Kobayashi*
- *Saitoo*
- *Nakamura*

When you arrive in Japan and begin meeting people, you may be overwhelmed at all the new faces and names to remember. If you know a little bit of vocabulary, then you can get a mental picture of what some of the names represent, thereby making them easier to recall. Another technique is to associate something distinct about that person's appearance and try to tie it into his or her name. If all else fails, carry a notebook and pen and ask the person to write his or her name in *kanji*, then add the phonetic spelling above or below it. A great conversation starter is to get people to explain their names to you.

Japanese surnames usually incorporate a place or geographic location. The *yama* in *Yamamoto*, for example, means "mountain." The name *Yamamoto* means "mountain origin." If you meet someone with this name, try to imagine her ancestors living in a mountain village and associate that image with her.

The word *naka* is found in two of the most common names: *Tanaka* and *Nakamura. Naka* means "inside" or "middle," or sometimes, "out of." Therefore, *Ta* ("rice paddy") plus *naka* ("middle") may indicate that this person's ancestors were rice farmers or lived in the middle of a paddy. *Mura* means "village" and is another common surname in Japanese. The name *Nakamura* means "inside the village."

Once you are able to recognize some *kanji* characters, deciphering last names will become even easier. Also, the more time you spend in Japan, the more you will hear the same names over and over again. Repetition is a great teacher.

Common First Names for Women

Women's names often end in *–ko* ("child") or *–mi* ("beautiful"), so if you hear a name with one of those syllables in it, it is most likely a woman's name. Some examples of common female names are:

- *Yumiko*
- *Akiko*
- *Yuriko*
- *Tomoko*

- *Tomomi*
- *Hiromi*
- *Ayumi*

Remember, there are many different *kanji* to represent the same sounds, so *Tomomi* can be written in *kanji* in several different ways. Even *mi* and *ko* have various forms, but the characters for "beautiful" and "child" are the ones most commonly used.

FACT

There is a recent trend to write girls' names in *hiragana* instead of *kanji*. Some parents are doing this deliberately to avoid ascribing a meaning, and therefore expectation, to the name. Others see *hiragana* as Japan's exclusive language and so are using it for reasons of cultural or national pride.

Men's Given Names

Men's names are often long and may be difficult to remember. Four-syllable names are not uncommon, especially if the person is the oldest son. Luckily, names are often shortened to an easy nickname. Some male names you may run across are:

- *Takahiro*
- *Tomohiro*
- *Naoki*
- *Kentaroo*

- *Yuuki*
- *Hiroto*
- *Toshiaki*

Characters often used in male names are *hiro* ("wide," "expansive"), *ta* ("fat," "big"), *ki* ("tree," "standing"). Unusual names that express the hopes of the parents can be found in *Kokoro* ("heart," "mind"), *Shizuka* ("quiet"), *Kakeru* ("build," "span"), *Mamoru* ("protect"), and *Shinken* ("trust," "knowledge").

The Hometown

So you've mastered the ability to introduce yourself, and you have become familiar with Japanese names, including which comes first. Now how about some more personal information, namely, one's *shusshin,* or hometown.

You may meet people from all over Japan, depending on where you travel. Memorization of all forty-five prefectures is not necessary, but becoming familiar with the major islands might prevent future embarrassment. Also, knowing what somebody is referring to—prefecture, city, island, town, or village—will help you get a picture of his or her background.

The major islands of Japan are Hokkaido, Honshu, Shikoku, Kyuushu, and Okinawa. When referring to a prefecture, the word *ken* is added to the place name. The word *shi* is used for cities; for towns and villages, *machi* and *mura*, respectively. Islands are called *shima*, but this word is usually prefaced with the particle *ga* following the island's name, as in *Sado-ga-shima*. This is mostly true when referring to the hundreds of small islands that dot the coasts of Japan.

37

Watashi wa Hokkaido no Sapporo-shi no shusshin desu.
My hometown is Sapporo, Hokkaido.

Watashi wa Fukushima-ken kara kimashita.
I'm from Fukushima Prefecture.

Niibo mura ga shusshin desu.
Niibo Village is my birthplace.

Boku wa Shibata-shi kara kita.
I'm from Shibata City.

Notice the two different past-tense versions of the verb *kuru* ("to come"). The first one is polite, the second more informal.

Quizzes and Exercises

1. Guess the meaning of the following *katakana*-style English + *suru* verbal phrases.

    jaanpu suru   _____
    mikkusu suru   _____
    doraibu suru   _____

2. Number the following sentences in order from 1–4 to construct a proper self-introduction.

    Doozo yoroshiku onegai shimasu.
    Watashi wa Jiimu Teetto to mooshimasu.
    Hajimemashite.
    Amerika no Nyuu Yooku kara kimashita.

3. Which question refers to your place of birth?

   Hajimete desu ka.
   Amerika no shusshin desu ka.
   Arekkusu Sumisu desu.

4. Label the following family member terms "M" for "mine" or "O" for "others."

   haha   _____
   imooto-san   _____
   sobo   _____
   otto   _____
   okusan   _____
   kodomosan   _____

5. Unscramble the following words to make a sentence introducing your girlfriend: *kanojo no desu wa kore boku*

   _____

6. Draw a line to match each word with its definition.

mura	city
shi	town
ken	prefecture
machi	island
shima	village

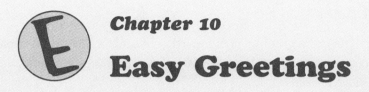

Chapter 10
Easy Greetings

Friendly efforts to communicate usually spawn deeper connections with people, whether they are new or old friends, acquaintances, or colleagues. The well-timed *aisatsu* ("greeting") is of utmost importance in everyday Japanese conversation.

Among Friends

Making friends with people who speak Japanese gives you inspiration to study and provides good listening comprehension practice. These friendships are the best way to develop your language abilities.

Topping the Charts

The most common greeting is the word *genki*. It is a shortened version of the phrase *o-genki desu ka*, "How are you?" Another, more casual, version is the abbreviated *genki ka*.

The most polite response to this question is, of course, *genki desu yo*, "I'm fine." (Notice you do not use the honorific *o-* in front of *genki* when referring to yourself.) But with friends, it is not necessary to be polite all the time. Other possible responses, perhaps more frank ones, to the question *genki* are listed in the following table.

Responses to *Genki*	
maamaa	so-so
bochi-bochi	so-so
ammari	not really
chotto kaze gimi	I feel like I'm catching a cold.
genki, demo isogashii	I'm fine, but busy.

If you look up *genki* in a dictionary, it will say "spirits, vigor, energy," but the general connotation of the word, especially when used in the phrase *o-genki desu ka,* is to inquire after someone's well-being. Therefore, it is best translated as "How are you?"

Other Options

Doomo itsumo o-sewa ni natte imasu. This is a doozy. It means, "Thanks for always looking out for me," and is reserved for the best of friends. You may also hear it between teachers and their students' parents, among neighbors, or business associates.

Friends often greet each other with a reference to the last time they were together. If you last met your friend at a dinner party, then you would start out with something like this:

Kono mae wa doomo gochisoo sama deshita.
Thanks for the great dinner the other night.

Or, if a friend had helped you rearrange your apartment you would say:

Kono mae wa doomo ne.
Thanks for the other day.

The phrase *kono mae* is directly translated to "the time before this," and is most often used in the following greeting:

Kono mae wa doomo o-sewa ni narimashita.
Thanks for doing me a favor recently.

Another word that means almost the same thing is *kono aida*, or informally, *konaida*. *Kono aida* also refers to "the other day," "recently," or "some time ago'" and can be found in the phrase:

Kono aida wa doomo gochisoo sama deshita.
Thanks for the great feast the other day.

Entering and Leaving Someone's Home

In Japan, the entryway of anyone's home, the *genkan*, is considered public space. Vegetable sellers, religious fanatics, and campaigning politicians, as well as family and friends, can open your front door and come right in. Most people call out a greeting upon opening the door and then wait for the owner of the place to come before actually stepping inside.

Friendly neighbors, and even people you have just met (especially in a festival situation) are sure to invite you in:

Doozo, agatte kudasai.
Please, come in.

Likewise, if you are entertaining people in your home, it is important to welcome them appropriately:

Doozo, agarimasen ka.
Won't you come in, please?

FACT

The verb *agaru* literally means "to come up." The design of most Japanese entryways is such that you must actually step up in order to enter. Note the command form of *agaru* with a double consonant is used in the first example: *agatte*. It is softened by the *kudasai* that follows. *Agarimasen* is the ultrapolite, nonassuming negative form of the verb.

Don't Mind if I Do

Once you have been invited into someone's home, the polite response is *ojama shimasu*. This phrase exudes humility in that you are literally calling yourself a hindrance. The *o* is honorific.

The word *jama* refers to something that is in the way, so *jama o suru* means "to create a disturbance or inconvenience." Japanese people tend to go all out for guests, so maybe, in a way, you really are creating a disturbance, but if you are a polite and respectful guest, your hosts will feel their efforts were not in vain.

This saying is also used when setting up a time to visit someone. You may call up a friend or someone may call you and say:

Ashita no asa o-jama shite mo ii desu ka.
Is it okay if I come over tomorrow morning?

When It Is Time to Go

After thanking your hosts and saying a parting *gochisoo-sama deshita*, you must once again call yourself a hindrance. Upon leaving someone's home, it is proper to say *ojama shimashita*. Changing *suru* to *shimashita* turns it into the past-tense form of the original greeting.

If you were the one doing the entertaining, you might end with the following:

> *Mata asobi ni kite ne.*
> Please come and play again.

If your guests brought a gift, it is appropriate for you to mention the present and say *o-miyage arigatoo* ("Thanks for the gift") or *kudamono gochisoo sama* ("Thanks for the fruit"). You may be seeing these people again at work the next day; in this case, *Mata ashita, ne* ("See you tomorrow") is a common parting phrase.

Of course, there are just plain goodbyes, too. If it is going to be awhile before you meet again, it is best to say *Sayoonara*. *Jaa ne* and *Mata ne* are casual "See you later"–type farewells. *Bai-bai* is mostly reserved for children and babies.

Ano Ne

The particle *ne* has several different uses. It can be utilized to emphasize an opinion, seek confirmation from the listener, elicit agreement, express emphasis, or as a way to get someone's attention.

38

> *Arigatoo, ne.*
> Thanks!

> *Ne, kore o mimashita ka.*
> Hey, have you seen this?

> *Kore o taberu, ne.*
> I'm going to eat this, okay?

Motteta hoo ga ii desu ne.
You had better hold onto it.

Long Time No See

What takes an entire sentence to communicate in English can often be said with one word in Japanese. The meaning of many formulaic expressions is determined by the context. A good example of this is the phrase *o-hisashiburi.*

O-hisashiburi is a phrase that is exchanged between people who have not seen each other for awhile. It means something like "It's been a long time." The *o* is there for honorific purposes, of course. The greeting can be repeated by the respondent with *ne* for emphasis: *O-hisashiburi desu ne!*

ALERT!

The past-tense form of "How are you?" is *o-genki deshita ka*. It is not necessary to alter the word *genki,* only the verb *desu* is conjugated to its past-tense form: *deshita.*

The last part of the phrase, *buri*, is a suffix that is often used in conjunction with a period of time. For example, an exchange between friends who are meeting after several years have passed may go something like this:

39

Friend 1: *O-hisashiburi!*
Long time no see!

Friend 2: *O-hisashiburi desu ne.*
Long time no see is right!

Friend 1: *Nan-nen buri desu ka ne.*
How many years has it been?

Friend 2: *Ni-nen buri gurai da to omoo.*
I bet it has been about two years.

Friend 1: *O-genki deshita ka.*
How have you been?

Friend 2: *Hai, o-kage-sama de.*
Fine, thank you.

The phrase *o-kagesama de* is an idiomatic expression. *Kage* means "behind" or "shadow," and *sama* is a polite version of the suffix *san*. It is similar to another phrase, *anata no o-kage de,* which means, "Thanks to you." Both have humble connotations.

Special Occasions

Birthday parties, Christmas parties, and recently even Halloween parties, are becoming more common in Japan. On the flip side, there are the less joyous occasions, such as funerals, where it is nonetheless important to show your support with some words of comfort.

Happy Birthday

The birthday greeting of choice for the birthday boy or girl is:

O-tanjoobi o-medetoo gozaimasu.
Congratulations on your birthday.

Though not much fuss was made about birthdays in the past, many Japanese households now celebrate "American-style," with cakes and candles. It remains a rather intimate family gathering, however, rather than a party with ten six-year-olds running around.

There are two ways to ask "How old are you?" in Japanese:

O-ikutsu desu ka.
Literally: "How many are you?"

Nan-sai desu ka.
How old are you?

The first example is more polite, although it is still considered rude to ask women of any age how old they are. The second example may be easier to remember because the response contains some of the same words:

> *Ni-juu roku sai desu.*
> I'm twenty six.

This sample answer can be used regardless of how the question is put. When referring to your age, the regular number words followed by *sai* are almost always acceptable. There is one exception, however, for twenty-year-olds.

Japanese can legally drink, smoke, and vote at the age of twenty. It is a time for coming-of-age ceremonies and recognition as an adult by members of the community. This may be why there is a special phrase for "I am twenty": *Hatachi desu.*

FACT

There is an old-fashioned way of determining age in which the time of birth is counted as one's "first birthday." This style of counting is called *kazoedoshi.* Using this method makes newborns one-year-olds and can get rather confusing, or depressing, from there on out. The currently used method of starting from zero at birth is called *mannenrei.*

Congratulations!

There are a variety of situations, aside from birthdays, in which you may want to say *o-medetoo gozaimasu.* In Japanese, congratulatory phrases are constructed by placing the reason for the special occasion in front of the "congrats."

40

> *Go-kekkon omedetoo gozaimasu.*
> Congratulations on your marriage. (formal)

Sotsugyoo omedetoo.
Congratulations on your graduation. (casual)

Go-shussan o-medetoo gozaimasu.
Congratulations on the birth of your child. (formal)

Another phrase that sounds like *omedetoo* is *omedeta*. This is used when asking about an upcoming special event, like the birth of a baby.

40 *Omedeta wa itsu desu ka.*
When is the happy event?

My Condolences

Hopefully, you will not need to use the following phrases, but in the event that you do, it is best to be prepared. If someone you know loses a loved one, the proper word of sympathy is *samishiku narimashita*. Literally translated, this phrase means, "You have become lonely." *Samishii* is a word that describes the combined feelings of sadness and loneliness. The *ku* is an adjective modifier, and *narimashita* means, "have become." Another possible phrase to express your condolences is *go-shuusho-sama-deshita*. This mouthful of a phrase means, "You must be sad."

Japanese funerals are predominately Buddhist, although several sects exist, so the ceremonies vary greatly. Gifts of money are common, presented in envelopes that are decorated with black and silver bows.

ESSENTIAL

If you see flowers laid by the side of the road, it may indicate that someone from a house in that area has recently passed away or that someone died from a traffic accident there. Flowers may also be placed anonymously at the end of a driveway as an offering of sympathy for the family members of the deceased.

Throughout the Day

Concern for the decline in polite behavior among young people has led to "greeting" campaigns being launched at schools all over the country. Entryways are festooned with banners that say *Genki-na aisatsu o shiyoo* ("Let's greet each other energetically"). The banners include examples of polite phrases used in everyday conversation: *o-hayou* ("good morning"), *konnichiwa* ("good afternoon"), *sumimasen* ("excuse me"), *gomennasai* ("I'm sorry"), and *sayoonara* ("goodbye"). The effects of these signs are yet to be determined.

Good Morning

Step out onto the street, flip on your radio or TV, and you will hear *o-hayou gozaimasu* being said everywhere and by everyone in Japan. It is the standard greeting among family members, coworkers, TV talk show hosts, and friendly neighbors. Family members may also use a shortened form, *o-hayou*, when stumbling out of bed in the morning.

To accompany the greeting, there are many words to describe the act of waking up, or being wakened. The verb *okiru* means "to get up," or "rise." But the verbs *sameru* and *okosu* have closely related meanings. *Sameru* is most often used in the phrase *me ga sameru* ("my eyes open"). *Okosu* means "to waken."

Hayaoki suru is the act of getting up early or being an early riser. In this phrasal verb, the adjective *hayai* ("early," "fast") and the noun form of *okiru* (*oki*) create a compound word that is then combined with *suru*.

41

Kesa no roku-ji-han ni okita.
I woke up at 6:30 this morning.

Mai asa shichi-ji ni me ga sameru.
My eyes open every morning at seven.
(I wake up at seven every morning.)

Boku no shigoto wa otooto o okosu.
My job is to wake up my younger brother.
(I'm in charge of getting my younger brother up.)

O-nee-san wa itsumo hayaoki shinai.
My older sister never gets up early.

Note the difference in meaning between the command forms of *okite* and *okoshite*. The former is demanding that someone wake up. The latter is requesting that someone wake you up.

41

Hayaku okite kudasai.
Please hurry and wake up.

Gozenchuu ni ikitai kara, hyame ni okoshite kudasai.
I would like to go in the morning, so please wake me up early.

When you meet a friend for the first time on a given day, it is not uncommon to use a shortened version of *o-hayou gozaimasu: o-hayou*. This is true even if it is past noon.

F A C T

After Noon

Following the noon meal, *hirugohan*, greetings change to *konnichiwa*. Broken down into its *kanji* elements, *kon* means "now," *nichi* means "day," and *wa* is the subject indicator. Veteran Japanese speakers will emphasize both *n* sounds, savoring the enunciation of each one individually. *Konnichiwa* can be likened to "hello," in English, and is therefore appropriate in most situations regardless of what time of day it is. If you cannot remember any other greeting, *konnichiwa* is the one to keep in your back pocket.

The root word for day, *hiru*, can be found in many different sayings when talking about the afternoon. *Hirumeshi* is another name for lunch or the noon meal. *Hiruyasumi* is a lunch break or noon recess. A *hirune* is an afternoon nap. People may talk about having something to do in the afternoon using either *hiru* or *hiruma*:

> *O-hiru kara shigoto ga arimasu.*
> I have to work this afternoon.

Go is another link to after-lunch activities. *Shoogo* means "twelve noon" and *gogo* means "afternoon":

> *Ranchi wa shoogo ni tabemasu.*
> Lunch is at noon.

> *Gogo kara wa hima desu.*
> I'm free this afternoon.

When the Sun Goes Down

It is rare to hear the phrase "good evening," in English anymore, but its Japanese counterpart, *konbanwa*, is still in circulation. Like *konnichiwa*, the *kanji* for *konbanwa* can be broken down into "now," "evening," and the subject indicator *wa*. This greeting is appropriate when visiting someone's home, talking on the phone, attending a night class or meeting, and any other activity that takes place in the evening.

At what time of day does it become appropriate to use the phrase *konbanwa*? Some identify the start of evening with the five-o-clock whistle. Others identify the onset of evening with the sunset: *yuuhi* or *hinoiri*. As the seasons change, however, many will start using "good evening" as soon as it starts getting dark: *kuraku natte kara*.

Following a greeting with a comment about weather or nature is very Japanese. Here are two common ways to reference the onset of evening:

> *Konbanwa. Kyoo wa hinoiri ga hayakatta desu.*
> Good evening. The sunset seemed early today.

> *O-ban desu. Kyoo wa go-ji gurai ni kuraku natte kita, ne.*
> Good evening. It got dark about five o-clock today, didn't it?

Notice that the adjective *hayai* ("fast," "early") in the first example is changed to its past-tense form by first dropping the *i* and then adding the suffix *–katta*, similar to the way a verb is conjugated. The following verb *desu*, therefore, is not changed into its past-tense form. This pattern can be found in many adjectives that end in *i* including *oishikatta* ("it was delicious"), *omoshirokatta* ("it was interesting"), and *kawaikatta* ("it was cute").

FACT

Another, more idiomatic and old-fashioned way of saying "Good evening" is *O-ban desu*. This phrase seems to be heard more often coming from men than from women. Literally translated, it simply states, "It is evening." There is something kind of poetic in the simplicity of this greeting.

The adjectival phrase in the second example, *kuraku natte kita* contains the verbs *naru* and *kuru*. *Kurai* ("dark") is modified first by dropping the *i* and then adding *ku*. *Naru* is changed to its participial form (*–te* ending) and *kuru* is put in the past-tense form. If you practice it a few times, the whole thing will roll off your tongue like one big word.

Daily Terms	
asa	morning
hiru	afternoon
ban, yuugata	evening
gozen	A.M., morning
gozenchuu	the time between sunrise and noon
gogo	P.M., afternoon
yoru	night
kesa	this morning
yuube	last night
okiru	rise, get up

Daily Terms (continued)	
sameru	wake up
ohirune, ohirune suru	nap, take a nap
neru	go to bed
nemui	sleepy
o-hi-sama	sun
o-tsuki-sama	moon

Before Going to Bed

Saying "good night" in Japanese is uncharacteristically aggressive, as you are literally insisting that someone take a rest. *O-yasuminasai* ("good night") is a combination of the regular form of the noun *yasumi* ("rest") and the command form of the verb *nasaru*. *Nasaru* is an honorific equivalent of the verb *suru* ("to do"). The prefix *o* is also honorific, but you will rarely find this greeting without it, even in the most casual situations. One variation, among family and friends, is to shorten the phrase to *o-yasumi*.

The suffix *–nasai* is commonly attached to verbs to make a stern, yet polite imperative. Parents, not to mention teachers, can be heard scolding their children and students in public with various combinations of a verb and *nasai*. This form sounds more respectful than the plain command form of the verbs: *Okite* becomes *okinasai* ("Get up!"), *suwatte* is transformed into *suwarinasai* ("Sit down!"), and *tabete* gets refined to *tabenasai* ("Eat!").

Here are some comments you may hear from those who are about to retire for the evening:

42

Sumimasen, kyuu-ni nemuku natte kita.
Excuse me, I suddenly became very sleepy.

Watashi mo nemui desu.
I'm sleepy, too.

Nemutai desu.
I want to sleep.

Kore kara neru tsumori desu.
I intend to go to bed soon.

Notice how the adjective *nemui* is conjugated by dropping the *i* and adding a *ku* before adding the verbal phrase *naru kuru*. In the third example, the same adjective is conjugated with the suffix *–tai* as another way to say "I'm sleepy."

Quizzes and Exercises

1. Match the greeting with its English translation.

    konnichiwa   good morning

    o-hayou gozaimasu   hello

    doomo, itsumo o sewa   good night
    ni natte imasu

    o-ban desu   thanks for always taking
                                                       care of me

    o-yasuminasai   good evening

2. Fill in the missing word: _____ *agatte kudasai*

3. Rearrange the words to make a sentence: *ii mo ka no asa ashita o-jama shite desu* _____

4. What does *mata ashita ne* mean? _____

5. Circle the more polite commands: *tabenai, nenasai, ikinasai, tabete, nete, ike.*

6. Conjugate the adjective *nemui* ("I'm sleepy") to convey that you have become sleepy: _____

Chapter 11
Making Friends

Being friends with someone from another culture who speaks an entirely different language and successfully communicating with that person is an incredible feeling. You may feel silly at first, answering questions about your favorite color and season. These introductory questions, however, will lay the foundation for deeper conversations.

Can You Speak English?

There are a number of people who are dying for a chance to practice what they have learned in school, so you may be accosted by eager English-speakers in bars, grocery stores, schools, and on the street. These potential conversationalists may require a little probing from you:

> *Eigo o wakarimasu ka.*
> Do you understand English?

This is a straightforward way to get the ball rolling. But even if the person you're talking to has passed the highest level of the proficiency exam with flying colors, she may deny her ability:

> *Eigo ga dekimasen.*
> I cannot (speak) English.

> *Eigo ga wakarimasen.*
> I do not understand English.

Somone with a little self-esteem may reply:

> *Eigo wa hon-no sukoshi shika wakaranai.*
> I only understand a little English.

If you want the potential form of most verbs, like *yomimasu* ("to read"), just change the second syllable to its correspond *e* form: *yomemasu* ("can read"). But with the verb *shimasu* ("to do"), the potential form is actually a totally different verb: *dekimasu* ("can do"). People often use the negative construction *dekinai* when speaking of their ability—or lack thereof—to speak English.

The word *shika* ("only," "nothing to do but . . .") followed by a verb is a way of stating something in the negative. It communicates an inability or a lack of something. The phrasing may seem rather roundabout, much like a double negative in English. Directly translated, *Eigo wa hon-no sukoshi shika wakaranai* means "English just a little only cannot understand." This way of stating a negative is very, very common in everyday conversations.

43

Watashi wa kono jikan shika nai.
I only have this time right now.

Kono heya ni wa go nin shika inai.
There are only five people in this room.

Saifu no naka ni wa ni-sen en shika nai.
I only have 2,000 yen in my wallet.

This same phrase is also used to make a recommendation, or when reconciling oneself to a lack of options.

43

Yaru shika nai ne.
I have no choice but to do it.

Kiru shika nai.
There is nothing to do but cut it.

Uru shika nai.
There is nothing to do but sell it.

FACT

The final verb in each of these examples ends with the suffix *–nai. Nai* is the negative form of the verb *arimasu.* These statements are all fairly casual. To make them more formal, you must replace the *–nai* with *ari-masen,* but this form of the verb is much less common.

Commonly Asked Questions

Whether you enjoy being the center of attention or shy away from the limelight, be prepared for a barrage of questions regarding your background.

And You Are . . .

Two things people will want to know right away is who you are and where you are from.

44

O-namae wa nan desu ka.
What is your name?

Go-shusshin wa doko desu ka.
Where were you born?

O-sumai wa doko desu ka.
Where is your home?

O-kuni wa dochira desu ka.
Which country are you from?

Amerika no nani shuu desu ka.
Which state in the U.S.?

Sore wa doko desu ka.
Where is that?

These examples follow a common pattern with their *–doko desu ka* endings. Note the two question words *nan* and *nani*. In the previous examples, *nan* means "what" and *nani* means "which." Use *nani* when the answer involves choosing from a class or group. The question *Amerika no nani shuu desu ka* asks which state—of all fifty—that the respondent is from. *Dochira* also means "which." It can stand alone, whereas *nani* is accompanied by a noun.

Once it has been determined that you are definitely not from Japan, people will wonder why you are there.

45

Nihon ni kita no wa ryokoo desu ka.
Did you come to Japan to travel?

Nihon de wa o-shigoto o shite imasu ka.
Are you working in Japan?

Nihon ni wa dore gurai imasu ka.
How long will you be in Japan?

Nihon ni wa itsu kimashita ka.
When did you come to Japan?

Nihon ni iru no wa moo nagai desu ka.
Have you already been in Japan for a long time?

Nihon ni iru no wa nan nen gurai ni narimasu ka.
How many years have you been in Japan?

Look at the use of *de* and *ni* in these examples. Do you notice the difference in the way that they are used? In the second question, *de* is used because *Nihon* is a site of action (*shigoto suru*). In the first question, *ni* is used because the action is moving towards *Nihon* (*kuru*). In the third question, *ni* is used because *Nihon* is the site of a state of being (*iru*).

Look at the last two questions. In those questions, *iru* is followed by *no wa*. This construction turns the verb into the subject of the sentence, somewhat like a gerund in English. The literal translation of the last question is: "Living in Japan, how many years has it been?"

Determining Categorical Preferences

Another way to get to know people is by finding out what they like. Depending on who is doing the asking, you may be asked to decide on a favorite color, animal, food, and season, among other things. You may also be quizzed on other preferences.

46

Nani iro ga suki desu ka.
What color do you like?

Doobutsu no naka de wa dore ga suki desu ka.
What kind of animal do you like?

Furuutsu wa suki desu ka.
Do you like fruit?

Kisetsu no naka de wa dore ga ichiban suki desu ka.
Which season do you like the best?

Pan to gohan wa dotchi ga suki desu ka.
Which do you like, bread or rice?

The first and third questions establish the basic pattern:

(Object of question) *wa* (or *ga*) *suki desu ka.*

In the second and fourth questions, the phrase *no naka de wa* identifies a group or class of things as the object of the question. *Doobutsu no naka de wa* means something like "of all the animals," and *kissetsu no naka de wa means* "of all the seasons." Using this pattern, you can replace *doobutsu* or *kissetsu* with any other class or group, such as *iro* ("colors"), *dezaato* ("desserts"), *nihon-ryoori* ("Japanese food"), or *hana* ("flowers"), to name just a few.

FACT

The question words *dore* and *dotchi* are very useful when asking about preferences. *Dore* is used in cases where there are three or more things to choose from. *Dotchi* is a more casual form of the word *dochira*. It is usually used when there are only two things to choose from, or when the speaker wishes to make the question more focused.

Easy Responses

All these questions may overwhelm you, or you may be flattered by the attention given to your background, likes, and dislikes. Once you have deciphered the questions, you can begin to think about responses.

Geographic Generalities

How familiar are you with Japanese prefectures? Do you know where Chiba is? How about Aomori? Aside from the occasional geography genius, Japanese people are no more familiar with the location of states within the United States (other than the famous ones like California and New York, or nearby ones like Hawaii, Alaska, and Washington) than the average westerner is with Japanese prefectures. Citing general directions like north, south, east, west, and center should suffice to provide an image of your home territory's location.

47

Sumai wa Amerika no higashi kaigan desu.
My home is on the East Coast of the U.S.A.

Tekisasu wa minami no hoo ni arimasu.
Texas is in the South.

Mishigan wa kita no hoo desu.
Michigan is in the North.

Yuujiin wa nishi kaigan ni arimasu.
Eugene is on the West Coast.

In the fourth example, look at the particle *ni*, which is used instead of *hoo* to indicate direction. The name of the country (in this case, America) is not explicitly stated, probably because it has already been determined by context. If you were to rephrase the statement to include this information, the sentence would look like this: *Iuujiinu wa Amerika no nishi kaigan ni arimasu.*

Further observation of these examples illuminates the use of two different verbs with almost identical meanings: *desu* and *arimasu*. Note that when *arimasu* is used, it is prefaced by *ni*. *Desu* does not require the presence of *ni*.

Remember the possessive *no* from earlier chapters? Here it is again, with a twist. When it connects two geographic locations, *no* indicates that one region or location is situated within a larger region, state, or country. Because in a sense the East coast "belongs" to America, *no* retains its possessive function. When *no* connects the name of a region with *hoo*, it means "in the direction of."

Testing Your English Skills

Jumping at the chance to hear some *nama eigo* ("raw English"), many people may ask you how to say certain things in English. Pointing to the object in question, speak slowly and clearly. You may have to repeat the word or phrase several times. On some occasions, you may not be familiar with the items in question. The following sentence patterns will help you out in all these different situations.

48

Kore wa eigo de apple *desu.*
This is "apple" in English.

Sore wa eigo de dish *desu.*
That is "dish" in English.

Kore wa eigo de wakarimasen. Nan desu ka.
I don't know what that is in English. What is this (anyway)?

Iku wa eigo de "go" *to iimasu.*
Iku means "go" in English.

An affirmative response like one of the following will encourage your conversation partner to further develop his or her English expertise. Kids, especially, will be overjoyed that you appreciate their efforts to communicate with you.

48

Chotto matte, "aka" wa eigo de red *desu ne.*
Just a minute, you're right; *aka* is "red" in English!

Sugoi, ne!
Wow, that's great!

Atari!
You're right!

In the following examples, you can see yet another function of the particle *de*. You can use it whenever you want to signal that something is being communicated in a particular language. Examples:

48

Kore wa nihongo de nan desu ka.
What is this in Japanese?

Kono ko wa supeingo de hanashi ga dekiru.
This child can speak Spanish.

The words for different languages are formed by combining the name of a country with the word *go,* which means "language." *Furansugo,* therefore, means "the language of France," or "French." The component parts of *nihongo* are fairly clear, but can you dissect the word *eigo*? The *ei* stands for "England," and the addition of *go* turns it into "English."

Do not confuse this *go* with other words you know that have the same pronunciation. The honorific *go,* for example, and the word for "five" are represented by completely different *kanji.* The *kanji* that is used to write the *go* in *nihongo* means "word" as well as "language." For example:

Kono go no imi wa nan desu ka.
What is the meaning of this word?

Favorites and Others

If you do not have a favorite color, season, flower, or fruit, now is the time to start thinking about it. Japanese children, especially, will delight in quizzing you on all of your preferences. Adults will be more interested in your preferences for food, drinks, and music. Here are some sentence patterns that will help you express your likes and preferences:

49

Hai, murasaki wa suki desu.
Yes, I like purple.

Aki ga ichiban suki desu.
I like fall the best.

Yappari, pan ga ii desu ne.
Well, I guess I prefer bread.

Saru ga suki desu.
I like monkeys.

Kaapentaazu wa amari suki janai desu.
I don't really care for the Carpenters.

To be amicable, it is nice to state things in the positive. But there are some things that cannot be tolerated (like bad music). In that case, it is necessary to be honest and say *amari suki janai*. This is a very gentle, albeit negative, statement. A more forceful way of saying you don't like something is to use the word *kirai*. *Kirai* is an adjective that includes the suffix *–na* when it is used to modify a noun. Its meaning ranges from "unpleasant" and "distasteful" all the way to "hateful." Remember, adjectives have a verb-like quality in Japanese. In the first two examples, notice how *kirai-na* is translated into English as a verb:

49

Kirai-na tabemono wa nan desu ka.
Are there any foods you don't like?

Kirai-na doobutsu wa imasu ka.
What animals do you dislike?

Kirai-na iro wa nani iro desu ka.
What is your least favorite color?

Kirai, like many other adjectives in Japanese, can take the place of the main verb in a sentence. In these cases, note that the *–na* is unnecessary.

49

Orenji-iro wa kirai desu.
I hate the color orange.

Ka wa kirai desu.
I hate mosquitoes.

Hometown Comparisons

Another great topic of conversation involves making comparisons between Japan and your home country, state, or town. Questions concerning weather, population, scenery, and seasons will have your head spinning. You may even find that you gain a whole new perspective on your hometown.

Weather

Japanese people will often refer to your homeland as *mukoo*. The dictionary defines its meaning as: "the other [opposite] side; over there." It may seem rather vague to hear your home country referred to as "over there" countless times, but it is an extremely common expression.

50

Mukoo no tenki wa doo desu ka.
How is the weather over there (in the U.S.)?

Mukoo ni ame wa ippai furimasu ka.
Does it rain a lot over there?

Mukoo ni yoku hare no hi wa arimasu ka.
Do you have lots of clear days over there?

Mukoo wa attakai desu ne.
Isn't it warm over there?

Mukoo wa koko yori samui desu ka.
Is it colder over there than it is here?

In the first and third examples, *no* is connecting *mukoo* and *tenki* (literally, "over there's weather"), and *hare* and *hi* ("the days of clear"). The second and third examples utilize *ni* to signify "where the weather is."

When answering these questions, it is not necessary to repeat the word *mukoo*, which has already been established. "Variables" in the question should be highlighted in your response, however.

50

Ame wa yoku furimasu.
It rains a lot.

Ame twa amari furanai desu ne.
It really doesn't rain that much.

Yoku haremasu, ne.
It is often sunny (clear).

Ondo wa koko to onaji gurai da to omou.
I think the temperature is about the same as here.

Notice how the verb *furimasu* is conjugated into the negative by changing the *–ri* to *–ra* and adding *–nai*. These verbs that pertain to weather, *furimasu* and *haremasu*, actually describe the falling of the rain and the clearing of the sky. Their noun forms are, respectively, *amefuri* ("rainy weather") and *hare* ("clear weather").

FACT

Hare is also used to describe something auspicious or grand, while *hareru* can refer to being cheered up or refreshed. These parallels between weather and feelings will hit home with people who find their own moods mirrored in the sky.

Population

Both city-dwellers and small-town citizens may discover similarities when comparing characteristics of the daily life of either setting in Japan.

51

Jonson-san no furusato no jinkoo wa dore gurai desu ka.
What is the population of your hometown, Mr. Johnson?

Jonson-san wa toshi ni sunde imasu ka.
Do you live in a city, Mr. Johnson?

Inaka ni sunde imasu ka.
Do you live in the countryside?

Note the present-tense version of the verb *sumu* ("to live") is created by replacing the ending *–mu* with *–nde* + *imasu*. The *–nde* (as opposed to *–te*) is necessary due to the *–mu* ending on *sumu*.

51

Furusato no jinkoo wa hyaku-man nin gurai desu.
My hometown population is about 100,000 people.

Watashi wa toshi ni sunde imasu.
I live in a city.

Watashi wa inaka ni sunde imasu.
I live in the country.

Watashi wa chiisai machi ni sunde imasu.
I live in a small town.

Scenery

Your hometown scenery will be of great interest to many people, especially those who have little or no experience with places beyond Japan's borders.

 52

Mukoo no keshiki wa doo desu ka.
How about the scenery over there?

Mukoo ni yama wa arimasu ka.
Do you have mountains over there?

Umi wa chikai desu ka.
Is the sea close by?

ALERT!

When addressing people you are just getting to know, it is polite, even among friends, to use that person's last name, plus the suffix *–san*. The Japanese word for "you," *anata*, is mostly reserved for lovers or married couples.

Depending on where you are from, there are many different ways to describe the scenery of your homeland.

52

Watashi no furusato wa tottemo heitan desu.
My hometown is very flat.

Watashi no furusato wa sabaku desu.
My hometown is a desert.

Watashi no furusato ni wa mizuumi ga arimasu.
My hometown has a lake.

Words for Where You Live	
toshi	city
inaka	countryside
machi	town
jinkoo	population
furusato	hometown
sunde iru (*sumu*)	living (live)
seikatsu	daily life

Words for Scenery	
keshiki	scenery
yama	mountains
kawa	river
umi	sea
mizuumi	lake
heitan	flat, level
hiroi	wide, open
semai	narrow

Words for Scenery (continued)	
sabaku	desert
mori	forest
chikai	nearby
tooi	far away

Words for Seasons	
ima	now
fuyu	winter
haru	spring
natsu	summer
aki	fall, autumn
yuki	snow
kanji	sense, feeling
kanjiru	to be impressed, sense

Talking about Your Family

The question of family always comes up in conversation when you're in Japan. Use the following sentence patterns to talk about your family members; if you have some family photos to show as well, all the better!

53

O-baa-san wa o-ikutsu desu ka.
How old is your grandmother?

O-too-san wa nan no shigoto o shite-imasu ka.
What does your father do for a living?

Kyoodai wa nan nin imasu ka.
How many kids in your family?

Imooto-san wa doko ni sunde imasu ka.
Where does your younger sister live?

O-ko-sama no namae wa nan desu ka.
What is your child's name?

QUESTION?

How should I answer the question *nan nin kyoodai desu ka*?
When describing the number of siblings in your family, include your-self in that number. Japanese people usually ask for the total number before asking how many brothers and how many sisters you've got, and whether they're younger or older.

When answering these questions, remember to use terms that refer to your own relatives, which are completely different from the terms that are used to talk about members of a family other than your own:

53

Sobo wa hachi-juu nana sai desu.
My grandmother is eighty-seven years old.

Chichi wa shinbun kisha desu.
My father is a newspaper editor.

Yon nin kyoodai desu.
There are four children, including myself, in my family.

Imooto wa Kariforuniya ni sunde iru.
My sister lives in California.

Musume no namae wa Eba desu.
My daughter's name is Ava.

THE EVERYTHING CONVERSATIONAL JAPANESE BOOK

Hobbies and Opinions

Shumi is a term used to describe anything you do in your free time, over a long period of time, or with intensity:

> *Sumisu-san wa shumi arimasu ka.*
> Do you have a hobby, Ms. Smith?

You are already familiar with the phrase *doo desu ka*. When seeking opinions, the same phrase is used as a sentence tag. For example, if you are interested in knowing how someone feels about baseball, you would just say *beesuboru wa doo desu ka*. The literal translation is "Baseball, how about it?" The following sentences all follow the same pattern. In each case, the English equivalent has an equally casual, conversational tone:

54

> *O-sakana wa doo desu ka.*
> How do you like fish?

> *O-sushi wa doo desu ka.*
> Have you ever tried sushi?

> *Nihon wa doo desu ka.*
> What's your impression of Japan?

> *Supootsu wa doo desu ka.*
> Are you interested in sports?

Doo desu ka can be likened to the English phrase "What do you think about . . . ?" It is very useful when asking open-ended questions about first impressions. You may find that many Japanese will ask for your opinion regarding Japanese arts, traditions, and customs such as *sumo*, *sushi*, chopsticks, *kimono*, and so on. Here are some possible answers:

54

Nihon wa omoshiroi desu.
Japan is interesting.

O-sakana wa oishii desu.
Fish is delicious.

Supootsu wa amari suki janai desu.
I do not really care for sports.

O-sushi wa maa-maa suki desu.
I sort of like sushi.

Quizzes and Exercises

1. What is the potential form ("can do") of the verb *suru*? _____

2. What does *o-sumai* refer to?

    _____

3. Organize the following words into a question: *ka sore nan wa desu*

    _____

4. What does *nihongo* refer to?

    _____

5. Translate the following sentence into Japanese: "Do you like sushi?"

    _____

6. How do you say, "I do not like pink," in Japanese?

    _____

Chapter 12

Letting Loose: Party Dialogues

There is nothing quite like a Japanese party. Designed as a way for people who work together to relax, let off steam, and get to know one another more intimately, *enkai* ("dinner/drinking party," "banquet") are a common occurrence in many schools and companies in Japan. *Enkai* are mini-festivals, held to boost office morale, give transfers a rowdy sendoff, or to conclude a culture/sports day at school.

Pouring Etiquette

At an *enkai*, as at most gatherings, the drinking can't begin until the *kampai* (the toast). Once the cue has been given, people will start popping beer bottles and passing around glasses. It is customary to make sure everyone around you has a glass (or plate or bowl) before accepting one yourself.

Doozo *and* Doomo

It is proper etiquette to hold the glass while someone is pouring for you. The person pouring will say *Doozo*, and you answer back *Doomo*. Once your glass has been filled to its frothy brim, you must then take the beer bottle from the pourer and say *Doozo*. She or he will in turn answer back *Doomo*. Designated drivers will observe the same etiquette while pouring their *uuron-cha* ("oolong tea") and *juusu* ("juice").

Once everyone's glass has been filled, someone will give a short speech stating the purpose of the *enkai*, thanking the organizers, and congratulating the staff on a job well done. Depending on the occasion, he or she may also bid farewell to a beloved colleague or make some other personal address. Then another person, previously designated as the official "cheers" leader, will give a short toast and shout out *Kampai!* Before throwing your drink down the hatch, join with the others by calling out *Kampai!* This formulaic expression means "bottoms up," which is why you will see many people drain their glasses. If you don't drain your glass, someone will soon be at your elbow saying *Doozo* again. Respond to this by taking a tiny sip from your glass, and then holding it out, saying *Doomo*.

When You Have Had Enough

If you are working in Japan, this *enkai* may be held partially in your honor, so your glass is likely to be filled several times over. It is difficult to gauge how much you are drinking in these situations and you may soon find you have had enough. People will want to welcome you by pouring beer into your glass, however, so it is best to humor them by taking tiny sips before humbly receiving more.

Pouring for yourself is taboo at an *enkai*, but you can hint strongly that you would like something to drink by filling the glass of someone else. The person you are pouring for will inevitably notice that your own glass is empty and ask you what you are drinking. This is a good opportunity for you to change beverages if you feel you have had enough alcohol.

Making the Rounds

After a while, you will want to stretch your legs a bit. This is a perfect time to circle the table with a bottle of beer, pouring for each person around the table: *Doozo; Doomo.* Make sure to note what is in each person's glass, just in case it is not beer. Tea, juice, and *nihon-shu* are also popular *enkai* drinks, and you should offer to pour whatever the person is already drinking.

Chatting briefly with each person is perfectly acceptable as you make your rounds. When you are ready to move on, just grab another bottle from the table and continue circling around until you have poured for each member of the party. This is a very humble act, and will get your stint in the Japanese work force off to a good start.

ALERT!

Make sure to circle around in back of people rather than passing in front of them as you make your way around the table pouring beer. Use both hands: Whether you're pouring juice or beer, have one hand supporting the bottom of the bottle while the other tilts the opening toward the glass.

The Drinking Party Speech

If the party you are attending is in your honor, you will be expected to give a short speech. It is a good idea to bow first, and it is perfectly fine to have a cheat sheet. Formal speeches at graduation ceremonies and other events in Japan are often read verbatim from a fancily folded paper.

To begin, stand up and make sure to bow to the people across from you, as well as those to the right and left. You may want to restate parts of your self-introduction and add a sentence or two about your new workplace, colleagues, or home.

55

Kono kaisha no mina-san wa shinsetsu-na hito da to omoimasu.
I think everyone in this office is really kind.

Koko de hataraku no wa tanoshimi ni shite imasu.
I'm really looking forward to working here.

Ima made doomo arigatoo gozaimashita. Kore kara mo yoroshiku onegai shimasu.
Thanks for everything you have done for me up until now. Please continue to look out for me from here on out.

The conjunction *no* in these phrases has two separate purposes. The first phrase uses *no* to connect the two nouns: *kaisha* ("company") and *mina-san* ("everyone") to make the phrase "this company's personnel." In the next example, *no* joins forces with *wa* to identify the verb *hataraku* ("to work") as the subject ("working here").

It's a Pleasure

The verb in the second example is actually a combination of *tanoshimi* ("pleasure") and *shite imasu* ("doing"). This is a colloquialism used to describe the feeling of looking forward to something: *tanoshimi ni shite imasu.*

The word *tanoshimi* has an adjectival form. To get form the adjective, simply drop the *–mi* and add an extra *i. Tanoshii* is the adjective used to describe something enjoyable or fun, but may also be used as "happy" or "cheerful":

Biiru o nomu no wa tanoshii desu.
Drinking beer is fun.

When *tanoshii* is placed in front of a noun, add *–ku*:

Kyoo wa tanoshiku paatei shimasu.
Today we will have an enjoyable party.

When changing it to its past-tense form, *–katta* is needed:

Kino no paatei wa tanoshikatta desu.
Yesterday's party was a blast.

FACT

Tanoshii also has a verbal form: *tanoshimu*. Conjugate this verb as you would other verbs that end in –*mu*. For example, the present-progressive tense is *tanoshinde imasu,* and the past tense is *tanoshinda.*

Encore

When called upon to give a speech more than once at an *enkai*, it is fine to repeat the same things you said earlier. Or, challenge everyone to listen to you give your self-introduction in English:

Eigo de itte mo ii desu ka.
May I say it in English?

If you feel comfortable doing so (in Japanese or English), you can add a few comments about your impressions of Japan so far, thank your supervisor for his or her hospitality, and express your appreciation for the food. Here's a sample *enkai* speech that you might want to use as a model:

56

Minna-san konbanwa. Watashi wa Kurisu Potta to mooshimasu. Amerika kara kimashita. Nihongo wa umaku dekimasen ga, yurushite kudasai. Kyoo no enkai wa tottemo tanoshii shi, o-hanashi mo omoshiroi shi, tabemono mo oishii desu. Ima made doomo arigatoo gozaimashita. Kore kara mo yoroshiku onegai shimasu.

Good evening, everyone. My name is Chris Potter. I am from the U.S.A. Please forgive my terrible Japanese. Today's party is not only fun, the conversations are interesting, and the food is delicious, too. Thank you for all you have done for me up until this point. Please continue to take care of me in the future.

Can You Drink Nihon-shu?

Your jaw may drop as you enter the banquet room filled with low tables heaped with large platters of raw fish, bottles of beer, juice, and tea. Locations for *enkai* vary as each person in the office takes a turn at being the party-planner, but most tend to be held at Japanese-style places.

Once the *kampai* has been uttered and drinks are flowing freely, work tensions and job-related issues are hashed out among coworkers, managers, and bosses alike. As the conversation gathers momentum, and the imbibing of spirits diminishes inhibitions, you may find that someone who has yet to speak a word to you at work is now bubbling over with questions. He or she may be particularly interested in your familiarity with Japanese customs and traditions.

57

Nihon-shu wa daijoobu desu ka.
Are you fine with drinking Japanese rice liquor?

Natto wa taberaremasu ka.
Can you eat *natto?*

O-hashi wa tsukaemasu ka.
Can you use chopsticks?

Umeboshi wa taberaremasu ka.
Can you eat pickled Japanese apricots?

Kanji o kakemasu/yomemasu ka.
Can you write/read Chinese characters?

Nihongo wa dekimasu ka.
Can you [speak] Japanese?

Sashimi o taberaremasu ka.
Can you eat sliced raw fish?

Only one of these phrases actually incorporates the verb *dekimasu* ("can do"). The rest of the verbs have "can do" built into their conjugations. Remember, for verbs that end in *ku* and *mu* (like the above *kaku* and *yomu*) simply change the final ending to its *–e* form and add *–masu*. For the verbs that end in just plain *–u*, like *tsukau*, the final "u" is changed to an "e" before adding *–masu*.

Verbs that end in *–eru*, like *taberu*, need a little more work to change into the potential "can do" form. First, substitute the final *–ru* with its *–ra* version, then add *–re* before sticking on the final ending *–masu*. This rule applies to verbs that end in *–eru* and any of its variations: *–seru*, *–keru*, *–heru*, and so on:

> *Kore o miseraremasu ka.*
> Can you show this?

Verbs that end in *–iru* (and *–kiru*, *–biru*, *–miru)* also follow this rule:

> *Kono kimono wa kiraremasu ka.*
> Can you wear this kimono?

When's the Party?

If the first *enkai* you attend is a party in your honor, you may not have to pay. In order to be polite, you should definitely attend a second time (so that you can help pay for the guest of honor) whenever the occasion arises. If you have a schedule conflict with the night of the *enkai*, you can politely decline the invitation:

> *Sumimasen, sono hi ni yotei ga haitte imasu no de, ikemasen. Mata kondo yoroshiku onegai shimasu.*
> Sorry, I have plans on that day. Please ask me again next time.

If this is a party being held in your honor, it is best to attend. Most places will do you the courtesy of coordinating the party with your schedule before setting up a date. Here's a sample dialogue for setting up an *enkai* date.

58 **Supervisor:** *Pottaa-san, sumimasen, raishuu no kin-yoobi no yuugata ni yotei wa arimasu ka.*
Excuse me, Mr. Potter, are you free next Friday evening?

Potter: *Raishuu no kin-yoobi desu ka. Nanimo nai to omoimasu.*
Next Friday? I don't think I have anything planned.

Supervisor: *Yokatta. Pottaa-san no uerukamu paatei o yaritai to omoimasu.*
Good. We would like to have a welcome party for you.

Potter: *Hontoo ni? Arigatoo gozaimasu.*
Really? Thank you!

Supervisor: *Biiru wa daijoobu desu ka.*
Are you able to drink beer?

Potter: *Hai, daijoobu desu.*
Yes, I can drink beer.

Supervisor: *Jaa, mukae ni ikimasu. Sore nara ippai nomemasu.*
Alright, then I'll pick you up. That way, you can drink a lot.

Potter: *Sumimasen. Nan-ji gurai ni kite moraemasu ka.*
That is very kind of you. What time can I expect you?

Supervisor: *Go-ji han de yorishii desu ka.*
How does 5:30 sound?

Potter: *O-machi shite orimasu.*
I'll be waiting.

New Vocabulary

There are a few new terms used in this dialogue. The use of the word *daijoobu*, which means "okay," is a good example of the indirectness of the Japanese language. Instead of directly asking Potter-san if he drinks beer, the supervisor asks if beer is okay ("Do you like to drink?" is the implied question).

Another new phrase is *to omoimasu*. The verb *omoo* has several different definitions, including "to think," "to hope," and "to fear," or "to be afraid." *Omoo* is used to state beliefs, considerations, wants, expectations, and intentions. You will hear this phrase often in professional situations. It serves as a way to soften a personal statement or opinion.

In the previous dialogue, the polite from of the verb, *omoimasu*, is preceded by the word *to*. These two are rarely apart. *To* functions somewhat like the word "that" in the English phrase "I think that," except that the order of "think" and "that" is reversed in Japanese: *to omoimasu*.

Setting Dates

When discussing schedules and setting up party times, it is essential to know the following words and phrases. Days of the week are represented by basic *kanji* characters whose meanings may serve as a mnemonic device. You can remember, for example, that *nichiyoobi* is "the day of the sun," and that *getsuyoobi* is "the day of the moon."

Days of the Week		
Japanese	***Kanji* Character Meaning**	**English**
nichiyoobi	sun, day	Sunday
getsuyoobi	moon, month	Monday
kayoobi	fire	Tuesday
suiyoobi	water	Wednesday
mokuyoobi	tree	Thursday
kinyoobi	money, gold	Friday
doyoobi	soil, path	Saturday

In the following table, you will notice a certain pattern: *kon* refers to "this," or "the present," *rai* means "next," and *sen* means "last" or "previous." Note one irregularity: When referring to "this year," the word *toshi* is used instead of *nen*.

Time Talk	
kyoo	today
ashita	tomorrow
kinoo	yesterday
konshuu	this week
raishuu	next week
senshuu	last week
kongetsu	this month
raigetsu	next month
sengetsu	last month
kotoshi	this year
rainen	next year
kyonen	last year

ALERT!

When referring to the months of the year, the term *gatsu* follows the number word for each month. January, for example, is *ichigatsu*, and February is *nigatsu*. For "last month," "this month," and "next month," use *getsu* instead of *gatsu*: *sengetsu, kongetsu, raigetsu*, respectively.

The Afterparty

Enkai are semiformal events for which the organizer will make invitations, set up arrangements with the restaurant, and designate the speechmakers, taking care of all the details in general. It is customary for an *enkai* to have a predetermined start and finish time. You will know the party is over when everyone stands up and someone gives a short speech. What follows may catch you off guard at first, but just do what everyone else is doing and you will be fine. Three times, people will throw their hands over their heads and yell *Banzai!* followed by a single clap as the finale. This is the signal that the *enkai* has officially ended.

Karaoke, *Anyone?*

The *enkai* may then be followed by an afterparty, the *nijikai* ("second party"). The *nijikai* will be less formal, but still somewhat organized. Those who are interested will be informed of a predetermined location where there will be more drinking, and, most likely, *karaoke*. This is a preferred pastime of many people who are usually too shy to get up and sing in front of a group. Some *karaoke* bars even have special rooms where your little gang can serenade each other privately. Books with song selections are usually written in both Japanese and English (many of the songs happen to be by Madonna or Elvis), so you will have no trouble finding your favorite tune.

QUESTION?

Can you guess the original verb in the word *ikoo*?
It is *iku*, or *ikimasu*. This conjugation is the equivalent of saying "let's." It is used when recommending that an action or activity be done together. The polite version is *ikimashoo* ("let's go").

By this time, *yopparai* ("drunken persons") will have dissolved the filter between their brains and mouths with beer and may be using very informal terms to urge you to join the next party.

59

Ne, Pottaa-san, nijikai ni ikoo yo.
Hey, let's go to the next party!

Pottaa-san wa bijin desu ne.
You are beautiful.

Potta-san wa kakkoii ne.
You are cool.

Karaoke wa doo.
How 'bout some karaoke?

Most verbs can be easily conjugated into volitional ("let's") phrases by changing the last syllable to an elongated *–oo* form: *iku* becomes *ikoo*, *nomu* becomes *nomoo*. (The same policy goes for verbs that end in just plain "u," too.) For verbs that end in *–eru* and *–iru*, drop the *–ru* and add a *–yoo*. If you master the ability to perform this linguistic surgery, you can be as friendly as your vocabulary will allow.

59

Potta-san, biiru o nomimashoo.
Let's drink beer.

Potta-san, karaoke o utaoo.
Let's sing *karaoke*.

Potta-san, odoroo.
Let's dance.

Potta-san, raamen wo tabeyoo.
Let's eat ramen.

Snack Bars

Sunakku bars are places where you pay a set amount of money for a certain amount of time; 5,000 yen for two hours, for example. In the company of beautiful women who are party professionals, conversation is lighthearted and drinks are included (up to a certain point).

Often moonlighting as coffee shops during the day, you can easily identify a *sunakku* by its plush velvet booths or fancy chairs, as well as the neon *koohii* signs in the windows. It is possible for the third (or fourth) party to end up in a *sunakku* so you might want to ask your group where they are headed (and perhaps get a price estimate) before you tag along. Both formal and informal examples of how to phrase these questions follow.

60

Sumimasen, kondo wa doko ni ikimasu ka.
Excuse me, where are we going next?
Ne, kondo wa doko iku no.
Hey, where to next?

Koko wa o-ikura gurai ni narimasu ka.
How much does this place cost?

Watashi no o-kane wa moo nakunarimashita.
I'm out of money.

Quizzes and Exercises

1. Which sentence means "I enjoy working here"?

   Koko de hatarakitai-n desu.
   Koko de hataraku no wa tanoshii desu.

2. Change the verb *tanoshimu* to its past-tense form. _____

3. Match the following verbs with their "can do" form.

   suru   *nomeru*

   nemuru   *dekiru*

   taberu   *yomeru*

   nomu   *taberareru*

   yomu   *nemureru*

4. Fill in the missing word: *Raishuu ni* _____ *wa arimasu ka.*

5. Arrange the following words into a sentence: *omoimasu nai to mo nani*

    _____

6. Write each time reference in Japanese.

    today   _____
    tomorrow   _____
    next month   _____
    this year   _____
    last week   _____

Chapter 13

The Guest of Honor

Eventually, your Japanese coworker or friend will invite you for a visit. Here is your big chance to get a glimpse of the inside of a Japanese home. Bringing something special as a token of appreciation will get you quickly in the door. And when you are treated with gracious hospitality, it is okay to say say thank you, but it may take a few times before your hosts believe you are sincere.

Presenting a Gift

When you are invited to someone's home in Japan, it is customary to bring a gift. If you happen to have brought gifts from your hometown (chocolates, July 4th celebration pins, and other souvenirs), they will be appreciated. If you do not have anything special on-hand, stop by the local grocery store and pick up some fruit or grab a bottle of wine.

Just a Little Something

When presenting a gift, even if you think it is the most wonderful, delicious thing in the world, you must downplay it with humble words. There is a phrase in polite Japanese that always accompanies the presentation of a gift:

Kore wa tsumaranai mono desu kedo, doozo.
Please accept this small token of my appreciation.

This phrase is extremely humble and is likely to make a great first impression. Note that *tsumaranai* means "boring" or "not satisfying," but in this case, it means "small" or "trivial." Also, *kedo* is a shortened version of the more formal *keredo*, which means "but" or "however." When used in its original form, it has a sidekick, *mo*:

Soto wa samui keredo mo ie no naka ga attakai desu.
It's cold outside, but it's warm inside the house.

Other Options

Gifts of money are usually prefaced with this statement, especially when the gift-giver feels that the amount is too low:

Kore wa kimochi dake desu ga, doozo.
This is just a token of our appreciation.

Specific feelings can be expressed by pairing the word for "good" or "bad" with *kimochi*. If something feels good, you say: *kimochi ga ii.* If something feels bad, you say: *kimochi ga warui.* For example:

O-furo de kimochi ga ii.
Taking a bath feels good.

Niku no nioi de kimochi ga warui.
The smell of meat makes me feel sick.

Slippers and Shoes

Most Japanese homes are furnished with *tatami*, which are rectangular mats made of woven straw. Warm in the winter and cool in the summer, *tatami* provide a comfortable place to sit on the floor. *Tatami* are rather delicate, however, and must be cleaned a certain way and protected from bacteria and lice. They would never withstand the wear and tear wrought from people walking on them in shoes. Keeping *tatami* clean is one of the reasons for taking your shoes off as soon as you enter a Japanese home.

One thing you want to make sure to bring to Japan is a pair of shoes that can be easily slipped on and off. Shoehorns are often conveniently placed in many *genkan*, but you may end up feeling conspicuous if you are always bent over, tying up your shoes while everyone is waiting.

Line Them Up

After stepping out of your shoes, bend over and line them up neatly, toes pointing towards the door, so that they can be easily stepped into on your way out. (If you do not do this, your hosts will do it for you.) Your hosts will be impressed at the level of cultural sensitivity you possess. Because Japanese people rarely show their bare feet, especially in front of a guest, be sure you wear socks.

Your hosts will have set out a pair of guest slippers for you:

Surippa wo doozo.
Please use these slippers.

Surippa o haite kudasai.
Please put on these slippers.

Where to Wear Them

Whatever slippers you are presented with at the door will be yours to use for the duration of your visit. Use these slippers in the hallway and kitchen. Going to the bathroom, however, you will encounter another pair of slippers. Wear these while you are in the bathroom, but don't forget to change into the regular slippers before you return to your hosts. *Tatami* rooms do not require slippers. Using the backup method, step out of your slippers and onto the mats.

Inside a Japanese Home

Many Japanese decorate their homes according to the principles of feng shui, the Chinese art of organizing a harmonious living space. In Japanese, this is known as *fuu sui* and most carpenters in Japan have at least a rudimentary knowledge of this approach to building. The free flow of water lines and happiness are top priorities for carpenters and homemakers alike.

Dining Area

Depending on the season, you may be dining in the *ima* ("the family room") or the *zashiki*, a *tatami* room that can be likened to a formal dining room. If it is warm, the *zashiki* will have its doors thrown open to look out over the Japanese-style garden, or *niwa*. This room is especially reserved for guests, but will also hold the family's ancestral Buddhist altar, the *butsudan*. The *butsudan* is a shrine to the family's ancestors. It often holds a statue of the Buddha himself, *hoteke-sama*. Formal photographs of ancestors usually line the walls above the shrine. In front of the *butsudan* you'll probably see a drum and a small table with candles and incense that are used to sanctify offerings of rice and fruit.

Asking questions about the ancestors, or practices surrounding the *butsudan* are perfectly appropriate. Most Japanese people will be pleased when you display an interest in their culture.

61

Kono hito wa dare desu ka.
Who is this person?

Itsu gohan toka kudamono o okimasu ka.
When do you offer rice or fruit?

Taiko wa itsu tatakimasu ka.
When do you beat the drum?

FACT

If it is cold during your visit, you may eat around the *kotatsu*, an electrically heated table. A square *futon* skirts the *kotatsu* and you sit with your legs underneath the blanket to stay warm. In the olden days, square pieces of charcoal were placed in a wire cage and inserted into a holder beneath the *kotatsu*. Nowadays, most models are electric.

Compliments to the Hosts

You can show your appreciation for your hosts' home in a variety of ways.

62

Kono uchi wa tottemo kirei desu ne.
This house is very beautiful.

Kono uchi wa suzushikute kimochi ga yoi desu.
This house is nice and cool.

Kono uchi wa oshare desu ne.
This house is very fashionable.

Kono heya no fusuma wa suteki desu ne.
The paper doors in this room are pretty.

Kono kotatsu wa hontoo ni attakai desu.
This heated table is really warm.

The adjective *suzushii* ("cool") is an example of a special tense in Japanese. This tense is used to provide the reason or origin for the feeling or action that follows.

62

Koko no piza wa oishikute itsumo tabetai.
Pizza is so delicious, I always want to eat it.

Natsu wa atsukute kimochi ga warui.
Summer is so hot, it makes me ill.

Most adjectives that end in "i" like *atsui* ("hot"), *samui* ("cold"), *furui* ("old"), *chiisai* ("small"), and *urusai* ("noisy") drop the "i" and add *–kute*. If you have a good Japanese-to-English dictionary, you may even find *–ku* in parantheses next to the entry word as a clue to its modification.

Kono hon wa furukute dare mo shiranai desu.
This book is so old, nobody recognizes it.

Konya no konsaato wa yasukute dare demo ikeru.
Tonight's concert is so cheap, anyone can go (afford it).

However, not all adjectives can be adjusted with the suffix *–kute*. *Kirei* ("beautiful"), for example, cannot be changed to *kirekute*. Instead, you use the ending *–na*. For example, "very beautiful room" is *tottemo kirei-na heya*. *Hade* ("bold," "flashy"), too, does not become *hadekute*. If you want to say something is gaudy, you can say *hade-sugiru* (the suffix *–sugiru* is explained later on).

Kirei ends in "i" but it falls into the category of Japanese speech called *na* adjectives—those that can be used as adverbs to describe how something is done or moves:

Sore wa kirei-na odorikata desu ne.
That is a beautiful way of dancing!

Kare wa itsumo jissaiteki-na yarikata o suru.
He always does things in a practical way.

Again, a good dictionary will clue you in with an "i" or *na* next to entries that require modification. Some adjectives go either way. For example, *chiisai* and *chiisana* have the same meanings ("small," "little," "trivial"), but *chiisana* is only used attributively in front of nouns.

You are already familiar with the word *uchi* as a familial reference. It is also the term used to describe the actual structure of a home. Another word for referring to your home is *jitaku/otaku*. *Jitaku* is used in reference to your own home, while *otaku* is reserved for talking about someone else's home. You may overhear *otaku* used by someone speaking on the telephone: *Watanabe-san no otaku desu ka.* ("Is this the Watanabe residence?")

Chopstick Etiquette

Platters of sushi, boiled vegetables, lotus root, kelp, and *toofu* may greet your eyes when you enter the dining area. There may be beer, wine, juice, tea, or other beverages. Even private parties usually start like an *enkai* (with a *kampai*) if you can get the cook to sit down long enough to toast her. It is common Japanese hospitality to prepare a feast for guests, so you may hardly see the women of the household as they spend their time running back and forth between the kitchen and the party room.

The table will already be set with several dishes, bowls, glasses, and *o-hashi* ("chopsticks"). Traditionally, *hashi* are placed horizontally, closest to you, with the thick edges to the right. The thin edges rest upon a small platform to prevent them from touching the table. An obsession with cleanliness may move your hosts to use *waribashi* ("disposable chopsticks").

The First Point

At your place setting, you will have a relatively small plate called a *torizara*. When selecting things from the large platters, use the opposite end of your chopsticks (the end that does not touch your mouth) and feel free to bring the *torizara* as close to the main platter as possible. As long as you are using the fat ends of your chopsticks, it doesn't matter if you brush up against the other food. Using your chopsticks like a shovel should be avoided if possible. Also, try to refrain from licking the residual potato salad from the fat end once you have helped yourself.

Many Japanese people do not expect foreigners to know this unspoken rule to prevent germ-sharing. You will surely impress your hosts by maneuvering your chopsticks in such a polite way.

It is possible, too, that a "serving" set of chopsticks will accompany each platter or dish. In that case, you may use those to bring food to your *torizara*. It is not necessary to use the fat end of the "serving" chopsticks.

FACT

Napkins are not commonly found in either restaurants or Japanese homes. Tissues are usually available, but most people carry a small hand towel or handkerchief with them at all times. The practice of always having something with which to wipe your hands is a habit ingrained in Japanese children from preschool. Public restrooms are usually without paper towels (and sometimes toilet paper) so it is a good idea to get into the habit of carrying a tiny packet of tissues for emergencies.

The Second Point

As with most dinner parties, conversation mingles with drinks and food, and the pace is leisurely (aside from the cooks frying up baskets of *tempura* in the kitchen). You will, most likely, be sampling a variety of new and interesting dishes. In between mouthfuls, you will want to rest your *hashi*.

Lay your chopsticks across the top right-hand section of either your *torizara*, or your *gohan-chawan* ("rice bowl"). If you have a chopstick rest, it is perfectly acceptable to lay them there as well. Do not jab your chopsticks vertically into your bowl of rice and leave them there or lay them down on the table.

The Last Point

If your chopstick skills happen to need a little work, your hosts may take pity on you and try to help you get the things you want to eat. If someone grabs something from the main platter and offers it to you, hold out your plate to accept it. *Never* take something from someone else's chopsticks with your own set of *hashi*. Passing food around from *hashi* to *hashi* is only done at funerals. Japanese are relatively superstitious about performing acts that mimic funeral rituals and will probably involuntarily cringe if you try to take something from an outstretched pair of chopsticks.

Sitting Pretty as Long as Possible

The head of the household—either the grandfather, the father, or the eldest son—will most likely act as your entertainer, and will be seated at the head of the table. Chairs are not a common feature in Japanese homes. Instead, you will be offered a *zabuton* ("floor cushion") upon which to rest.

Start out on your knees with your bottom resting on your heels, if at all possible. This is a formal sitting position that is appropriate for the beginning of the meal. Try to stay in this position at least through the *kampai* and the *itadakimasu*.

Sitting cross-legged is fine for men, but is still considered rather crude for women, so many of them eventually slump to the side, sitting on their hip, with their legs folded underneath. Changing sides often helps to keep the pins and needles away. Be careful when you stand up after sitting for a while, however, as your legs may give out.

Your hosts will likely notice your effort to be polite and insist that you relax and make yourself at home:

63

Ashi o nobashite mo ii desu yo.
Go ahead and stretch your legs out under the table!

Sonna ni teinei-na koto o shinakute mo ii desu yo.
You do not have to be so polite.

You are familiar with the phrase *mo ii desu ka* in connection with requests. A common response to the request is, of course, *Doozo*. Another possible response is *Ii desu yo*. Look at the first sample sentence, for example. The speaker is telling you that it is okay to do something before you even ask. The *yo* at the end of the sentence is a verbal form of punctuation, like *ka*. *Ka* serves as a question mark, while *yo* serves as an exclamation point.

The verb in the second example, *shimasu* ("to do"), is modified like the adjectives above. Only in this case, the *–na* suffix puts it in its negative form. The *–kute* ending lets the listener know that this action is what is under scrutiny.

After insisting that you are fine a few times, it is okay to discreetly stretch out your legs under the table. Most Westerners are unaccustomed to sitting on the floor for long periods at a time and it may take some getting used to. Offering to assist with bringing food or drinks or clearing empty dishes will get you up and moving around. Visiting the restroom will also give you an opportunity to stretch your legs.

Politely Refusing Seconds and Thirds

So, you have sampled one of everything and are genuinely stuffed, yet your hosts keep bringing out more platters of food. With a gruff command from the head of the household, the women are up and scurrying back to the kitchen for *soomen* ("thin wheat noodles") and *mikan* ("tangerines"). Tea flows freely as well and you may feel as if you are about to burst.

Japanese hospitality requires that there be a feast and that no one's palate go unpleased. This attitude sometimes makes for interesting combinations: potato salad and raw squid, for example, or cheese toast and fried shrimp kabobs. When you have really had enough, it is fine to say so.

64

Sumimasen, kekko desu.
I'm sorry, but I'm fine.

Moo onaka ippai desu.
I'm full.

Tottemo manzoku desu.
I'm very satisfied.

Luckily, dessert is not a regular part of Japanese meals. Fruit and tea are the usual finish to a big meal. When these are brought out, you may safely assume the meal is close to being over. Your cooks may finally flop down and relax, as well. This is a perfect time to compliment the host without making anyone think you are still hungry. Refrain from using *Gochisoo-sama deshita* until you are ready to leave.

64

Tottemo oishikatta desu.
That was very delicious.

Hontoo ni ryoori ga umai desu ne.
You really are a great cook.

Notice how the adjective *oishii* ("delicious") is conjugated into the past tense, leaving desu in its simple form. Another, slightly less formal, word for "delicious" appears in the second example: *umai*. The way it is used in this sentence is not impolite, but you would not use it singularly with people you do not know very well, or in a restaurant. *Oishii* can be used alone anytime, anyplace.

When It Is All Over

After all of their great hospitality, you may be shocked when your hosts shove *o-miyage* into your hands as you are leaving. If there was a special dish you showed extra appreciation for, the leftovers wrapped in tin foil may be going home with you. Fruit or Japanese desserts and snacks are also common gifts to depart with. Aren't you glad you brought something when you came?

Now is the time to thank your new friends and repeat *Gochisoo-sama deshita* a few times. The following exchange is also common:

O-kaeri ni ki o tsukete kudasai.
Please be careful on your way home.

Hai ki o tsukemasu yo. O-yasuminasai.
I will be careful. Good night!

Quizzes and Exercises

1. *Kedo* is a shortened version of what word? _____

2. Fill in the appropriate expression: *Massaji de* _____ (Massages feel good.)

3. Where should you wear slippers? (circle all that apply)

   daidokoro　　　　　　　*zashiki*
   toire　　　　　　　　　*shinshitsu*
   genkan

4. Translate the following sentence into English: *Kono surippa wa attaka-kutte kimochi ga ii.*

   _____

5. Rearrange the following words to make an exclamatory sentence: *yo o nobashite ashi ii desu moo*

   _____

6. How do you politely let your hosts know you are full?

   _____

 Countryside Quaintness

Cities around the world have begun to resemble each other almost to a fault. Of course, there are still funky old buildings and old-world neighborhoods, even in Tookyoo. But if you want to get a glimpse of what life was like twenty, thirty, even fifty years ago, it is best to head out into the countryside.

The Next-Door Neighbors

Even in the countryside, there are a variety of living situations available. Apartment buildings house transferred teachers, administrators, and company workers. Housing developments that could have come out of any Midwest suburb cluster around commercial areas, providing single-family dwellings. Larger complexes are reminiscent of old farmhouses with barns and sheds, and are likely occupied by multigenerational families.

If you choose to live in Japan for a while, your *kinjo no hitotachi* ("neighbors") could be anyone: noisy kids, nosy retirees, friendly moms, bossy landlords, or generous gardeners. Whoever they are, you are going to have to learn how to get along with them for the duration of your stay.

Your Business Is Everyone's Business

If you have never lived in a small town before, you may not realize how much your comings and goings are going to be observed. It is probably not anyone's malicious intent to infringe upon your privacy, but Japan's population is only 0.5 percent non-Japanese. That makes you a pretty hot topic, not to mention an interesting sight, around town.

FACT

Hopefully, you will never overhear your name and the word *kinjo-mee-waku* (nuisance to the neighbors) in the same sentence. You may want to use it yourself, though, if you have a complaint about someone living next door. Keep in mind, however, that walls of apartment buildings, especially those that claim to be modern, are pretty thin, so some level of disturbance is unavoidable.

Dealing with some of the "concerns" for your personal life can be managed through a few white lies. If you are not married, but are expecting a visit from or traveling with a partner of the opposite sex, it may be best to introduce him or her as your fiancé or sibling (if you are same-sex partners, all the better, because rural Japan will not suspect a thing). Your neighbors will have an easier time adjusting to the fact that this person is staying with you if they can believe you will be getting married someday:

> *Kochira wa boku no fianse desu. Eemi to iimasu. Yoroshiku onegai shimasu.*
> This is my fiancée. Her name is Amy. Please keep her in your favor.

Garbage Policy Briefings

Another area in which to exercise extra consideration with regard to neighbors is garbage. There are strict laws about what goes in which color bags, where it is placed, and on which days it can be put out. Most garbage is divided into two categories: combustibles *(moeru-gomi)* and noncombustibles *(moenai-gomi)*. Here's a sample dialogue about figuring out the garbage policy.

65

Neighbor 1: *Sumimasen, chotto gomi no dashikata o oshiete kuremasen ka.*
Excuse me, could you explain when and where to put the garbage out?

Neighbor 2: *Gomi, ka. Jaa, moeru gomi-tte wakarimasu ka.*
Garbage, huh? Well, do you understand [the phrase] *"moeru gomi"*?

Neighbor 1: *Hai, wakarimasu.*
Yes, I do.

Neighbor 2: *Moeru gomi wa pinku no iro no fukuro ni iremasu. Getsu-, sui-, kinyoobi ni dashimasu. Asoko no kago ni irete kudasai.*
Put the combustibles in the pink bag. It goes out on Mondays, Wednesdays, and Fridays. Put it in that caged box over there, please.

Neighbor 1: *Hai, wakarimashita. Moenai gomi wa itsu dashimasu ka.*
I see. What about noncombustible garbage?

Neighbor 2: *Moenai gomi wa aoi fukuro ni irete, mai tsuki dai ni kayoobi ni dashimasu.*
Noncombustibles go in the blue bag and are put out on the second Tuesday of each month.

Neighbor 1: *Tsuki ni ikkai desu ka.*
Once a month?

Neighbor 2: *Hai.*
Yes.

Neighbor 1: *Dasu tokoro wa moeru gomi to issho desu ka.*
Do I put it in the same place as the combustible garbage?

Neighbor 2: *Hai, soo desu.*
Yes, that's right.

Neighbor 1: *Doomo arigatoo gozaimashita.*
Thank you so very much.

Neighbor 2: *Dooitashimashite.*
You're welcome.

Checking for Understanding

Look at the second sentence of the dialogue. *Moeru gomi* means "combustible garbage." The construction *moeru gomi-tte* shows that the phrase is being isolated for clarification or comment. When –*tte* is added to a word or phrase, it is as if that phrase were being surrounded by quotation marks. The speaker wants to know if you understand, or are familiar with, a certain concept or word. It is actually a shortened, –*te* ending version of the verb *iu* ("to say") and can be likened to the English phrase "speaking of which."

66

Uindouzu kyu-juu-hachi-tte wakarimasu ka.
Are you familiar with Windows 98?

Sakana-tte wakarimasu ka.
Do you understand [the word] *"sakana"*?

This same phrase can be used to check people's understanding of English words:

66

"Fish"-tte wakarimasu ka.
Do you understand [the word] "fish"?

"Illinois"-tte wakarimasu ka.
Are you familiar with [the state of] Illinois?

This is a relatively frank way of speaking, but communicates your point quickly and easily. To make the phrase more formal, it is necessary to use *to wa* instead of *–tte*:

66

Moeru gomi to wa nani ka wakarimasu ka.
Do you understand the meaning of the words *"moeru gomi"*?

Kayoobi to wa nani ka wakarimasu ka.
Are you familiar with the term *"kayoobi"*?

Being Polite

A young couple renting an old farmhouse has nearly daily visits from their neighbors. In the fall, those visits usually revolve around *kaki* ("persimmons"). A large *kaki* tree stands in front of the rented home and all the neighbors can see that the persimmons are ripening. Fearing that the renting couple is being polite by not picking and eating the *kaki*, the neighbors urge them to *enryo shinai*.

Enryo suru is the overtly polite act of restraining yourself. It is a sign of modesty. Almost all Japanese people, even close friends and family members, will politely refuse an invitation to help themselves to something the first two or three times. Because of this, it is often necessary to offer something three, four, even five times before it is finally accepted. It is up to you to decide how many times you will offer something before you take the person's response at face value.

In rural Japan especially, the art of *enryo* is alive and well. Hosts and neighbors alike may offer you gifts of all sorts. Politeness necessitates the refusal of these things once or twice. This display of modesty can be likened to the English phrase "Oh, you shouldn't have." If you just say "thanks" and receive the bounty immediately, the gift-givers may feel a little jilted. Here's how *enryo* works in action:

67

Host: *Koohii o moo ippai, doozo.*
          Please, have another cup of coffee.

Guest: *Sumimasen, moo o-naka ippai desu.*
          Oh, I'm full, thank you.

Host: *Chotto dake.*
          Just a little.

Guest: *Hontoo ni ii desu.*
          No, really, I'm fine.

Host: *Doozo.*
          Please.

Guest: *Jaa, itadakimasu.*
          Alright, thank you.

Gift-giving and Receiving

Waking up to a robust *konnichiwa* coming from their *genkan*, a young Australian couple teaching English in the Japanese countryside throw on their clothes and cautiously poke their heads out. Standing in his rubber boots, a neighboring farmer holds out a bunch of *daikon* radishes and a prettily wrapped box from the local cake shop. After apologizing for the early hour, he goes on to explain that his daughter is studying for the English proficiency exam and has written an essay. Would they be so kind as to look it over and correct any mistakes? Accepting the radishes and the cakes, the Australian couple can only agree to the request.

Complicated Thanks

Gifts in rural Japan are used as an extra layer of cream (on top of polite words) when requesting a favor. In our example, it is not necessary for the Australians to give a return gift, but there are occasions when it becomes almost mandatory. Your mother may have taught you to write "thank-you" cards, but it is not that simple in Japan. What and how much to give in return for receiving a gift, especially if it is not monetary, can be confusing. Thanks to the market's capitalization of this gift-giving custom, determining the required value of your return gifts is an available service at many stores.

FACT

You may have heard of the "Welcome Wagon" for new neighbors. In Japan, the policy is opposite. The new neighbor must bring a small something (usually a hand towel—something too fancy will make people think they have to give a return gift) around to each neighbor. You must take on the attitude that you are an intrusion and a nuisance, and request that your neighbors forgive you now for any inconvenience you may bring upon them.

Asking your neighbors or a friend who knows about such things (someone different than the gift-giver, of course) for assistance is also acceptable:

Kore o moraimashita. O-kaeshi wa doo sureba ii desu ka.
I was given this. What should I do about a return gift?

Yeah for Yen

As a rule, gifts of money require return gifts of at least half the value. One exception is a gift of money prior to going on a trip; these gifts are called *o-senbetsu*. If you receive *o-senbetsu*, it is fine to just bring back *o-miyage* ("a souvenir") for that person. Gifts of money can be expected on such big occasions as weddings, the birth of a child, graduations, and funerals. If you spend some time in the hospital, people may also give you money to help offset your expenses.

When receiving a gift, it is appropriate to refuse once or twice before accepting with a deep bow and an *Itadakimasu*. When the gift is in the form of *o-miyage,* it is not necessary to supply a return gift, but if you go on a trip somewhere, it is best to remember those who have remembered you. Keeping a list of benefactors may help you keep it all straight. If the *o-miyage* is simply candy, it is fine to just say *O-miyage o arigatoo* or *O-miyage gochi-soo-sama desu/deshita.*

Wading Through the Farmers' Market

Come market day, wagons, carts, and pickup trucks are piled with garden produce and hauled to the designated spot. Farmers set up tents and customers gather around to bargain for baby eggplants, oversized cabbages, and fat bunches of grapes. Grade-schoolers often frequent the market with their sketchpads, attempting to capture the essence of commercial-free commerce.

Haggling for Your Health

You may recognize some of the items at the farmers' market, or you may have seen pictures of them in Asian cookbooks. Names of other items may completely escape you:

Kore no namae wa nan desu ka.
What is this?

Farmers' Market Vocabulary	
nae	shoots (baby plants)
mame	beans
tane	seeds
nooyaku	pesticides
munnooyaku	organic
gennooyaku	one application of pesticides (semi-organic)
hatake	garden
tanbo	rice paddy
kingyo	gold fish
koi	carp
o-hana	flowers
tsukuru	to make
sodatsu	to grow, raise
maku, makimasu	to plant (seeds); to spray (pesticides)

Local Delicacies

Ichi, as these open-air markets are referred to, are also a good place to pick up some authentic local dishes. One such delicacy is the *tsukemono*. These Japanese-style pickles come in a variety of colors, shapes, and sizes, depending on the vegetable used to make them. Tiny eggplant, gnarly cucumbers, and the king of radishes, the *daikon*, are all popular *tsukemono*. *Umeboshi*, though made with the Japanese apricot, can also be lumped into the *tsukemono* category, as it often shows up in the center of *o-nigiri*, which is a rice ball that is flattened in the shape of a triangle.

In the case of the Japanese pickle, the name says it all. Simple and direct, *tsukemono* combines *tsukeru* ("pickle," "preserve") with *mono* ("thing"). The knowledge of how to *tsukeru* these *mono* may disappear when the *o-baa-chans* pass away, however. Ask your neighbors or the friendly market women for advice on how to *tsukeru* and you may get several different replies. As with a lot of traditional foods, people just make it the way they always have. If you take a particular liking to a certain pickle, be it the *takuwan* or the *rakkyo*, you had better interview the person you bought it from and get to pickling yourself.

68

Kono tsukemono wa doo yatte tsukeru no.
How do you make this pickle?

Kono tsukemono no tsukekata o oshiete kudasai.
What is the process for pickling this particular pickle?

Finding Out the Market Schedule

Markets organized for special occasions are usually advertised, but the ones that happen every week, or once a month on a certain day, are not. If you wander around enough you may eventually stumble onto one. Then, you can ask one of the stall owners what days the farmers gather.

69

Kono ichi wa itsu yarimasu ka.
When do you have this market?

Kono ichi wa nan nichi ni yaru no.
On what day do you have this market?

Market days may vary with the seasons, or they may be held rain or shine. Each town and farmers' group may be different.

69

Mai tsuki tooka ni yaru yo.
It's held on the tenth of each month.

Mai shuu mokuyoobi ni yarimasu.
Every Thursday, we do the market.

You may be able to guess from context that *mai* means "every." Note that the appropriate word for "month" in this case is *tsuki*, rather than *getsu* or *gatsu*.

If you happen to miss the market, another option is to locate a *hyaku-en sutando* ("100-yen stand"). These "mini-markets" often consist of a simple stall set up by the side of the road. Vegetables, fruits, flowers, and occasionally *tsukemono* can be found inside. There is usually a little fire-safety box where you insert your 100 yen coin—one for each item bought.

Local Dialects

Speaking in the countryside will not be a problem, but understanding the replies could take some practice. *Toshi totte iru* ("elderly"; literally, "taking years") people have a tendency to communicate in the local dialects, but young people are starting to reclaim these dialects as well.

New Question Indicator

In rural areas, you may hear the question indicator *ka* replaced by the more colloquial *no*:

> *Nasubi wa iranai no.*
> Don't you need some eggplant?

Get a group of people from different parts of Japan in the same room and the conversation will inevitably shift to dialects and their nuances. You may be surprised at the variation in terms as the comparisons make the rounds of regions. It is a great source of amusement and regional pride for the people involved to try and explain the history of their individual colloquialisms.

This way of asking a question is gentler and is more commonly used by women. *No* also shows up as an audible pause (like "um" or "uh") as people struggle to communicate the unique deliciousness of their *daikon* ("Japanese radish") or *kaki* ("persimmon"). In this way, it resembles the *ne* sometimes used when trying to get someone's attention:

> *Ano ne, kono daikon wa oishii yo.*
> Hey, um, this long radish is tasty!

Aside from these subtle semantic differences, there are entire words and phrases whose connection to standard Japanese is elusive, to say the least. Using contextual clues, most Japanese people can guess at the meaning of local vocabulary words.

Exiled Words

Travel to Sado-ga-shima, an island in the Sea of Japan, and you will find colloquialisms from all over the country. *Sado-ben* ("Sado's dialect") has many words in common with the area around Kyooto, referred to as "Kansai." There used to be a ship that traveled from Kansai to Sado and then north to the island of Hokkaido called the *Kitamaebune*. This ship loaded and deposited many colloquialisms from Kyooto to Sado.

For example, the phrase *tori ga utau* ("birds sing") is used in both Kansai and on Sado, but in other parts of Japan, people say *tori ga naku* ("birds cry"). Other Kyooto-influences can be seen in the words *tessho* ("dish") and *nekui* ("warm").

Another colloquialism from Sado is *daccha*. It is a twisted version of *desu* and is used to express emphasis.

70

> *Sore wa ii-n daccha.*
> That's good!

> *Soo daccha.*
> That's right!

Sometimes this shortened form of *desu* is further abbreviated into a just plain *cha*. It can also be attached to verbs, adjectives, or adverbs to create interesting new words. Recent resurgences of local pride have moved people to highlight this unique phrase by adding it to roadside signs, community newsletters, and T-shirts.

70

Kore wa umeeccha.
This is scrumptious.

Tabeeccha.
Eat!

FACT

Efforts to preserve *Sado-ben* can be seen most distinctly in the work of *Sooei Kodama*. His hobby is collecting Sado folktales and then making them into children's books. By recording the stories in Sado's dialect and enlisting local wood-block print and paper collage artists to do the illustrations, Kodoma has helped to preserve local storytelling traditions.

Quizzes and Exercises

1. What is a *kinjo meewaku?*

2. Change the following verbs to their "how-to" versions.

   dasu _____
   tsukau _____
   taberu _____
   nomu _____

3. Translate the following sentence into English: *O-sake-tte wakarimasu ka.*

4. Read the following conversation, then answer the question:

Chotto oshiete kudasai. Moeru gomi wa nan yoobi ni dashimasu ka.
Moeru gomi wa maishuu ka to mokuyoobi ni dashimasu yo.
Arigatoo gozaimashita.
Doo itashimashite.

On which days do you put out combustible garbage?

_____

5. If you receive *o-senbetsu,* what should you do?

_____

6. Which of the following words combine to make the word for Japanese pickles? (Circle two words, one from each column.)

tsukuru   *daikon*

tsukau   *mono*

tsukeru   *ringo*

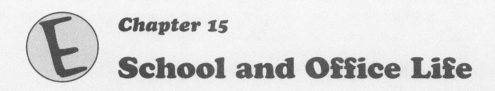

Chapter 15

School and Office Life

Working in Japan for any period of time will pose a variety of situations that may be new and unfamiliar. The unquestioning attitude with which your coworkers go about their jobs may surprise you. What westerners have a tendency to consider private sometimes ends up being an office-determined policy. Conforming to some extent may help you ease into your new workspace. Developing good relationships with your coworkers will help to make the transition a smooth one.

Morning Rituals

Whether you are a jump-out-of-bed-and-do-ten-pushups kind of person, or you need at least three cups of coffee before you open your eyes fully, getting to work on time should be a major priority. In exchange for your devotion to your job, your office or school will look out for you in a variety of ways. Making sure you are healthy and adjusting well to life in Japan will be a top concern for your coworkers and supervisors.

Morning Meetings

Tardiness is extremely discouraged in Japanese schools and offices. Reinforcement of this policy seems to be limited to peer pressure, a common force in shaping behavior in Japanese society, but it's effective—people are seldom late for work. Morning meeting times may vary with location. 8:00 or 8:15 A.M. on the dot is a common starting time for schools and government-related offices.

Morning meetings start with everyone standing at their desks. When everyone is ready, the vice principal or office secretary initiates a bow and everyone says *O-hayou gozaimasu* ("Good morning") in unison. The date is announced along with any special events going on that day. After the initial greeting, the leader will ask if anyone has any announcements.

When you are a newcomer, and later, when there are other newcomers, you may be asked to give a short self-introduction, or *jiko shokai.* If there is not much time, you may be limited to just a quick one, *hito koto.*

> *Kore kara Buraian-san kara hito koto ga arimasu.*
> Now, we will have a quick word from Brian.

> *Buraian-san onegai shimasu.*
> Brian, please go ahead.

In this situation, simply stating your name followed by a *doozo yoroshiku onegai shimasu* will suffice. If you are asked to give a *jiko shokai,* then a more complete self-introduction is appropriate.

ALERT!

If you are working as an English teacher in Japan, your students and maybe some of your colleagues will refer to you as *sensei* ("teacher"), but you cannot refer to yourself this way and your superiors will not use this term to address you. Even in modern-day Japan, the title of *sensei* has connotations of great respect, so it would be considered very egotistical to refer to yourself as *sensei*. If you are indeed an English teacher, you can describe your job by saying *Eigo o oshiete imasu* ("I'm teaching English").

Morning Exercises

Many offices also require group participation in an exercise that is famous throughout Japan: *rajio taiso*. This is a short routine with various stretches, deep knee-bends, and arm swinging. These exercises are believed to contribute to good health.

71

Kenkoo no tame ni mai asa rajio taiso o yarimasu.
For our health, we do radio exercises every morning.

The phrase *no tame ni* identifies the reason or purpose for something. In the previous phrase, *kenkoo* ("health") is the reason for performing these calisthenics. Other words can be substituted for *kenkoo* to create statements about things that are important to you.

71

Benkyoo no tame ni Nihon ni kimashita.
I came to Japan to study.

Shigoto no tame ni koko ni hikkoshite kimashita.
I moved here because of my job.

Similarly, you can also show that an action is being performed for the sake of a particular person.

O-kaa-san no tame ni mai toshi Amerika ni kaerimasu.
For my mother's sake, I go home to America every year.

Minna no tame ni ganbatte imasu.
I'm trying my best for everyone's sake.

> Don't forget about the Japanese custom of giving *o-miyage* ("souvenirs"). If you're going to Japan to start a new job, it's best to bring lots of souvenirs from home. Penny stamps, chocolates, lapel pins, and pens or pencils with your town logo on them are just a few ideas for appropriate *o-miyage*. Your new supervisor can help you determine the number of people needing gifts in your workplace.

Bonding with Coworkers

Aside from the occasional *enkai*, there are many opportunities throughout the day in which to develop relationships with your coworkers. Conversing during coffee breaks or while taking lunch gives you a chance to get to know them. Scheduled meeting times, too, provide a chance to communicate. Even simply being present, working at your desk, fosters a sense of camaraderie.

The School Lunch

If you will be teaching English in Japan, you may have the option of eating at the school cafeteria. If you have strict dietary regulations, it is probably wise to bring your own lunch. Many Japanese elementary schools have adopted the slogan:

Nan demo taberu to joobu-na karada o tsukuru.
Eating a wide variety of food is the way to make a strong, healthy body.

Kids are expected to eat everything that is served and teachers, therefore, must model this behavior. Note that the phrase *nan demo* literally means "anything," so *nan demo taberu* means "to eat anything." Substituting other verbs for *taberu*, you can make sentences with phrases such as *nan demo nomu* ("drink anything"), *nan demo suru* ("do anything"), and so on.

72

Kare wa nan demo dekiru.
He can do anything.

Kanojo wa nan demo tsukureru.
She can make anything.

Watashi wa nan demo yaru yo.
I'll do anything!

If you feel that you cannot eat all that you are served, there are several things you can do, but it's important to limit waste. You may notice some teachers shaving off the top half of their bowls of rice back into the pot. Other teachers may be willing to accept whatever is you don't wish to eat. It is considered polite and respectful toward hardworking farmers, however, to eat every last grain of rice in your bowl. It is fine to use your *hashi* to put the rice back or into someone else's bowl as long as they have not touched your mouth yet.

Your coworkers may comment on your use of chopsticks and wonder how or where you learned to eat with them.

72

O-hashi no tsukaikata wa joozu desu ne.
Your use of chopsticks is excellent.

Amerika de mo o-hashi o tsukaimasu ka.
Do you use chopsticks in the States, too?

O-hashi no tsukaikata wa dare ga oshiete kureta-n desu ka.
Who taught you how to use chopsticks?

Responses to these questions will vary depending on your experience with using chopsticks prior to coming to Japan.

 72

Uchi de wa o-hashi o tokidoki tsukaimasu.
We sometimes use chopsticks at my house.

Chuugoku no resutoran toka Ajia no resutoran de wa tsukaimasu.
I use chopsticks at Chinese restaurants or other Asian restaurants.

FACT

If someone approaches you with hands in prayer position and says, *Onegai ga aru,* he or she is looking for a favor. You may recognize *onegai* from the oft-used phrase *onegai shimasu.*

Scheduled Meeting Times

Meetings are an important aspect of Japanese work life. Whether you are team teaching or involved in a committee, organizing a club or helping with a project, *uchiawase* ("meetings") will be one of your job duties.

 73

Buraian-sensei uchiawase wa itsu dekimasu ka.
When are you able to have a meeting, Brian?

Nigakki no uchiawase wa raishuu no getsuyoobi ni onegai shimasu.
Please observe that the meeting for the second semester is next Monday.

Your coworkers probably do not speak much English so these meetings may involve the use of dictionaries, gestures, and, above all, laughter. Try to be aware of the group dynamics and follow suit. Some teachers enjoy team-teaching lessons, while others prefer to let you handle the activities. Pushing your own ideas relentlessly onto other people is not effective in any country, but will be especially ill-received in Japan.

Break Times

Breaks are another chance to get to know your coworkers a little better. Making yourself available during these times provides other people opportunities to interact with you. A few may be interested in practicing their English, while others will be curious about your life in your home country and how it compares to life in Japan. You may find yourself responding to the same questions over and over again.

74

Amerika to Nihon wa docchi ga samui desu ka.
Which is colder, the U.S. or Japan?

Nihon no tabemono wa doo desu ka.
How do you like Japanese food?

Naze Nihon ni kimashita ka.
Why did you come to Japan?

It is not uncommon for teachers to smoke in either the teachers' room near the exhaust fan or in the lounge. Most buildings also have a smoking area indoors. Rather than protesting directly, coughing or asking if you can close the door is considered a polite way to let people know you do not want them smoking around you.

Cleaning Time

O-sooji ("cleaning") is a daily activity for Japanese students and teachers. Unlike U.S. schools, where a custodial staff takes care of the building, Japanese schools are cleaned by their occupants. Everybody cleans, even the principal. Both teachers and students will appreciate your participation.

Which Room

If you are assigned to a cleaning task force, a specific area of the school will become your responsibility for the week or the month.

School Rooms	
taiikukan	gymnasium
seito genkan	student entrance
kyooin genkan	teachers' entrance
kyooshitsu	classroom
kyoomushitsu	teachers' room
toshoshitsu	library
ongakushitsu	music room
rooka	hallway

At the end of cleaning time, everyone lines up and the designated student leader checks to make sure each person finished the designated task. Teachers are also assigned to a specific cleaning team, but they often step back and allow the students to perform the managerial responsibilities.

Which Floor

The counter for floors has only one oddball: three. When referring to the first and second, and then fourth on up, the counter is *kai*. For "third floor," *gai* is used instead of *kai*.

Ni kai no ongakushitsu de o-sooji o shite kudasai.
Please clean the second floor music room.

San gai de o-sooji o shite kudasai.
Please clean on the third floor.

Cleaning Supplies

Cleaning supplies are generally located in several different places throughout the school. They usually consist of only a few things, however.

Cleaning Supplies	
bakettsu	bucket
zookin	rag for the floor
fukin	rag for tabletops, counters
o-mizu	water
hooki	broom
chiritori	dustpan
gomibako	trashcan
gomibukaro	trashbag

Cleaning time usually only lasts about fifteen minutes, and there is often music being played over the loudspeaker to keep people "whistling while they work." A member of the broadcasting club will keep track of the time and announce when there are five minutes remaining. This is a cue for the student managers to get everyone to line up for reporting.

When planning your mini-vacations either within Japan or abroad, keep in mind that Japanese people usually use their paid vacation time for when they are ill and rarely to take time off from work for fun. Concerned that an absence will adversely affect the school or company, most Japanese people refrain from traveling except during designated holidays.

Rag Racing

Many places still practice *zookin gake,* the Buddhist monk style of cleaning the floors. The act consists of grabbing a damp *zookin* with both of your hands and placing it on the floor. At the signal, start running, pushing the rag in front of you to wipe the floor. When you get to the other end, turn around and head back.

With large rooms, usually several people perform this floor-cleaning routine at once, so the job is quickly finished. Supposedly, being on all fours stimulates parts of your brain that you do not always use. It takes some getting used to, but once you get the hang of it, you just might start enjoying yourself. You may even end up taking this custom back with you to clean your own floors.

Sports Days and Culture Festivals

Dating back several generations, *undookai* or *taiikusai* ("sports days") and *bunkasai* ("culture festivals") are celebrated on a variety of levels. Public schools at all levels spend a considerable amount of time and energy organizing events to compete with each other physically or to display artistic and creative talents.

A Day of Activity

In the shade of awnings erected specifically for the festival, grandmas and grandpas can stretch out on woven straw mats and enjoy the *o-bentoo* ("boxed lunch") brought from home. Parents are often roped into participating in a few events themselves. It is a busy day for some, but relaxing for others. In exchange for coming to school all day on a Sunday, the following Monday is awarded as a day off.

For the sports festival, students are divided into two teams: *akagumi* and *shirogumi* ("red team" and "white team"). For weeks leading up to the actual day, students practice running, tugs-of-war, three-legged races, hurdles, high jumps, and long jumps. More traditional activities like climbing a bamboo pole barefoot to retrieve the flag of the opposing team, or working as a team to get as many balls as possible into a basket held high, are also rehearsed.

In addition to these physical challenges, students must practice organized cheerleading and marching-band formations. Each team has a designated cheerleader, *ooendancho*, or group of leaders, *ooendan*, who conduct a call-and-response type of cheer. These cheers might be original, or they might be passed down from previous years. Though sports festivals date back to before World War II, some elements were adopted from the western world following the war.

Sports Day Terms	
undookai	sports day
taikusai	sports day
guraundo	playground
renshuu	practice
ooensuru	cheer
ooendan	cheerleader
ooendancho	head cheerleader
kotekitai	marching band
seifuku	uniform
rikujoo kyoogi	track and field events

Showing Off

Culture festivals also take place on Sundays so that everyone can attend. Students and teachers set up displays of pottery, paintings, sculptures, collages, and original work the week before. The school is cleaned from top to bottom, and festive red and white banners are draped along the walls of the gymnasium.

Some *bunkasai* also have a *happyookai* element (a recital or talent show of sorts) where students perform skits, dances, and musical numbers, or give presentations on things they have studied throughout the year. After the performances, visitors can wander the hallways and into the classrooms to see the artwork on display. The PTA (parent-teacher association) often sells a variety of lunch items like curry rice, *mochi* ("rice cakes"), *yaki-soba* ("stir-fried noodles"), and *o-nigiri* ("rice balls").

The whole community may also celebrate its very own culture day with similar activities. There is even a national holiday called *bunka no hi* ("Culture Day") on November 3. It is one of the few times that you can see Japanese flags flying in front of stores.

Dress Codes

Standards for professional wear in Japan are similar to those in the United States. Standard celebration fare for men is a black suit with a white necktie and shirt. Women wear skirts and jackets or sometimes *kimono* or *hakama* (traditional Japanese wide-legged pants that tie above the waist with a broad sash).

Teachers will often start out wearing something professional for the morning meeting, but will then change into sweats or sportswear for the rest of the day. Their responsibilities range from physical education coach to music conductor, so optimal freedom of movement is a consideration. Principals and vice principals, too, will start out with suits, but may be in more casual clothing by lunchtime. You will know special guests are expected that day if everyone stays dressed up. Someone will, hopefully, let you know when you are expected to dress formally.

> *Ashita ni seisoo de kite kudasai.*
> Please come dressed formally tomorrow.

> *Kuroi suutsu ga areba, sore o kite kudasai.*
> If you have a black suit, please wear that.

Offices tend to be more formal on a day-to-day basis. Women usually wear heels and nylons with a skirt or suit. Men wear neckties and suits. After working somewhere for a while, you can see what other people in your office wear to work and follow their lead.

QUESTION?

Did you notice the word *kite* has two different meanings in the previous examples?

In the first example, *kite* is the imperative (*–te*) version of *kuru* ("to come"). In the second example, *kite* is the imperative form of the verb *kiru* ("to wear"). *Ki o tsukete ne!*

Leaving Before Everyone Else

Technically, work hours are 8:15 to 5:15, but usually only the ALTs (assistant language teachers) actually observe those hours. Bogged down with paperwork and planning for extra events such as sports days and culture festivals, teachers often put in overtime without receiving extra pay. Likewise, if a teacher is sick, he or she will opt to take paid vacation leave rather than paid sick leave; it has something to do with end of the year bonuses, which take sick days into account.

The Part-Timer's Hours

If you are working in a Japanese school as an assistant English language teacher (ALT), your hours may be part-time or full-time, depending on whether you are municipally or independently employed. Even thirty-five hours a week is considered part-time, however, so do not fill out your moonlighting application just yet.

It is unlikely that you will be given responsibility for a homeroom class, so your job will consist of planning lessons, making materials for those lessons, and meeting with the homeroom teachers. Some schools may have already designed a curriculum, but other districts will leave it up to you to determine your lesson objectives. The bottom line is, you may find yourself with plenty of time on your hands. What are appropriate activities for your paid "free time"?

1. Lesson-related, Internet-based research is fine in small doses.
2. Making games, flashcards, puppets, and other materials is great.
3. Studying Japanese is also an admirable activity.
4. Trips to the local library may provide supplementary lesson material.

Things that should be avoided are:

1. Excessive e-mailing.
2. Reading novels or magazines.
3. Sleeping at your desk (unless it is during a designated break time).

Quitting Time

After a busy, productive day, you may be anxious to leave. When the appropriate time comes, you are free to go home. It is likely, however, that no one else will be leaving before you. Therefore, there is a set phrase that you must use as you head out the door.

75

Mina-san, o-saki ni shitsurei shimasu.
Everyone, please excuse me for being rude by going home first.

Mina-san is the term that can be used to address a group of people in both casual and formal circumstances. The honorific form is *mina-sama* ("ladies and gentlemen"). It is also sometimes pronounced with an extra *n*, *minna-san*.

Shitsurei shimasu is a phrase you will hear often in the school or office setting. Students will say it upon entering the teachers' room, and will repeat it in past-tense form upon exiting: *Shitsurei shimashita*. You may also hear it used when someone is passing in front of you or trying to get around you: *Chotto shitsurei shimasu.* It can often be used interchangeably, or in conjunction with, *Sumimasen* ("Excuse me").

ALERT!

If you happen to be a few minutes late when reporting for work in the morning, it is appropriate to use the past-tense form of the phrase, "I was rude": *Shitsurei shimashita*. If you really want to impress your boss, go straight to her desk, bow, and say: *O-kuremashite sumimasen deshita. Shitsurei shimashita.*

If you politely excuse yourself to go home, whoever is in the office at the time of your departure will likely respond with *O-tsukare-sama deshita* or *Go-kuroo-sama deshita*. Both are expressions of appreciation for hard work.

O-tsukare-sama deshita can be broken down into four parts. The "O" is honorific, of course. *Tsukare* means "fatigue," or "tiredness." *Sama* is a polite version of the suffix used after peoples' names (*san*). And *deshita* is the past-tense form of the verb "to be." All four separate elements combine to make a phrase that lets you know your efforts are being acknowledged.

Go-kuroo-sama deshita, or the less formal *Go-kuroo-san,* essentially means the same thing: "Thanks for your trouble." People may say it to you as a parting expression, even when you are not working. It is not appropriate, in either form, to say this phrase to a superior.

FACT

When leaving a room, it is most polite to bow and back out of the door. Acknowledging the people in the office still working as well as showing respect for the space in which you are employed are the main feelings behind this demonstration.

Quizzes and Exercises

1. What is the difference between a *jiko shokai* and a *hito koto*?

2. Rearrange the following words into a sentence: *ni tame no kaimono o shite imasu yuhan*

3. Fill in the missing phrase: *Burain-sensei wa _____ taberu ne!*

4. What is *uchiawase*?

5. Translate the following sentence into English: *Ongakushitsu wa san gai ni arimasu.*

6. What is the difference between *undookai* and *bunkasai*?

7. What are two things you should remember to do as you leave to go home?

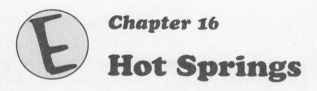

Chapter 16

Hot Springs

O nsen is translated as "hot spring," but this term can be misleading. *Onsen* are not always fed by a natural hot spring. Some places heat their water with a wood fire, while others simply use a boiler. If you smell sulfur, you will know you have found the real thing. Often, different minerals will be added to the bath water to make it more beneficial. Most people come to an *onsen* for the atmosphere rather than their health, however.

House Policies

Different *onsen* have different layouts, hours of operation, rules, and benefits. Prices and ways of buying tickets also vary, depending on the place.

Sara's Story

Anxious to try out the *onsen* up the street from her new home in rural Japan, an assistant language teacher stepped through the automatic doors and into the lobby. The three men in suits standing behind the counter looked surprised to see her. In her limited Japanese, she asked for directions to the *o-furo* and inquired, *O-ikura desu ka.* The men appeared concerned and Sara eventually realized that there seemed to be no one else in the building.

It dawned on her that the *onsen* must be closed and she began to back out of the door. At this, the men protested vehemently and insisted that she take a bath, free of charge. Acting out of kindness, the managers opened the women's bathing area. They may have feared that she was a traveler and that this was her only chance to bathe at the *onsen*. For Sara, however, the situation became a mixture of embarrassment and discomfort at bathing alone in a deserted *onsen* while three men in suits waited outside.

Being able to determine whether a business is operating, or not, on a particular day could save you from some potentially disconcerting situations.

76

Ima wa aite imasu ka.
Are you open now?

Kyoo wa yatte imasu ka.
Are you operating today?

Ima wa shimatte imasu ka.
Are you closed now?

Yasumi no hi wa itsu desu ka.
What day are you closed?

Nan-ji kara nan-ji made yatte imasu ka.
What are your hours?

In the last example, the duo *kara* and *made* combine to identify the operating hours of the *onsen*. An answer can be formed by replacing *nan-ji* ("what time") with a specific time. For example: *Ku-ji kara juu ichi-ji made yatte imasu.* If you want to discuss something that will occur between those times, it is necessary to add the words *no aida.* The sentence then becomes: *Ku-ji kara juu ichi-ji made no aida ni yarimasu.*

FACT

Yatte imasu, or *yaru,* is an informal version of the verb *suru* ("to do"). It can also mean "give" as in *ame wo yaru ka* ("Would you like some candy?"). A verb in *–te* form followed by *yaru* indicates something is being done as a favor and often carries the connotation of social superiority. It is most often used by an older person when speaking to someone younger.

How to Pay

Some *onsen* have a reception counter where you pay anywhere between 300 and 700 yen for a ticket. Other places have machines where you insert your money and push a button that indicates how many tickets you need. There are different buttons for adults and children, so you may want to ask for assistance.

77

Sumimasen, kono kikai no tsukaikata o oshiete kudasai.
Please show me how to use this machine.

Otona futari to kodomo san nin no kippu onegai shimasu.
We need tickets for two adults and three children, please.

Minna de o-ikura ni narimasu ka.
How much will it be for everyone?

Sumimasen otona hitori wa docchi o oseba ii desu ka.
Which one should I push for one adult?

Remember, when *–kata* appears at the end of a verb, it may indicate "how to." In the first example, *tsukau* ("to use") is changed to *tsukai* ("use") and then, when the suffix *–kata* is added, becomes *tsukaikata* ("how to use"). Being able to change verbs into this form makes it easier to get people to teach you things.

ALERT!

In two of the verbs in the previous examples, removing the suffix *–kata* reveals the noun form of the verb: *odoru* ("to dance") becomes *odori* ("dance") and *kangaeru* ("to think") becomes *kangae* ("thought"). This does not necessarily apply to all verbs, however. For example, *tabe* does not mean "food." The word for food is *tabemono*, which is formed by adding *mono* ("thing") to the root.

Which One Is Which

Unlike bathroom doors, the entrances to the separate bathing areas for men and women do not have little figures in a skirt or suit. You can always ask a manager or another bather for assistance:

Sumimasen, otoko no hito no araiba wa dotchi desu ka.
Which one is the men's bathing area?

It is more polite to use *otoko no hito* and *onna no hito* rather than just *otoko* or *onna*. Another (simpler) way to refer to male and female is *danshi* and *joshi* or *josei*. In this case, it is not necessary to add *hito*. *Danshi* and *joshi* are often used by teachers in school when talking to or about their students. Changing *hito* to *ko* changes the reference to indicate children. *Onna-no-ko* and *otoko-no-ko* are the words for "girl" and "boy."

Follow the Rules

Behavior and things that are not allowed in the *onsen* are similar to those reserved for poolside. Smoking in the bathing area is forbidden, as is alcohol and any glass containers. Running is also against the rules.

Different places may have different rules. If you happen to break a rule unknowingly, you may be reprimanded by the manager, or by other bathers.

78

Koko de suenai yo.
You cannot smoke here.

Kore wa dame yo.
This is not allowed.

Sono koto o yatte wa ikemasen.
You can't do that here.

If you ever hear the verb *ikemasen*, you will know that what you are doing is not allowed. It is the polite version of *ikenai* ("bad," "wrong") and can be likened to saying "You must not (do)." This message is most often expressed with the "forbidden" verb in its *–te* form followed by *wa* (to identify the behavior as the subject of the sentence), plus *ikemasen*.

Getting Settled

An authentic *onsen* experience requires special supplies. Getting undressed and dressed require special words. Despite these complications, keep in mind that relaxation is the main objective.

Buying a Bath Set

Most people bring their own towels and other bathing necessities to the *onsen* from home. Some *onsen* double as a type of *ryokan* or hostel and may have towels or an *o-furo* set (which usually includes toothbrush and toothpaste, razor, comb, and body towel) for sale:

O-furo setto wa o-ikura desu ka.
How much is the bath set?

"Towel," in Japanese, is just the *katakana*-style English version: *taoru.*
Several towels are often necessary when visiting the *onsen.* You need one
to wash with (in place of a washcloth, Japanese use a long, thin towel), one
to wrap your head in, and one to wipe yourself off with when you are done.
You can specify which towel you need with other *katakana* English words:

baasu taoru	bath towel
hando taoru	hand towel
fuesu taoru	face towel

If you forget the name for bathing area (*araiba*) you can just use the
phrase *no wa* as in *Sumimasen, onna no hito no wa docchi desu ka.*
("Which one is the women's?") *No wa* is a great substitute for forgotten
nouns. It is like saying "thing" or "stuff."

Keep Your Pants On

The verb for "to get dressed" depends on the type of clothing. With a scarf
or apron, you must *suru.* For jackets, sweaters, dresses, and shirts, the verb
is *kiru.* For pants, underwear, and shoes you must *haku.* Cold weather gets
even trickier as you *hameru* your gloves and *kaburu* your hat. Accessories
have their own standards as well: Glasses require you to *kakeru,* but you
tsukeru a ribbon and *shimeru* belts and neckties.

Luckily, getting undressed is simpler—use the verb *nugu* for all of the
above.

 79

Fuku o nuide kara, kago ni irete kudasai.
After you take off your clothes, please put them in the basket.

Koko de surippa o nuide kudasai.
Please remove your slippers here.

The first example illustrates a new compound verb conjugation. Like other compound verb sentences, the first verb is changed into its –*te* form, but this time the word *kara* ("from") comes after the verb. Translated verbatim from the Japanese, the sentence would look like this: "Clothes take-off from, basket in put please." *Kara* can be used after most verbs in the –*te* form to indicate the order of action to be taken.

79

Yuhan o tabete kara, ikimasu.
After I have eaten dinner, I will go.

Kutsu o katte kara, hakimasu.
After I have purchased the shoes, I will put them on.

Where to Wash First

As with many first-time experiences, it is always helpful to have a guide, or at least someone to model the appropriate behavior. Unless you have entered the *onsen* when it is closed, there will most likely be others whom you can watch and learn from.

It is important to make sure you're fully clean before you step into the bath. Some visitors simply take a shower prior to heading over to the big bath area, but if you want to go native, grab a scoop-bucket and go straight to the bath. Squat down next to it and dip your bucket into the piping hot water. Start by pouring water over your hands and feet to get used to the temperature. Once you have adjusted to the *oyu* ("hot water"), continue dipping and dousing until your whole body has been thoroughly cleaned and rinsed. It is now safe for you to step into the bath.

If you want to give your circulation a workout, alternate between the *o-furo* and the *mizuburo* ("cold-water bath"). You may see people going back and forth between the sauna and the *mizuburo* as well. Some places have a thermometer advertising the temperature (in Celsius) of the different pools, so you can make an educated decision about which ones to enter and which ones to avoid.

If you wash your hair, it is proper *onsen* etiquette to wrap your head in a towel before entering the communal pool. This prevents hair from trailing in the water and clogging the drains. Even if you do not wash your hair, it is still common courtesy to keep it out of the water.

Naked Talk

Onsen hold different significance for different people. Some go only a few times a year, others are weekly dippers. If you live in Japan and begin to go to the *onsen* on a regular basis, you will certainly start to recognize some faces. You may even find yourself conducting English lessons in the bath or sauna. *Eikaiwa buro* ("English Conversation Bath") can be a fun way to get to know people and an easy way to bridge the communication gap.

Comments from Fellow Bathers

As if communal bathing weren't intimate enough, conversations in the bath may probe any remaining privacy you have left. Again, of course, it depends on the situation and where you are located in Japan, but questions are likely to arise with a foreigner in the midst.

80

Onsen wa suki desu ka.
Do you like hot springs?

Sauna ni haite mo daijoobu desu ka.
Is it okay for you to go into the sauna?

Nihon ni sunde imasu ka.
Do you live in Japan?

Nihon ni kite kara nan nen ni narimasu ka.
How many years have you lived here?

Nonbiri de ii kimochi desu ne.
It feels good to relax and take it easy, doesn't it?

In a room where everyone is naked, body comparisons (either voiced aloud or kept to yourself) are inevitable. People who have grown up in this atmosphere, however, may more readily recognize that there are all different shapes, sizes, and colors.

Body Parts	
kao	face
atama	head
kaminoke	hair
kubi	neck
me	eyes
mimi	ears
hana	nose
kuchi	mouth
ude	arms
te	hands
senaka	back
koshi	lower back
oshiri	behind, buttocks
ashi	legs
hiza	knees
ashi	feet

While You Are Washing

Because of our busy lives, we have a tendency to multitask even when we are supposed to be relaxing. Chatting while washing your hair or sweating in the sauna does not have to be stressful. Describing the action of doing more than one thing at a time in Japanese, though, may be.

To show that one action is happening simultaneously with another action, add the suffix *–nagara* to the verb stem of the main verb. *Nagara*, in this case, means "while."

81

Atama o arainagara kiite imasu.
I'm listening while I wash my hair.

Terebi o minagara, tabete imasu.
I'm eating while watching television.

Sauna ni hairinagara, hanashimashoo.
Let's talk while we are in the sauna.

Kare wa unten shinagara, tabako wo sutteimasu.
He is smoking while he is driving.

There is even a type of dental hygiene called *nagaraburasshingu,* brushing your teeth while doing something else.

If Someone Offers

Like the atmosphere at an *enkai*, normal societal rules of interaction seem to be stripped off with peoples' clothes at an *onsen*. Voices are often boisterous, laughter echoes off of the tiles, and frank statements are common. It may be a setting that sends you fleeing home, never to return, or one that brings you back time and again.

Visiting the *onsen* can be a great cure for homesickness as the friendly, intimate ambiance and relaxing mood release your tensions and put things into perspective.

Sign of Respect

On either side of the wall that divides the men's and women's bathing areas, there is a traditional demonstration of respect and friendship. This gesture is washing someone's back for him or her. You may see it happen between complete strangeers.

If someone offers to wash your back for you, it is wise to humbly accept, even if you do not know the person very well. The gesture, between strangers, is meant to be an extension of friendship or goodwill:

> *Senaka o aratte ageyo ka.*
> Shall I wash your back for you?

In this case, it is not necessary to *enryo*. A simple, accepting *arigatoo* will acknowledge that you recognize the significance of this gesture. If you agree, the scrubber will take your towel and soap and give your back the cleaning of a lifetime. If you feel comfortable doing so, it is nice to return the favor by washing this person's back, too:

> *Kondo wa watashi ga aratte agemashoo ka.*
> Now, shall I wash you?

Giving and Receiving

Verbs for giving and receiving in Japanese can get a little tricky at times. With the verb *ageru*, for example, you might think that changing it to its *–te* form and adding a *kudasai* will get you what you want, but the Japanese are way too polite for that. If you want something, you must use *moraitai, itadakitai, hoshii,* or a special form of *kudasai*.

If you want someone to do something for you, there are more than a few verb combination options available. These duos can also be used to describe someone's act of kindness, such as a massage, backwashing, or other favor.

82

Yatte moraimasu ka.
Will you do it for me?

Yatte kureru?
Will you do it for me? (informal)

Senaka o aratte kudasaru.
She will wash my back for me. (honorific)

Kare wa gohan o tsukutte kureta.
He made dinner for me.

Asonde itadaita.
She played with me.

Kudasaru ("to give") is the honorific version of *kureru*. *Itadaku* ("to receive") is the humble form of *morau*. When accepting something from someone who is older than you, or of a higher position, it is polite to use *kudasaru*. When describing something that was (or is being) done for you by an older person or someone of a higher rank, it is necessary to use *itadaku*.

Notice how the first verb is changed to a –*te* ending and that the "receiving" verb reflects the tense of the sentence. *Yatte* is a common first verb for this combination, but any verb in its –*te* form will fit. For example:

Sensei ga omiyage o katte kudasaimashita.
My teacher bought me a souvenir.

O-jii-san kara maki okitte itadakimasu.
My grandfather will cut the firewood for me.

ALERT!

Getting out of the bath, like entering someone's home, is referred to as *agaru*. If someone says to you, *Moo agarimasu ka,* he is asking if you are getting out. Do not confuse it with *Ageru ka* and think that he is trying to give you something.

Side Businesses

For a while, *onsen* were losing popularity in Japan. Recently, however, they are enjoying a resurgence in favor. This may be due to their expanded inclusion of health and recreation-related services. People can now spend an entire day at the *onsen* bathing, eating, getting massages, and shopping.

Eats and Drinks

Once you are fresh and clean, you will want to replace all those fluids you sweated out in the sauna and bath. Vending machines are a regular fixture nearly anywhere in Japan and you can easily get a cheap can or bottle of something to drink. You may be surprised to find out that hot drinks are also available from vending machines. If you are not sure whether the drink you are selecting will be hot or cold, please ask for assistance:

> *Kono nomimono wa attakai desu ka.*
> Is this drink warm?

> *Kono nomimono wa tsumetai desu ka.*
> Is this drink cold?

Notice how the words that describe the temperature of beverages differ from those used to describe a room. *Attakai* is preferred in this sense because it has a more positive connotation than *atsui* ("hot"). *Tsumetai* can be used in either a positive or negative way, depending on what is being described. *Kaze ga tsumetai* ("The wind is chilly") is obviously not a good thing, but *tsumetai o-cha* ("cold tea") in the heat of summer can be a blessing.

Miniature restaurants with *soba, raamen, udon, katsudon,* and *karee raisu* are also an option at many new *onsen* establishments. Ice cream, puddings, sweet breads, and fruit are also usually available for hungry bathers. Some families bring *o-bentoo* from home and enjoy eating together in the communal chill-out room.

FACT

Most *onsen* establishments have self-serve complimentary tea available for customers. Whether the tea is hot or cold usually depends on the season. Hot is usually served in cool weather and cold for warm weather.

Getting a Massage

Massage therapists have also become regular fixtures at many *onsen*. Acupuncture (*hari*), aromatherapy (*aromaserapi*), reflexology, and *shiatsu* (a traditional form of Japanese massage involving pressure points) are just a few of the available services. If you are interested in getting a massage, you can inquire at the front desk for open time slots and costs.

The massage therapist will probably ask you a variety of questions about your body and where you would like to be massaged.

83

Doko ga itai-n desu ka.
Where do you feel pain?

Doko ni massaji shite hoshii desu ka.
Where would you like to be massaged?

Itakattara oshiete kudasai.
If it hurts, please tell me.

Ashi o sawatte mo ii desu ka.
May I touch your foot?

If you have a specific part of your body that needs attention, you can let the therapist know.

83

Kata kori desu.
I have stiff shoulders.

Koshi ga itai.
My lower back hurts.

Ashi no ura ni massaji shite hoshii desu.
I would like you to massage the bottoms of my feet.

Throughout the massage, it is important to communicate how you feel. *Chotto itai* or *ii kimochi* will give the therapist important feedback. When the massage is finished, you can also let her know whether you feel better or not.

83

Yokatta yo.
That was great.

Kimochi ga yoku narimashita.
I feel much better.

Mada chotto itai-n desu kedo.
I still have a little pain.

Yokatta and *yoku narimashita* are past-tense forms of the adverb *yoku* ("well"). *Yoku* combines with *narimashita* ("to become") to describe a complete recovery.

Quizzes and Exercises

1. What are the hours of operation according to the following sentence?
   Juu-ji kara roku-ji made aite imasu.

2. Define the following words.

   nomikata _____
   araikata _____
   tsukurikata _____

3. Put the words in order to make a sentence: *yatte koto ikemasen sono o wa*

   _____

4. Match the item of clothing with the verb for wearing it.

   scarf   *hameru*

   shoes   *kiru*

   sweater   *haku*

   underwear   *shimeru*

   belt   *suru*

   gloves   *haku*

5. Fill in the missing verb. *Koko de kutsu o _____ kudasai.*

6. How would you convey that a massage feels good?

Chapter 17

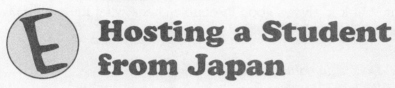

Hosting a Student from Japan

Hosting a foreign-exchange student can be a great experience for you and your family. Providing a variety of new experiences to introduce your hometown and the surrounding areas will take some planning. Taking measures to avoid accidents and emergencies will also ensure that everyone has a good time.

Getting Names Straight

Cross-cultural sensitivity calls for heroic efforts in getting names pronounced right. Sounds and combinations, as well as the names themselves, may be unfamiliar. With a little practice, though, they will be rolling off your tongue.

Students visiting the United States may recite their names in the western fashion, but it is always good to double-check what the child's given and family name are:

> *Docchi ga namae desu ka.*
> What is your given name?

> *Docchi ga myooji desu ka.*
> What is your family name?

You may want to write out the name phonetically for better recall. Having the Japanese student write it in *roomaji* is fine if he or she has studied English privately or is at least nine years old:

> *O-namae wa doo yatte kaku-n desu ka.*
> How do you write your name?

Asking a few questions will help to clarify the pronunciation of a Japanese name written in Roman letters:

> *Chiisa-na "tsu" wa haite imasu ka.*
> Is there a small *"tsu"* character?

A small *"tsu"* character indicates a short stop before the following consonant, but it is not commonly found in given names. It is more likely to show up in nicknames. You may hear kids referring to each other as *Ma-cchan* or *Te-cchan*. These are shortened versions of given names like *Masahiro* or *Tetsuya*. Even small children use the polite suffixes *–chan*, *–kun*, or *–san* after their friends' names. Lately, it is trendy for kids to add *–ppi* after girls' names: *Ayaka-chan* becomes *A-ppi*, *Runa-chan* becomes *Runa-ppi*, and so on.

Students who have learned the *Monbusho roomaji* method will write the sound *shi* as "si," *chi* as "ti," *zu* as "du," and *tsu* as "tu." Syllables that are formed with *ya, yo,* or *yu* will be written as "sya," "syo," and so on.

Using the *Monbusho* method, a child may write his name "*Syotaro,*" but it should be pronounced *Shootaroo*. The double "oo" indicate an elongated vowel sound that can make all the difference. You may meet many boys named *Yuuki* and several girls named *Yuki*, the subtle difference being in the elongation of the "u." If you address the boy as "Yuki," however, he may be embarrassed and other students will most likely be amused:

O-namae wa Yuuki-san desu ka. Sore tomo Yuki-san desu ka.
Is your name Yuuki or Yuki?

FACT

The verb *iu* is often pronounced with a *y* sound in front. *Iu* comes out sounding like "yuu," and *itte* sounding like "yutte." Likewise, *itta* will often be heard as "yutta."

Checking Vital Signs

Your efforts to welcome and befriend your guests are met with blank stares. Smiles seem to be last on everyone's list. You try to get them to relax and make themselves at home, but having a conversation seems out of the question. With time, though, kids' natural curiosity is sure to beat out shyness and soon you will be initiated into the unique phrases of "kidtalk."

Soooo Shy

For some reason, most young Japanese children are very shy at first. If their mother is present, they will often hide behind her as she apologizes and explains:

Hazukashigari desu.
He is shy.

If she is not present, they may have a hard time meeting your gaze or speaking in an audible voice. You may want to reassure them that there is no reason to be shy:

> *Hazukashigaranai de ne.*
> Don't be shy, okay?

Extra quiet responses to your questions may make it difficult to understand what is being said, more so because it will be in Japanese or non-native English:

> *Moo chotto ookii-na koe de itte kureru?*
> Could you say that a little louder?

Older children may be shy at first, too, but not to the same extent as their younger siblings and friends. This shyness may manifest itself in giggles or pleading looks for help directed at their friends.

Another way to set your guests at ease is to use a colloquial phrase. *Doo shita no,* when directly translated, means "How happened?" A more useful translation, however, would be "What happened?" or "What is the matter?"

Better in Groups

"Safety in numbers" is a common philosophy in Japan. Students in school are often allowed to consult with the people around them before giving an answer and will do so either out of lack of confidence or to double- and triple-check even if they really do know the correct answer. Teachers must often choose someone to answer a question rather than asking for volunteers. Fear of saying the wrong thing seems to be a common concern.

For this reason, kids visiting the United States will definitely do better if they are in a small group with other Japanese kids. Separating individuals and sending them to different host families may have disastrous results and should be avoided for the sake of the students' comfort.

Kidspeak

You will know that your guests have started to adapt to their new surroundings when you hear them speaking freely with their friends or siblings. Japanese students from preschool on up are known for their special slang and other variations on regular words. One of the most popular ways to alter adjectives into slang is by changing the ending *i* sound to an elongated *e* sound. This makes the word *kitanai* ("dirty") into *kitanee*. *Takai* ("expensive") becomes *takee*. *Kusai* ("stinky") becomes *kussee*.

Another phrase commonly used by kids when they do not want to do something is *iya da*. It seems to be one of the first words that toddlers learn and you hear plenty of it from two-year-olds. If your guests seem reluctant to try something you have prepared or arranged for them, you can ask:

> *Iya desu ka.*
> You don't want to do this, do you?

If the person you are talking to is too shy to answer directly, you can ask his or her friend:

> *Kare wa uma ni noru no o iyagatte-imasu ka.*
> Is he unwilling to get on the horse?

In Japanese, responses to a yes/no question don't have to be either completely positive or completely negative. For example, in response to the question "You didn't forget anything, did you?" the answer might be *Hai, nanimo nai.* The literal translation of that answer is "Yes, I didn't forget anything," because the answer is in agreement with the speaker's question which, in this case, is stated in negative terms.

After warming up to you, some kids may let you know directly, *Iya da*. The *da* is actually a shortened, informal version of *desu*. Others have probably been warned by their parents to be polite and that includes trying everything.

When changed to the negative, as when parents scold their kids, the informal negative version of *desu* is used: *ja nai. Iya ja nai yo,* is a common phrase uttered by parents and teachers.

Generating Conversation

Getting to know people involves a little detective work. Good conversations often resemble a quick game of catch. Someone throws out a question, another person catches it, answers, and tosses back the same question (or maybe a new one). In this way, personal histories, past experiences, and future dreams slowly reveal themselves.

Experiences

Hosting people from another country is a great opportunity to show off your own culture. You may have many fun things already planned for your guests, or you may want to wait until they arrive to see what they are interested in doing. Hopefully, the activities you have lined up will be new experiences for the students. You cannot know what they have and have not done before, though, unless you ask.

The phrase, "Have you ever . . . ?" in Japanese is created by combining the past-tense form of the verb with *koto arimasu ka.*

84

Uma ni notta koto arimasu ka.
Have you ever ridden a horse?

Piza wa tabeta koto arimasu ka.
Have you ever eaten pizza?

Nyuu Yokku ni wa itta koto arimasu ka.
Have you ever been to New York?

As previously explained, *hai* is used to show agreement with a yes/no question, whether or not the following statement is negative or positive, and *iya* or *iie* are used to show disagreement:

84

Iie, notta koto nai.
No, I haven't.

Hai, tabeta koto arimasu.
Yes, I have eaten (pizza) before.

Iie, itta koto arimasen.
No, I have never been (to New York).

While You Are Here

You may have to take the initiative to see if there is anything special your guests are interested in trying during their visit:

Nanika yaritai koto wa arimasu ka.
Is there something you would like to do?

Easy proximity to famous people is a common misassumption about Americans, but if you do have access, you might ask:

Dareka aitai hito wa imasu ka.
Is there someone you would like to meet?

The question words *nani* and *dare* paired with *ka* create the words "something" and "someone," respectively. Other interrogatives paired with the particles *ka, mo, de,* and *mo* make up a variety of useful words.

Question Word Combinations	
dareka	someone
daremo (with positive verb)	everyone

Question Word Combinations (continued)	
daremo (with negative verb)	no one
daredemo	anyone
dokoka	somewhere
dokomo (pos. verb)	everywhere
dokomo (neg. verb)	nowhere
dokodemo	anywhere
itsuka	someday
itsumo (pos. verb)	always
itsumo (neg. verb)	never
itsudemo	any time
nanika	something
nanimo (neg. verb)	nothing
nandemo	anything

FACT

If you hear the phrase *Mata yaritai,* you will know your plans were successful. *Mata* means "again," and *yaritai* means "want to do." It's possible that while doing the activity or when it is time to go home, your guests might say *Mada yaritai.* Mada means "still" or "continue." *Mada* and *mata* are easy to mix up.

Likes and Dislikes

Sharing and preparing meals with and for your guests, you may get an idea of their likes and dislikes. Children, especially, can be extremely picky eaters. Mixing in familiar items with stuff they have never had before (*tabeta koto nai*) may help them feel more at ease.

85

Suki-na tabemono wa nan desu ka.
What foods do you like?

Daisuki-na tabemono wa nan desu ka.
What is your favorite food?

Amari suki ja nai tabemono wa nan desu ka.
What foods do you not really care for?

Kirai-na tabemono wa nan desu ka.
What foods do you hate?

ALERT!

A sudden change in diet can be one of the most trying aspects of traveling. In order to keep your guests' digestive systems running smoothly, make rice available at least once a day. Some Japanese kids are used to eating rice for almost every meal and could be adversely affected if this staple of their diet were entirely eliminated.

Specific answers depend on the individual and you may want to have a dictionary in the house in case you are not sure what it is your guests will and will not eat. Easygoing kids, or those who have been instructed by their parents to be polite guests, may give any of the following responses.

85

Zenbu suki desu.
I like everything.

Nandemo ii desu.
Anything is fine.

Kirai-na mono wa nanimo nai desu.
There is nothing I don't like.

Answering Questions

Your guests will probably be on sensory overload when they first arrive. This, plus jetlag, might delay the initial onslaught of inquiries, but once the questions start, you may find yourself answering nonstop. Being aware of some typical questions that commonly arise when comparing Japanese and American practices in daily life will assist you in preparing your answers.

There are usually two verbal indications that what is being said is a question: an interrogative appears at the head of the sentence, or a question indicator brings up the rear. Note that kids may be more likely to use the colloquial *no* instead of *ka* as a question indicator.

Why Ask Why

Kids of all ages are likely to be full of questions, even more so when surroundings and cultural practices are totally new. The polite form of "why" is *naze*. But there are a couple of kidspeak versions you may encounter: *nande* and *dooshite*. (Adults can use these versions, too, but usually do so only among close friends or family.)

86

Naze ie ni hairu toki wa kutsu o nuganai no.
Why don't you take off your shoes when you enter your house?

Nande toire to o-furo wa onaji heya ni arimasu ka.
Why are the toilet and bathtub in the same room?

Dooshite o-furo no naka de karada o arau.
Why do you wash your body in the bathtub?

Answering questions like these may be difficult and will, of course, vary according to the individual. Here are a few suggestions:

86

*Koko de wa isu toka sofa de suwaru kara shita ga kittanaku natte mo
daijoobu desu.*
We sit on chairs or couches here so it doesn't really matter if the
floor gets dirty.

*Mukashi, toire wa soto ni arimashita. Mizu o tsukau mono wa onaji
heya ni aru to daiku-san no shigoto ga raku ni naru ka naa.*
In the past, toilets were outside. Putting all the things that use water
in the same room makes the carpenters' job easier, maybe.

Nande da roo.
Good question. I'm not sure why.

FACT

When you are not convinced that what you are saying is totally true,
you can add *ka naa* on the end and cock your head to one side. This lets
the listener know you are simply proposing this as an idea and that it
should be "taken with a grain of salt."

May I?

Generous hospitality is not only the domain of Japanese hosts. If you
have already gone to the trouble of arranging to have guests from another
country in your home or school, you are likely to go all out to provide a
good experience. Your guests may not quite believe their luck in scoring a
homestay with you.

87

Moo ikkai yatte mo ii desu ka.
Is it okay to do it again?

Kore o tabete mo ii desu ka.
Can I eat this?

Hontoo ni moratte mo ii desu ka.
Can I really have it?

Older students will be cooler in their excitement, not letting it show so blatantly. Younger students are new to the thrill of being away from home, in the care of people who are free to spoil them a little. Your affirmative responses to these animated requests for permission can be simple and direct.

87

Doozo.
Go ahead.

Mochiron.
Of course.

There maybe be situations, however, in which other responses are necessary. The following phrases are gentle enough to use everyday without invoking tantrums (hopefully).

87

Moo chotto matte kudasai.
Please wait a little longer.

Minna ga kite kara ni shiyo.
Let's wait until everyone has arrived.

Gomen ne, sore wa dame desu.
I'm sorry, but that's not possible.

Ato de ne.
Later, okay.

A Few More

Once they feel more at home, your guests may begin to inquire about things more freely. Kids everywhere have shorter attention spans than their adult counterparts (Japanese and U.S. kids possibly even more so than other countries due to the popularity of video games), and that drives them to be both curious and impatient.

88

Mada desu ka.
Are we there/done yet? Should I continue?

Kooen wa arimasu ka.
Is there a park?

Kono hen ni wa nani ga arimasu ka.
What do you have around here?

Make the daily schedule or plans clear. Providing students with an idea of what is available will allow them to make more educated decisions when choosing an activity.

88

Ato moo sukoshi.
After a little bit. A little further.

Kooen wa arimasu yo.
Yes, we have a park!

Mizuumi ga atte, sakana-tsuri mo dekiru shi, oyoide mo ii yo.
Well, there is a lake; you can go fishing and swimming there.

Family Dynamics

Families function in ways that are influenced by culture, environment, individual personalities, and the number of people sharing a home. It is becoming more rare, but many Japanese children still live in multigenerational homes with grandparents and sometimes still unmarried aunts and uncles.

When speaking about your own mother to someone else, you call her *haha*. When you speak to her directly, a variety of terms are possible. *O-kaa-san* and *kaa-chan* seem to be the most often used names for mothers. Some families use the term *Mama*, or sometimes *Mama-chan*, but that is a recent trend.

FACT

Solving disputes between siblings and classmates is easy in Japan. You have to play a game of *janken* ("rock, paper, scissors"). *Janken* is the accepted, ultimately fair arbiter of disputes. You will often see groups of students whipping out one of the three hand gestures: *gu* ("rock"), *choki* ("scissors"), or *pa* ("paper") to settle any problem.

Other family members, as a sign of intimacy, are referred to with the suffix *–chan* instead of *–san*: *too-chan* ("father"), *nee-chan* ("big sister"), *nii-chan* ("big brother"). Sometimes kids attach these familial terms onto the sibling's name: *Yumi-nee-chan*. Using the terms *baa-chan* or *baa-baa* ("grandmother") and *jii-chan* or *jii-jii* ("grandfather") instead of *o-baa-san* and *o-jii-san* also reflects a familiar relationship.

Younger siblings may be addressed by name, but no suffix will follow. Often, a more casual version of "you," like *kimi* or *omae*, is used in place of a little brother's or sister's name. You would never use either of these words when speaking to someone older than you or of a higher status than you.

Rarely will you see Japanese parents disciplining their children in public. Kids can sometimes be overheard describing their moms as demons, however, so you know that parents are disciplining their children at home. Mothers, too, describe getting angry as *tsuno ga deru* ("my horns come out"). If you need to discipline one of your guests, it is best to do it privately if at all possible. A public reprimanding will likely embarrass the child and make the rest of the trip rather miserable.

Emergency Situations

Sometimes there is nothing you can do to prevent an emergency, but there are things you can do to be better prepared for one. Precautions can make a big difference in how quickly things improve.

Reactions

Being aware of things like food allergies or medical conditions beforehand can help to prevent an emergency situation, or provide you with background upon which to make crucial decisions in the event of a reaction to something. The number of Japanese kids with conditions like asthma or eczema has been increasing in recent years. Restrictions on activities or daily application of topical creams are things you should know about.

89

Arerugi wa arimasu ka.
Do you have any allergies?

Taberarenai mono wa arimasu ka.
Is there anything you cannot eat?

Chooshi ga warukunareba, oshiete kudasai no.
If you start to feel unwell, please let me know, okay?

Even small children with chronic conditions are aware of them and can often self-monitor things they should not have or do. Just to be on the safe side, seek as many details as possible. Here are some possible responses to your questions:

89

Tamago to bataa wa taberarenai desu.
I cannot eat eggs or butter.

Atopi ni naru kara choko wa dame desu.
I cannot have chocolate due to my eczema.

Tori no hane o sawaru to kushami ga deru.
If I touch bird feathers, I will sneeze.

These trips are often short and it would be a shame for someone to pass the time sick in bed because of a silly mistake. Your guests may be too shy to tell you that they can't eat something or that they feel ill. You should assure them that they should let you know if they have any pain or discomfort.

89

Dokoka ga itaku nareba, hayaku oshiete kudasai.
If you develop pain anywhere, please let me know right away.

Note the modification of the adjective *itai* combined with *naru* in its "if," or potential, form. As you can see, *itaku* is conjugated with *ku*, not *ni*.

FACT

When they come down with a cold or have flu symptoms, many Japanese opt to wear a facemask to help prevent the spread of germs. Concern for others' health is the main reason for the mask.

Medical Terms

If the problem is not a previously known diagnosed medical condition or an allergic reaction, then you may have to investigate other possible reasons for your guest's discomfort.

90

Itami wa tsuyoi desu ka.
Is the pain strong?

Itai tokoro wa doko desu ka.
Where does it hurt?

Netsu o hakatte miru ne.
I'm going to take your temperature, okay?

The adjective *itai* has a related noun form: *itami* ("pain"), which appears in the first sample sentence. In the second example, the adjective *itai* modifies the noun *tokoro*. The literal translation, *hurt place,* is translated into English as a relative clause: "place that hurts."

In some cases, as previously mentioned, the sudden change in diet can cause digestive systems to go berserk. Becoming constipated or having diarrhea is a common problem for many travelers.

90

Unko wa demasu ka.
Are you having bowel movements?

O-naka/atama wa itai desu ka.
Does your stomach/head hurt?

Kaze o hiita ka mo shiranai.
You may be coming down with a cold.

Like *ka naa, ka mo shiranai* helps to disclaim or downplay a prediction. It is another way to say "maybe." *Shiranai* is the negative version of *shiru* ("to know").

Terms for Playing Doctor	
netsu	fever
itami	pain
o-naka	abdomen, belly
unko	bowel movement
kaze	cold
hakike	vomit
hakuge	nausea
chooshi	condition
kimochi warui	feel bad, sick
kigen ga warui	bad mood

Terms for Playing Doctor (continued)	
kizu	cut, scrape
nodo	throat
seki	cough
hanamizu	runny nose (snot)
kushami	sneeze

Like most of the rest of the world, Japan uses the metric system. Celsius, rather than Fahrenheit, is the preferred temperature gauge. Average body temperature using the Celsius scale is around thirty-six degrees. Therefore, announcing to a parent or chaperone that the patient has a temperature of 101 degrees Fahrenheit could be momentarily alarming.

Quizzes and Exercises

1. What is the likely kidspeak response to something undesirable?

2. Please answer the following question in Japanese: *Sushi wa tabeta koto arimasu ka.*

   _____

3. Match the words with their English definition.

   itsumo (neg. verb)   anywhere

   dareka   something

   nandemo   never

   dokomo (pos. verb)   someone

   nanika   anything

4. Fill in the appropriate word: *Kono geemu wa tanoshikatta desu.*
   _____ *ashita yaritai.*

5. What are three words for "why"?

6. Rearrange the words to make a question: *tsukawanai hashi nande no o*

   _____

7. What words for "you" should you avoid using with a superior?

Chapter 18

Especially for Vacationers

All travelers are looking to make the most of their vacation time. Keeping an open mind about all types of experiences is essential. People who are good with languages may enjoy picking up some colorful vocabulary. Testing out those new terms in spontaneous conversations will keep you on your toes.

Making Fast Friends

Whether your travel pace is leisurely or rapid, there are a variety of reasons to establish ties with the people you come across. Natives of any area are bound to know more about it than you. Tapping into local resources can make your trip all the more special as the secret spots and homemade delicacies are revealed to you by your newfound friends.

Pay Compliments

Flattery, when it is sincere, can be a great opener for developing quick connections with people. Complimenting someone's town or country, culture or dress, performance, or presentation is easy even when you do not know the person. Demonstrating appreciation for Japan and its culture is the quickest way into most Japanese people's hearts.

91

Kono kimono wa kirei desu ne.
This kimono is pretty.

Koko no keshiki wa tottemo utsukushii desu.
The scenery here is really beautiful.

Kono machi no mina-san wa yasashii desu ne.
Everyone in this town is so kind.

Nihon no onna no hito wa hada ga kirei de urayamashii desu.
Japanese women have such pretty skin, I'm jealous.

One challenge in complimenting people is knowing how to refer to them. In Japanese, the word *anata* means "you," but it is rarely used. It is preferable to use the person's name, if you know it. If not, you can always use familial titles. Someone who seems to be about your aunt's age could be referred to as *oba-san*, someone your older brother's age could be addressed as *o-nii-san*.

Ask Questions

Inquiries about a place, its history, language, and people also demonstrate an interest that will be flattering to many Japanese people. Ask around enough and you may end up with a personal tour guide who also happens to be a local historian or winner of the most recent chrysanthemum-growing contest.

92

Koko no ichiban yuumei-na tokoro wa doko desu ka.
Where is the most famous place in this area?

Koko no ichiban oishii mono wa nan desu ka.
What is the most delicious thing here?

Koko no ichiban omoshiroi koto wa nan desu ka.
What is the most interesting thing here?

Ichiban can mean "number one," "first," "top," "best," or "most." Together, *ichiban* and an adjectival phrase form a superlative construction, as in the above examples.

E ALERT!

Ichiban can be used to describe an amazing experience, the best food, and other things that occupy the top notch, but when referring to your personal "number ones," the phrase *dai suki* is preferred. *Dai suki* literally means "big like," but it is translated into English as "favorite."

Keeping the Culture

Upon hearing you speak Japanese, many people will be impressed:

Nihongo wa joozu desu ne.
Your Japanese is great!

Even if you can barely squeak out *konnichiwa*, some people might say your Japanese is wonderful. They are probably just being polite. How you respond to this compliment gives you a chance to change that politeness to genuine awe.

Remember, the most essential element of Japanese culture is humility. All compliments, therefore, must be deflected with self-deprecating comments. In Japanese society, the humblest person always wins. Responding to a compliment in a way that reflects your knowledge of Japanese culture will impress your listeners.

93

Mada heta desu.
I still have a long way to go.

Nihongo wa tottemo muzukashii desu.
Japanese is extremely difficult.

Mada wakaranai koto ga ippai arimasu.
There are still many things I do not understand.

Minding Your P's and Q's

When it is time to part, you will want to thank the person who assisted you during your visit. If you have some memento from home you can pass on, it will be humbly received. A simple *Doomo arigatoo gozaimashita* will do, but if the person went all out for you, you may want to be more specific.

94

Doomo, o-sewa ni narimashita.
Thank you for taking such good care of me.

Hontoo ni tasukarimashita.
You really saved me.

Moshi, Amerika ni kitara, uchi ni yotte kudasai.
If you ever come to the States, please visit my home.

The word *moshi* is another way of saying "if" or "in case." It is almost always paired with a verb in its potential form, as in *kitara* ("when/if you come"). *Moshi* can also be paired with the particle *mo* to give the potential situation more emphasis.

94

Moshi mo yasumii o torereba, ryokoo ni ikimasu.
We are going on vacation if I can take some time off.

Responses to your gratitude may include some of the following phrases. Remember, humbleness is a common characteristic, so people are likely to downplay their role, and may even be too embarrassed or shy to acknowledge your appreciation.

94

Iie.
It was my pleasure.

Nandemo nai.
It was nothing.

Iya iya.
Don't think of it.

Dooitashimashite.
You're welcome.

Mata asobi ni kite kudasai.
Please come and visit (literally "play") again.

The phrase *asobi ni kite* is an example of a verbal phrase. In this case, *asobi* ("play" or "playing") and *kite* ("come") are connected by *ni*. The order is the reverse of that in English. The purpose comes first, and the verb follows. In most cases, the verb is either *kuru* ("to come") or *iku* ("to go").

94

Kare wa pan o tori ni kuru.
He will come to pick up the bread.

O-too-san wa o-baa-chan o mukae ni itta.
He went to pick up Grandmother.

Watashitachi wa aka-chan o mi ni kita.
We came to see the baby.

ALERT!

When going to pick up something (a book at the library, for example) the verb *toru* is appropriate. If you are picking up a person (your daughter, for example), the verb *mukaeru* is preferred. It is considered rude to say: *O-baa-chan o tori ni ikimasu.*

Being a Good Sport

Traveling is exciting, but can also be exhausting. There are times when you may feel that you need a break from sitting on the floor or just want to be left alone to enjoy the view. Your patience is likely to run thin when it comes to food, especially meals prepared in festival times.

Festivals are a great way to get a glimpse of Japanese traditions. Traditional clothing, food, hairstyles, and customs all reveal themselves during festivals. Attend enough festivals in Japan and you will start to see patterns in these customs, especially where food is concerned.

Boiled vegetables, kelp, and *toofu*, arranged artfully on large platters can be found sitting next to equally attractive trays of *futomaki* (fat sushi rolls) with iridescent ingredients. Hot or cold *soba* noodles (depending on the season), only-for-special-occasions-*sekihan* (*mochi* rice cooked with *adzuki* beans, topped with black sesame seeds and salt), *sashimi* (sliced raw fish), and local delicacies like *igoneri* (a kind of seaweed gelatin) may also adorn the tables.

For guests with a sweet tooth there are milk *kanten* (another gelatin-type dish), *kurumi yookan* (sweet walnut candy), and, of course, *daifuku* (sticky rice cakes with sweet bean jam inside). Your host may fill a plate for you, or simply hand you a pair of chopsticks and let you fend for yourself:

> *Doozo, o-agari kudasai.*
> Please, help yourself.

Aside from being used for entering a home and getting out of the bath, the verb *agaru* is also a polite way to invite someone to eat or drink. The example above uses the honorific version in its root form, but you can also say:

> *Doozo, tekitoo ni meshi agatte kudasai.*
> Please take it easy and join us for a meal.

FACT

Meshi can mean "cooked rice" or "a meal," depending on the circumstances. The same goes for the word *gohan*. It can refer to rice or the whole meal itself. *O-kome* is the term used for rice before it has been cooked and when it is still in the paddy.

Tricky Treats

The textures of various Japanese foods may make trying new things a challenge for those with weak stomachs. In Japan, there seems to be an abundance of slippery and gooey foods. Instead of trying to tone down the gooey-ness, it is sought out, and even celebrated for its beneficial effects. The name for this texture even feels slimy when spoken: *neba-neba*.

How you are introduced to these things (and Japanese people *love* to introduce foreigners to native dishes such as *natto*) can make all the difference in the world. There are a variety of ways to prepare these slimy ingredients. If your *neba-neba* guide has a benevolent heart, you may be able to develop an appreciation for the texture, eventually. If not, you may never enjoy wrapping spider web-like strings around your chopsticks in an effort to keep them from sticking to your chin.

Foods that may overload your sliminess receptors are *natto, nagaimo,* satoimo, mozuku, and mekabu. Natto is fermented soybeans, usually eaten with rice, rolled in sushi, or even mixed with daikon radish and spaghetti. Bacteria used in fermenting the beans are supposedly good for digestion, and the big intestine, especially. If you can stand to try it more than once or twice, you just may develop a taste for natto and impress your colon.

Mozuku and mekabu are sea plants or the roots of sea plants; nagaimo and satoimo are potato varieties, starchy, gooey ones whose tough skins bely their innards. To release the ooze, many of these foods are scraped over graters before being dolloped on top of a bowl of rice and doused with karashi ("yellow mustard") or shooyu ("soy sauce").

Funny Onomatopoeias and Other Expressions

Japanese is full of words that feel ticklish in your mouth. They are fun to say and cleverly evoke the sounds, flavors, actions, and textures they represent. For example, feelings of excitement, nervousness, or intense emotion are described as doki-doki and waku-waku.

When used in a sentence, however, these expressions are often followed by the word suru ("to do"):

> *Kareshi ga kitara mune ga doki-doki shita.*
> My chest started pounding when my boyfriend arrived.

Other variations can be created with *to* plus another verb:

> *Hebi ga nyoro-nyoro to hatte itta.*
> The snake slithered away.

These words can be used in a variety of situations where the verb needs describing. When combined with *to* and *shita*, doki-doki can be modified slightly and used to describe a reaction to hearing something shocking:

> *Sore o kiitara, dokkitto shita.*
> Upon hearing that, I was startled.

Words for textures also abound in Japanese. You are already familiar with *neba-neba,* but how about *nuru-nuru* to describe wet noodles or *tsuru-tsuru* to describe someone's smooth cheeks? *Pasa-pasa* pertains to flaky skin or shredded coconut. *Gasa-gasa* describes calloused toes and fingers. Sand feels *sara-sara.*

Actions, too, are more easily imagined when described with an onomatopoetic flare. Elephants walk *noshi-noshi.* Acorns tumble *koro-koro.* Merry-go-rounds and ballerinas go *guru-guru.* Snakes move across the grass *nyoro-nyoro.*

QUESTION?

Do tongue twisters or other word games exist in the Japanese language?
Yes! Try this one five times fast: *Nama mugi, nama gome, nama tamago.* ("Raw barley, raw rice, raw eggs".) *Rensoo* is a word game in which players pose onomatopoetic riddles. "Magic banana" is a fast-paced word-association game. More linguistic entertainment can be found in the game *shiritori,* where the final syllable of the first word must be the first syllable of the second word, and so on.

Onomatopoetic expressions are used to describe sounds in Japanese, just as in English. *Kari-kari* is the noise *tsukemono* make when you chew them. *Para-para* describes the first drops of rain, or marbles falling down a staircase. A chilly winter wind may *pyuu-pyuu* outside your window. Anyone who speaks a foreign language impressively will earn the compliment *pera-pera*: *Eigo de pera-pera to hanashita.* ("They spoke English fluently.")

The many different ways of smelling aren't sufficiently evoked in Japanese, as in English. The word for sniffing, though, is *kun-kun.* A few expressions, such as *pika-pika* ("sparkling") describe the way that things look. A wobbly chair may be described as *gura-gura.* *Chika-chika* describes the on-again-off-again flashing of Christmas-tree lights.

Surefire Conversation Starters

Once the initial connection is made, you will want to keep the conversation lively and interesting. With limited vocabulary skills on either side, both parties may find that they quickly run out of things to say. It will put your mind at ease if you have a few fallback topics.

Animal Sounds

If you think that roosters crow the same way all over the world, you are mistaken. Ask any Japanese person to mimic the quintessential "early bird" and you will hear an unfamiliar squawk. Frogs say *gekko-gekko,* cats say *nyan,* and dogs go *wan-wan.* These sounds can be found in songs and baby talk.

Conversations comparing the cries of animals in the United States and Japan are entertaining and may even border on performance art in some arenas. If you have any theatrical talent in you at all, broach this topic at any gathering for hilarious results:

> *Niwatori wa donna fuu ni nakimasu ka.*
> In what manner does a rooster crow?

Any time you are interested in finding out the style, appearance, or manner of something, you can include the phrase *donna fuu.* For example:

> *Kaminoke wa donna fuu ni shimasu ka.*
> How will you style your hair?

ALERT!

Another phrase that is sometimes used in place of *donna fuu,* but that means almost the same thing is *doo iu fuu.* Like *donna fuu, doo iu fuu* shows how something is done or prepared: *Doo iu fuu ni yomeba ii desu ka.* ("How should I read this?")

Making Comparisons

Another way to keep the conversation lively is by comparing lifestyles in Japan and your home country. You can make these comparisons using the verb *kuraberu* ("to compare"). Food, as usual, is a great way to start. Here's a sample dialogue for making comparisons:

95

Oda-san: *Nihon de wa gohan ga shushoku desu. Amerika de shushoku wa pan desu ka.*
In Japan, the staple food is rice. Is the American staple food bread?

Frank: *Hito ni yoru kedo, uchi de wa jagaimo no ryoori ga ookatta desu.*
It depends on the person, but in my house, we ate a lot of potato dishes.

Oda-san: *Demo nihon to kuraberu to pan o taberu hito ga ooi-n ja nai.*
But, if you compare it with Japan, there are more people who eat bread, aren't there?

Frank: *Sore wa soo ka mo shirenai.*
That is probably true.

Oda-san: *O-sakana wa doo desu ka.*
How about fish?

Frank: *Taberu hito wa ippai iru to omoimasu dakedo uchi de wa amari tabenakatta.*
I'm sure that there are a lot of people who do, but in my house we did not eat much fish.

Counting Everything

As you may remember, Japanese is very particular in its way of counting. A special counter is used for different classes of objects or things. For non-Japanese, remembering which counter goes with which item can be baffling. Luckily, there is one factor that lends some sense to the madness: shape.

Bowls and Round Containers

Hai, which is sometimes pronounced *pai,* is a counter that applies to round containers. Cups and bowls then, are counted this way: *ippai* ("one bowlful"), *ni hai* ("two bowlfuls"), *san bai, yon hai, go hai, roppai, nana hai, happai, kyu hai, juppai.* The counters for "one," "six," "eight," and "ten" are irregular in this category, so they are spelled, in *roomaji,* as single words. Otherwise, counters are separated from the class or category markers. Ultimately, any way of representing Japanese in *roomaji* is arbitrary. This way of representing the Japanese counting system has been chosen to make the counters more salient. Here is an example of a counter in action:

> *Itsumo, yuhan ni gohan wa san bai tabemasu yo.*
> I always eat three bowls of rice at dinner.

Concerns about your caffeine consumption can also be quelled with the response:

> *Asa wa koohii ni hai o nomimasu.*
> I drink two cups of coffee in the morning.

Balls and oranges are counted in the following way: *ikko, ni ko, san ko,* and so on. Note that only "one" is irregular. They are round, but they are not containers, which is why they are counted differently than cups and bowls.

Tall, Long, or Slender

Pencils, pens, dowels, towels, chopsticks, and long, slender roots can all be counted the same way: *ippon, nihon, sanbon, yonhon, gohon, roppon, nanahon, happon, kyuhon, juppon.* As long as it is tall and rounded or long and slender, this counter applies:

> *Enpitsu o roppon kaimashita.*
> I bought six pencils.

Bottles, too, can be counted in this way, but they also have a second, slightly more old-fashioned, counter, usually only used for one or two bottles: *hitobin* and *futabin* use the word for bottle (*bin*) so there is no question about what is being counted:

> *O-mizu o futabin kudasai.*
> Two bottles of water, please.

FACT

Though long and slender, snakes are not counted in the same category as pencils and towels. If you want to make people laugh, though, you might say, *Hebi wa ippon imashita yo.* (Snakes should be counted like other small animals: *ippiki, nihiki,* etc.)

Animals, Big and Small

Small animals such as raccoons, dogs, cats, squirrels, and fish have their own special counter. When you see a mama *tanuki* run across the road with her four babies, you can say:

> *Tanuki ga go hiki ita!*
> There were five raccoons.

As with many other counting patterns, the terms for "one," "six," "eight," and "ten" start with "p"; the terms for "two," "four," "five," "seven," and "nine" stick with "h" and for "three" it's "b": *ippiki, ni hiki, san biki, yon hiki, go hiki, roppiki, nana hiki, happiki, kyu hiki, juppiki.*

Cows, elephants, pigs, and other large animals are counted with *–too: ittoo, nitoo, santoo,* and so on—the counters are regular. (This counter is actually a reference to the animals' massive heads.) When counting birds and rabbits, too, if you can remember *ichi, ni, san, shi,* etc. and the suffix *–wa*, you will be fine: *Ichi wa, ni wa, san wa,* and so on.

Flat Things

If you were hoping for one counter for all flat things, you will be disappointed. Beds and futons, pieces of paper, napkins, plates, envelopes, and sliced bread can all be counted with *mai*. However, books and bills must be counted with *satsu*:

> *Kami o roku mai kudasai.*
> Six pieces of paper, please.

> *Kono ni satsu o karitai-n desu.*
> I'd like to borrow these two books.

FACT

There used to be a time when killing rabbits was illegal in Japan. People still did it, though, because the rabbits were garden pests. If the police questioned you about what you had in your gunnysack (bunnysack), you could evade arrest by saying you had *"go wa,"* which meant you had five birds. This is why birds and rabbits still have the same counter, even though they do not have the same shape.

Taking Care of Business

Even the most carefree vacationers have to perform some housekeeping duties. Getting to all of those little temples in the mountains will require a few tanks of gas, even if you have only rented a mini-car. Picturesque views will prompt you to take pictures and send them to friends, or do the next best thing and buy postcards.

Getting Gas

Japan has several easily recognizable service stations conveniently referred to as *gasorin sutando*. If you are low on cash, you can ask for any amount specifically and still get great service:

> *Ni-sen en dake onegai shimasu.*
> Please put in 2,000 yen worth.

On Sundays, however, it may be a challenge to find an operating station. Most stations function on a rotating schedule, taking turns offering services on Sunday. You may need to ask around to find out whose turn it is on the day you need gas:

> *Kyoo wa doko no gasorin sutando ga yatte imasu ka.*
> Where can I find a gas station that is open today?

If you do find someplace open on a Sunday, you may want to take advantage of the opportunity to fill up your car:

> *Mantan ni shite kudasai.*
> Fill it up, please.

At the Post Office

Some people buy souvenirs, some send postcards, some do both. Letters sent to friends and family members are more authentic when affixed with stamps from your travel location:

> *Hyaku-juu en no kitte o juu mai kudasai.*
> Ten 110 yen stamps, please.

Japanese post offices recently went private. They are no longer federally run, but still offer most of the same services. You can have a savings account, pay bills for mail-order stuff, and get certified checks and money orders in addition to all the other regular postal services.

Quizzes and Exercises

1. What is a humble response to a compliment on your Japanese proficiency?

   _____

2. Translate the following sentence: *Moshi ashi ga itakattara yasunde kudasai.*

   _____

3. Fill in the missing particle: *Ashita, kippu o kai* _____ *iku.*

4. What does *meshi agatte* mean?

   _____

5. Fill in the missing verb: *Sakkaa o miru to waku-waku* _____.

6. Which expression would you use to describe the following?

   a rickety endtable   _____
   fluent Spanish   _____
   a spinning top   _____
   chapped lips   _____
   a flashing neon sign   _____

7. Match the following items with the appropriate counter:

   one horse   *roppiki*

   eight rabbits   *ittoo*

   six dogs   *go satsu*

   five books   *hachi wa*

   two bottles   *san bai*

   three bowlfuls   *futabin*

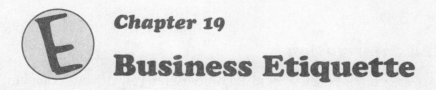

Chapter 19

Business Etiquette

Even when the United States and Japan are in economic slumps, opportunities to exchange business cards can arise in unexpected times and places. Knowing how to interact on a professional level can come in handy anywhere. Major cultural differences are becoming more widely known and respected. Be assured, your Japanese hosts are probably worrying about *echiketto*, too.

Preparing and Exchanging Business Cards

Meishi ("business cards") are a staple for many Japanese people, even those who are not in any particular business. They are an easy way to exchange information and are convenient to carry. With new computer programs that do all the work for you, designing unique and memorable *meishi* is becoming a snap.

Essential Information

Designing a business card that represents you or your company in a straightforward and positive manner can pose some challenges. Essential information must be easily and clearly recognized, or the card will not serve its purpose.

If you plan to be living in Japan for a while, you might consider getting cards printed up with English on one side and Japanese on the back. Having your name and address in Japanese will make future negotiations easier for your Japanese counterparts. You may find that people who work in companies or other offices that have a lot of contact with foreigners will also have bilingual business cards. Consider your own feelings of relief when you receive a card with the person's name and other information in English.

FACT

Japanese *meishi* usually have the company name written most prominently. Rank is also a big concern for many Japanese businesspeople, so the person's title will usually appear somewhere on the card. Traditionally, Japanese names are written vertically from right to left, but recently, with e-mail and homepage additions, many people are going *yoko* ("horizontal") and from left to right.

Who Goes First

Whoever is hosting the meeting should offer his or her card first and present it with the side that has the native language version of the recipient.

It can be given over with one hand, but should not be upside down from the recipient's standpoint. Stand first, then bow before saying *Yoroshiku onegai shimasu* and handing over your *meishi*.

If you are receiving the card, use two hands and bow when accepting. Treat the card as if it were a newborn baby or your favorite candy bar. Look it over carefully before putting it in your chest pocket. Never put it in your back pocket and then sit on it; that is very insulting to the person who gave it to you! Japanese consider *meishi* as part of themselves and handle them with utmost care and respect. Putting the card in your wallet is acceptable, but pressing it into your notebook or memo pad is also fine.

Tips for Keeping Names with Faces

Receiving several cards at once can be overwhelming; more so if the names are in a language that you are still in the process of mastering. In a country where eye and hair color tend to be similar (if not identical), distinctive characteristics at first glance may be limited to noticing who wears glasses, sports a colorful necktie, or has a unique hairstyle. Utilizing *meishi* to remember which name goes with which face is a wise tactic.

Lining up the cards on the table in the same order as people are sitting is one option. It is not the most polite act, but acceptable in extreme situations. Another idea is to insert the cards in your front shirt pocket, keeping them in the same order as they were presented. Then, you can discreetly pull out each card and double-check them before people by name.

When addressing people in a business setting, it is essential to use the person's last name followed by the word *–san*, as in *Watanabe-san*. You do not, however, refer to yourself as *Smith-san*. It is also appropriate to use *–sensei* instead of *–san*, especially in connection with an official title. For example, you may refer to the vice principal of a school as *kyootoo-sensei*.

Opening and Closing Statements

First meetings have a tendency to be slightly awkward, even between people from the same country. Crossing cultural differences and language barriers can make initial conversations challenging, to say the least. Starting with safe and easy topics like weather, sports, and travel can set a jovial foundation for further discussions.

Small Talk, Japanese Style

Japanese tend to ease into negotiations as into a hot bath. *Maefuri* ("small talk") provides everyone with an opportunity to relax for a few minutes before jumping into business-related conversation. Comments about the weather are common openers.

96

Kyoo wa ii o-tenki desu ne.
Today the weather is fine, isn't it?

Kyoo wa samui desu ne.
It is cold today, isn't it?

An easy response to either of the above comments is:

Soo desu ne.
It is, isn't it.

Sports are another common topic. *Yakyuu* ("baseball") and *sakkaa* ("soccer") are the most popular sports in Japan.

96

Beesuboru wa suki desu ka.
Do you like baseball?

Sakkaa wa shimasu ka.
Do you play soccer?

Most Japanese are familiar with the English words for many sports, so a Japanese pronunciation of "baseball" may be used instead of the traditional word, *yakkyu*.

Of course, travel is another great topic of small talk. If you came from far away, your hosts will want to know how the journey went.

96

Kuru toki wa doo deshita ka.
How was the trip over?

Hikooki no naka de wa nemuremashita ka.
Were you able to sleep on the plane?

Since these are really just polite inquiries, you do not have to go into great detail about the turbulence on the plane or the horrible food. Simple responses that reflect an easygoing attitude are most appropriate.

96

Daijoobu deshita.
It was fine.

Chotto shika nemurenakatta.
I was able to sleep only a little.

As the *maefuri* winds down, the host will inevitably say, *Sore de wa*, an introductory phrase that means something like "Let's get down to business, shall we?"

ALERT!

Try not to confuse the verbs *neru* and *nemuru*. The former means "to rest," while the latter means "to sleep." (Even though Japanese people often use *neru* when they actually mean *nemuru*.) In the previous example, notice how *nemuru* is conjugated in the negative, past-tense form. This is done by adding *–nakatta* to the verb stem.

Ending the Meeting

There are only a few possible outcomes to business meetings. You may have a sense of how things are going without anyone saying anything at all. If you hear either of the following sentences at the end of your meeting, however, you will know that the answer is either "no" or that a decision has not yet been made.

97

Mata denwa shimasu.
We will call again.

Kochira kara denwa shimasu.
Do not call us, we will call you.

Maemuki ni kentoo shimasu.
We will continue to study this with a positive attitude.

Maemuki can be broken down into two parts: *mae* ("front") and *muki* ("facing," or "direction"). Perhaps you can see how these words combine to create a term for positive thinking. These three examples are all pretty vague, indirect ways of saying "no" or "We'll think about it." For fear of conflict, not wanting to disappoint the guests, and a variety of other reasons, most Japanese people find it difficult to say "no" directly.

If the meeting was successful, a party atmosphere may develop. Any of the following statements are sure signs that your negotiations went well.

97

Kondo wa itsu aimasho ka.
When shall we meet again?

O-shokuji ni ikimasen ka.
Shall we go for dinner?

Nomi ni ikimasen ka.
Shall we go for a drink?

"A drink," in Japanese, is really *nomimono*, but you would not say *Nomimono ni ikimasen ka*. The third example features an idiom in which *nomi* is used as a substitution for *nomimono*, even in formal situations.

FACT

Wining and dining, Japanese-style, may involve a trip to a club in the flashy Ginza district of Tokyo. It is said that some clubs charge 50,000 yen just to sit next to a pretty girl.

Seating and Introductions

Well thought-out organization of a room and strategic seating assignments have been known to have psychological effects on people's attitudes. When conducting business, seating arrangements can be as important as the agenda. In Japan, these arrangements are determined by custom.

Seating Arrangements

If you are the guest of a Japanese company, you will most likely be treated like royalty from start to finish, and this includes occupying the seat of honor. If the room is *washitsu* (Japanese style with *tatami* mats), the guest or the highest-ranking member of the party will be seated near the *tokonoma*. The *tokonoma* is a kind of alcove with a slightly raised floor, usually decorated with calligraphy scrolls and *ikebana*. The seat in front of the *tokonoma* is the *kamiza* ("seat of honor") and will always be reserved for the president of the visiting company, an honored guest, or the most important person in the room:

> *Doozo, kochira e suwatte kudasai.*
> Please sit here.

If the room has a table and chairs rather than *tatami*, the seat farthest from the entrance is the place of honor. Once it has been determined who will occupy the *kamiza*, other members of the company should sit in order of rank, with the lowest ranking person seated in the *shimoza* ("worst spot").

The *shimoza* is usually closest to the door and will most likely be occupied by the person who arranged the meeting.

In a car, the philosophy that the point furthest from the entrance is the place of honor persists. This means that the highest-ranking individual will be given the seat behind the driver. You may often see grandmothers proudly occupying this spot in the family car.

Who Does the Talking

Much like companies in the West, Japanese businesses are organized according to a hierarchy. The *shachoo* ("president") obviously runs the show. The *buchoo* ("division managers") help keep things organized, while the *kachoo* ("supervisors") keep the *tantoosha* ("workers") in line.

The designated *tantoosha* is responsible for setting up the meeting. This will usually be done by phone. When making a formal inquiry by phone to see if someone is in the office, the honorific form of *imasu* is used:

> *Tanaka-san wa irasshaimasu ka.*
> Is Ms. Tanaka there?

Note the double elongated *sh* sound in *–ssha*. You may also hear this honorific verb when you arrive. The *tantoosha* will greet the guests at the door (or sometimes even pick them up from their hotel) and bring them to the meeting room:

> *Yoku irasshaimashita.*
> I'm glad you have come.

He or she will also make the initial introductions:

> *Kochira wa uchi no shachoo desu.*
> This is our company president.

Sono tonari wa watashi no kachoo desu.
Next to him is my supervisor.

Notice how the word *uchi* is used to describe the company boss. In this instance, it does not refer to the person's home, but rather the person's company and is another way of saying "my" or "our."

Two Major Differences

Throughout your time in Japan, you will most likely notice many things that are unique to Japanese culture. Bowing, not wearing shoes indoors, sitting on the floor, eating with chopsticks, and bathing rituals are some of the more obvious examples. Exposure to and experience with the Japanese language, itself, will give you even greater insight into these cultural differences.

Order of Delivery

It took Shoo Kamei forty years of being Japanese and a trip to Europe before he discovered why conversations in Japan take so long. While conducting business with European and American companies, he noticed that the conversations seemed to be over quickly. He also found that what was being said by both parties, even in his self-described "broken English," was easily and clearly understood. After the meetings, he returned to his hotel where a Japanese tour guide was waiting to show him around. In conversing with the guide, Kamei-san realized a crucial communication difference.

When Japanese people speak, especially when they are saying "no" to something, they often give several *ryuu* ("reasons") before delivering the *ketsuron* ("conclusion"). There are a few speculations as to why this is so.

One theory is that because Japan is crowded, people have to be extra careful in the way they communicate with each other. This means taking care to say things gently, so as to avoid conflict. Some people, like Kamei-san, feel that this practice goes too far:

Nihonjin wa ki o tsukaisugiru.
Japanese people are too careful.

Hanashi ga nagasugiru.
Conversations take too long.

FACT

Method of payment is often an issue in business dealings. In Japan there is a kind of late check called the *tegata*. This check is slow to turn into cash, sometimes taking as long as six months, and yet *tegata* is a commonly used payment method in Japan.

The suffix *–sugiru* can be added to verbs as well as adjectives to show that something has gone over the limit. In the two examples above, *–sugiru* is translated as "to exceed." To combine this suffix with a verb, reduce the verb to its stem and then add *–sugiru*. *Sugiru* is a verb in itself, so it is conjugated, not the root:

98

Yuuhan o tabesugita.
I ate too much dinner.

Karera wa itsumo nomisugiru.
They always drink too much.

Ima kangaesugite iru.
I'm thinking too much right now.

Likewise, when attaching *–sugiru* to an adjective like *muzukashii* ("difficult"), you must first identify the stem of the adjective:

98

Muzukashisugi.
This is too difficult.

Sono denki wa akarusugiru.
That light is too bright.

Another explanation for the roundabout nature of Japanese responses involves the language itself. Verbs come at the end of a Japanese sentence. It makes sense, then, to put anything that might deliver a punch toward the end of a conversation, too.

Beautiful "No"s

Few people actually enjoy turning someone down. Finding a way to do it gently, yet firmly, is a challenge. Disguising a rebuff in a beautiful package of verbosity is one option. Be warned, though—Japanese legend has it that the negotiator who can deliver a beautiful "no" and smile the whole time is the fiercest of them all. The rejected party may not even realize it until later.

QUESTION?

What is the difference between humble and honorific forms of speech?
Honorific forms of speech elevate the status of something or someone. Adding the prefixes *o* or *go* to any number of words is a way of paying respect, although the meaning isn't changed in any substantive way. (There are exceptions to this, especially with some verbs.) When speaking with a superior, or with someone you respect a great deal, it is necessary to use verbs that are particularly associated with humble forms of speech.

The following examples are all extremely eloquent refusals. Even dissecting the sentences and translating them word for word will not uncover a single straightforward "no." Each example, however, demonstrates a way to *kotowaru* ("refuse," "decline," "reject"):

> *Naruhodo osshatte iru koto wa yoku wakarimasu ga shikashi watashidomo wa koo kangaete orimasu.*
> While I understand what you are saying, we are thinking this way about the matter.

> *Kangaete orimasu.*
> We will give it some thought.

Kentoo itashimasu.
We will consider it.

Naruhodo is another great Japanese word. It simply means, "I see," or "I admit," but it can constitute a response to a variety of situations, depending on the tone of voice. Aside from *naruhodo*, the first example is filled to the brim with other honorifics. *Osshatte iru koto* is a really fancy way to refer to what is being said. The word *koto* on the end changes the "–ing" form of the verb (*osshatte iru*) to a noun. *Watashidomo* is the business-appropriate "we" (as opposed to the *watashi-tachi* "we" you would use with family and friends). *Orimasu,* too, is the humble version of *iru* (the "to be" verb for animate things).

Expressing Opinions and Backing Them Up

The meat of a meeting, of course, is the discussion. Ideas are presented, tossed, and tasted before being given further consideration, or discarded. Expression of opinions, therefore, is inevitable. If you can remember a couple of phrases, you will be able to share your personal views on different matters, as well as present any facts you have acquired, without offending anyone or coming across as a *waga mama* ("self-centered") Westerner.

In English, when you express an opinion, it is often unnecessary to say, "I think," because it is assumed that you are expressing your own thoughts. In Japanese, however, adding the equivalent of "I think," *da to omoimasu,* will soften your statements for the ears of your listeners.

99

Sore wa muzukashii to omoimasu.
I think that is difficult.

Tottemo ii kangaekata da to omoimasu.
I believe that is a great way of thinking.

Moo chotto benkyoo shita hoo ga ii to omoimasu.
I think it is a good idea to study a little more.

Using this expression when stating an opinion will lead to a more positive reception of your ideas.

Another way to express your knowledge without stepping on anyone's toes is with the phrase *tonokoto desu*. It is a polite way of saying *soo da* ("I hear that," or "They say that"). When *tonokoto desu* is added to the end of a sentence, it's not necessary to make any changes to the rest of the sentence; just leave it the way it is:

99

Sono horitsu wa rainen ni kawaru tonokoto desu.
I hear that law will change next year.

Chuugoku no sanbutsu o takusan yunyuu suru tonokoto desu.
I hear they import many Chinese products.

Notice how the verbs *kawaru* and *suru* are unaffected, so to speak, by *desu*. Using *tonokoto desu* is a good way to support personal opinion. When using the phrase, however, the source of the information is not usually given.

Unexpected Divisions of Labor

For some it was when your family moved before you started sixth grade, for others it was the first day on the job. Being the new face can be exciting and intimidating. Fortunately, most people will go out of their way to welcome you, show you around, and make you feel at home.

FACT

In Japan, newcomers can expect flowers on their desks, decorations on their lockers, and maybe even an invitation to an *enkai*. After a short honeymoon-like period, however, the tough-love phase starts.

Fresh Meat

It will not happen right away, but as the newcomer to the office or the youngest member of a group, you will eventually be given tasks that no one else wants to do. It may seem unfair that the new person is burdened with these jobs, but it is standard protocol in almost all Japanese institutions that the more experienced, older party is revered.

You will most likely hear the words *senpai* and *koohai* often while working in Japan. *Senpai* is the term used for superiors, which also includes upperclassmen. Junior high school first-year students frequently lament:

> *Senpai ga kowai.*
> The upperclassmen are scary!

Respect for superiors accounts for the sense of responsibility that many middle-aged Japanese feel for their aging parents. This kind of respect makes sense in a lot of ways. Earning your colleagues' respect through hard work and devotion may seem a little old-fashioned, but it beats being turned down for a top position just because you do not have a Ph.D. behind your name.

Still, always getting stuck cleaning the toilets or emptying everyone's wastebasket is no fun, either. As a foreigner in Japan, you will most likely not be subjected to the *senpai* and *koohai* routine (as long as you show respect for your superiors), but you may be asked to help with setting up tables and chairs for a meeting, or erasing the whiteboard:

> *Chotto o-tetsudai o moraemasen ka.*
> Could you give me a hand?

You can offer your assistance, as well, with the phrase:

> *O-tetsudai o ageyo ka.*
> Would you like me to give you a hand?

Notice how the verb *moraimasen* is used when the speaker needs help whereas *ageyo* (*ageru*) is used when the speaker is offering assistance.

The poor *koohai*, though, for the most part, must "earn his keep" so to speak:

> *Hitori de dekiru shigoto dattara yatte moraimasu.*
> If one person can do the job alone, then the newest, youngest person is expected to execute it.

The Role of Women

When you arrive at work, you may find a cup of tea waiting on your desk. In some places, *o-cha* (Japanese green tea) is served in the mornings; in other places, *mugi-cha* (barley tea) or *ban-cha* (roasted green tea) are the preferred choice. Who is the tea fairy? It depends on the office, but usually, the youngest woman is in charge of serving tea for all.

Even today, many companies in Japan still look to their female staff members to take care of cleaning the office, keeping fresh flowers in the *ikebana* vases, and serving tea to guests. Is the office an extension of the home?

Like the "supermoms" of the 1990s, many of these same women will return home after a day of work to cook supper for their families, draw the bath, bathe the children, and put them to bed. They often get up early to make *obentoo* ("packed lunch") for husbands and children before heading off to work themselves. No wonder Japanese women are, statistically, the latest in the world to marry.

Female foreigners working in Japan will most likely not be enlisted to serve tea or perform other housekeeping duties in the office, the lucky ducks. Offers of assistance will be welcomed, however. Helping out the person who seems to get saddled with undesirable jobs all the time may impress your *senpai*. Your colleagues, too, will be more likely to accept you as part of the group if you demonstrate a willingness to pitch in.

Quizzes and Exercises

1. What is *maefuri* and when is it appropriate?

   _____

2. What can you discern about your meeting from the following phrases:

   Maemuki ni kentoo shimasu.
   O-shokuji ni ikimasen ka.

   _____

   _____

3. What is the honorific form of *imasu*? _____

4. How should you introduce your boss?

   _____

5. Which of the following words means "does too much?" *tabesugiru, nomimasugiru, yarisugiru*

6. Rearrange the following words to make a beautiful refusal: *orimasu wa koo wakarimasu shikashi wa naruhodo osshatteiru koto yoku ga watashitomo kangaete*

   _____

   _____

Chapter 20

Putting It All into Practice

People are always saying, "If you don't use it, you lose it." This phrase is especially true when it comes to language. People who live outside of their home country and rarely use their native tongue often find their vocabulary shrinking. Likewise, students of foreign languages who fail to find conversation partners quickly lose precious skills. It is not enough to simply read and listen. You must find a way to incorporate Japanese language into your daily life if you want your efforts to stick!

A Japanese Embassy Near You

Depending on where you are located, it may be possible to contact a Japanese Embassy for helpful information. Certain branches of the United Nations, diplomats, and ambassadors should be able to direct you to different Japanese organizations around the country. Universities, too, may have a foreign-language department with professors willing to provide assistance.

Culture Clubs and Classes

The Japanese Embassy in Washington, D.C., has connections with various organizations that host cultural workshops for people preparing to travel, live, or work abroad. Daylong sessions with brief introductions to language, food, customs, and etiquette may supplement your studies and provide hands-on, interactive opportunities to practice what you have learned.

Of course, different people may interpret Japanese culture in different ways. Experiences within Japan are sure to vary with each instructor, traveler, or student. Try to avoid allowing someone else's viewpoint to entirely color your expectations. Remember to reserve a space in your mind for your own upcoming adventure.

Immersing Yourself in Japanese

Locating a place where Japanese is spoken naturally and parking yourself within that space for a few hours a week is a great way to expose your ears to various pronunciations, dialects, intonations, and vocabulary. Just as in the United States, Japan is full of dialects, colloquial phrases, and localized idioms.

Lots of listening is the first step in learning a language. Eventually, you will be able to distinguish individual words. From that point, you begin speaking it yourself. Words you have read over and over again on paper will slowly come to life. Once you start recognizing those words in conversation, their meanings become clearer. This is how your vocabulary expands. This is also where abstract rules of grammar begin to make sense.

Speaking in Front of the Mirror

If listening is the first step to learning a language, speaking is the second, and possibly, most important one. Practicing aloud what you have studied on paper is essential for the vocabulary, sentence structure, and grammar to take root in your brain. Everyday words and activities are a good place to start.

FACT

A technique often used with first-graders learning to read is labeling the room. Copy down essential vocabulary words onto note cards and attach them to corresponding things around your house. Sentences to accompany various activities could also be printed out and put up in appropriate places.

When You're Alone

Tape a chart of the Japanese sounds next to your bathroom mirror and run through them before or after you brush your teeth. Unlike English, Japanese does not require a lot of tongue or mouth movement when spoken. Try giving your self-introduction or experiment with various statements.

Pay attention to your facial expressions. Do they correspond with what you are saying? Sometimes you may get so caught up in getting the words right that your brow furrows and your face gives the impression that you are confused or upset even though you happen to be talking about your favorite color. Think about what you want to say, then smile at yourself and relax your shoulders before you begin speaking.

Take Note

Think about things you might want to share with people you meet in Japan. Try to guess what questions might be asked of you. How would you describe your living room? What color is your kitchen or your favorite coffee mug? What is your favorite TV show? What commercials make you laugh or cry? How would you summarize the lyrics to your favorite song?

Pretend you are an anthropologist and begin taking notes on the basic aspects of everyday life in your homeland. Actions you take for granted will be exactly the types of things people will be interested in knowing about. Practice describing, in Japanese, what you eat for breakfast, how you get to work, and what you and your friends do for fun. These notes will be invaluable to you when making comparisons or if questioned about how or why things are done in a certain way.

Practice Bowing

If you are from a small town, you may be familiar with friendly honks or waves people give from their cars. In Japan, it is the bow which is much more commonly seen, even with people you do not know. If you allow someone to enter into traffic ahead of you, expect a bow of thanks in return. You should respond in a similar fashion if someone shows you the same kindness.

Bowing comfortably will take some practice. You do not want to throw your neck out by dropping your head forward too quickly. Neither do you want to take your eyes off of the road for too long. The best bows are deliberate, not rushed, and sincere. It is best to practice when your car is in a stopped position.

As you go about your day, imagine times when common, humble Japanese phrases like *onegai shimasu, o-sewa ni natte imasu, doozo,* and *yoroshiku* may fit. Practice saying them mentally or out loud at these moments, and they will come out more naturally once you arrive in Japan.

Being able to bow properly is not only physical. Bowing often involves releasing your ego in order to demonstrate respect or reverence for someone you barely know. Prepping yourself for the modesty required in daily life in Japan may take some time. Westerners, and Americans especially, have a tendency to think the world revolves around them and it may be difficult to break that way of thinking. Humility is often thought to be a sign of weakness in Western culture. Take stock of your own thoughts on these matters and be prepared to respond accordingly.

Making a Game of Katakana-style English

As in any language, there are many loan words used in Japanese. They are "on loan" from French, Italian, Russia, Spanish, and English, just to name a few. You may hear quite a few words that sound familiar, but with a distinctly Japanese pronunciation. If you practice saying English words with a Japanese pronunciation, it may be easier for you to recognize them in conversation.

At Mealtime

Whether you are eating alone, or are joined by family or friends, mealtimes are a great opportunity to practice *katakana*-style pronunciation. Do not worry about total accuracy; just enjoy adding vowels. Putting one or two vowels after each consonant is a good way to get started. Remember, if the vowel is a long one, elongate it even more in *katakana*. If the consonant is rather hard-sounding, better make it a double.

Saying *Paasu za baataa* may get you some strange looks at the dinner table. *Miruku puriizu* may or may not get you what you want. *Puriizu paasu za peppaa ando saruto* will have everyone searching the table for the mysterious items.

This is not only excellent practice for your language skills—it is also a lesson in communication. Making yourself understood across language barriers requires patience and creativity.

At Work and School

Exposure to different cultures can make even the dullest job more exciting. Teaching someone else what you have learned is, also, a great way to improve your own knowledge of the subject matter. Why not pass on some of what you have gleaned from this book to your coworkers and classmates? Who knows, you may impress your boss, or spark someone else's interest in Japanese language and culture.

At first, people may think you are joking when you bow and say *Guuddo mooningu*. Likewise when you offer to fetch someone's *koohii*. Impromptu language lessons in the *kopii* room are a good way to break up the day. Incorporating a little *katakana*-style English into your daily routine is the perfect way to get your mouth and ears accustomed to the sounds you are likely to hear on your travels.

Becoming fluent in *katakana*-like pronunciation will come in handy when you introduce yourself. If you are able to smoothly *katakana*-cize your name, it be easier for others to pronounce.

Phone Practice

Speaking another language is challenging enough when you are face-to-face, but it is even more difficult on the phone. Without the clues provided by facial expressions and gestures, you may find yourself knee-deep in misunderstandings. This is where having someone to practice your Japanese with can save you a lot of trouble later on.

FACT

Moshi-moshi is the phrase used when answering the phone in Japanese. It is used by both the caller and the receiver and can be likened to "Hello?" Other than on the phone, the phrase *moshi-moshi* can be used when trying to get the attention of a stranger. If someone dropped his hat, you could say, *Moshi-moshi, booshi o otoshita yoo desu.* ("Excuse me, it looks as if you dropped your hat.")

Is there a place in your community where people put up personal ads requesting tutors, roommates, dog-sitters, and so on? Does your local high school host exchange students from Japan? You may want to scan these bulletin boards for potential Japanese-speaking phone partners. Or write up an ad describing your situation.

You may be able to locate someone who is willing to speak to you on the phone in Japanese a couple of times a week. This will improve your listening comprehension abilities and give you practice in thinking on your feet.

Don't Be Afraid to Make Mistakes

Gaijin-san is the word used to refer to foreigners in Japan. This is a shortened version of the term *gaikokujin* ("outside person"). It literally means "alien." It can be used in a derogatory way, but simply means "foreigner" when used respectfully (with the suffix *–san*). Although the term may seem insulting at first, it can actually be used to your advantage when attempting to communicate in Japanese.

You may make many mistakes, both linguistically and culturally, but you can always play the "*gaijin* card." Most Japanese people feel that their language and culture are so complicated that only Japanese people can truly understand them. Therefore, any effort to speak Japanese or emulate Japanese culture is treated as an act worthy of applause and most mistakes will be swiftly forgiven.

Everyone Is a Potential Teacher

While traveling in Japan, treat everyone as a potential instructor of Japanese language. Some "teachers" may be subtle in their instruction. A widely used technique is to repeat back to you the correct version of what you are trying to say, so pay close attention. The gas station attendant, your server at the restaurant, and the sushi chef can provide valuable lessons in grammar, vocabulary, syntax, and pronunciation.

Utilizing a few simple phrases will get you through a variety of situations:

Watashi no nihongo wa daijoobu desu ka.
Is my Japanese okay?

Kore wa nihongo de nan desu ka.
What is this in Japanese?

If you have questions about how to conjugate a verb, you can list the options and then add:

Docchi ga tadashii desu ka.
Which one is right?

Heart to Heart Communication

Grammar plays an essential role in all languages. It helps to discern requests from commands and identifies what is being done to whom. But when it comes down to real communication, sincerity and determination play the leading roles.

Many Japanese teachers of English, until recently, focused on the acquisition of vocabulary and boring grammar, causing many students to despise their English lessons. These same kids who slept through English class are delighted to find that when communicating with foreigners, earnestness counts much more than word order when conveying what it is they want to say.

The same goes for Japanese. Forget grammar if it gives you a headache. Draw on your creative resources when giving explanations. Use what you do remember and let the rest come through in your facial expressions and body language.

ALERT!

If you're an Asian American, a Japanese person may expect you to be fluent in Japanese. It can be frustrating to constantly explain your situation. Try to handle it in the way that is most comfortable for you. As the number of people in Japan with multicultural heritage grows, hopefully, so will understanding of the unique challenges involved with growing up with multiple languages and customs.

Relying on Gestures

A raise of an eyebrow, hands in pockets, shuffling feet—all of these are nonverbal clues that fill out your verbal communication, sometimes revealing more than you want your listeners to know. Some nonverbals are deliberate, however, packing in questions or commands without ever uttering a syllable. Though many translate across borders, some are unique to the culture they are embedded in.

Japanese Style

Most Westerners will touch their chests when saying "I" or "me." In Japan, when referring to oneself, people touch their nose. Usually, this gesture is made with a single finger touched to the tip of the nose and accompanied by one of the various words for "I": *boku, watashi, atashi.* Partnered with raised eyebrows, the gesture has the questioning effect of an innocent person being accused, or can be likened to the phrase: "Who, me?" When the nose is tapped successively, the effect is that of a confessor taking responsibility for a deed.

How do you indicate to someone across the room that you would like her to come to where you are standing? How do you call your children into the house for dinner? In Japan, the "come here" gesture is made with hand extended, palm facing down. The fingers flap out and back towards the gesturer. If more emphasis is required, a bent elbow may be enlisted to give the gesture greater visibility from far away. This gesture is often accompanied by the phrase *oide.*

Hands joined in prayer can mean any number of things. For this gesture, the accompanying phrase can make all the difference. *Onegai ga aru* indicates that a favor is needed. *Itadakimasu* and *gochisoo-sama deshita* (phrases used before and after eating) are almost always paired with a palms-touching gesture. When said with hands together, *arigatoo* deepens in its sincerity.

FACT

You may find that Japanese women, especially, have a tendency to cover their mouths when they smile or laugh. Seemingly self-conscious, this gesture may be left over from times when coquettish behavior was the norm.

Universals

You may find that you naturally incorporate gestures when speaking in another language, or as visual aids when attempting to explain something in English to a non-native speaker. References to numbers are easily supported by fingers (and sometimes toes). Size and shape are also more easily conveyed when arms get involved.

Facial expressions and the feelings behind them, too, are almost always understood across cultures. Smiles usually indicate friendliness or joy, but can also mask apprehension or uncertainty. Cocked heads and furrowed brows convey confusion. Nodding means "yes" or "I understand." Shaking of the head says "no" or expresses refusal. Tears may be contextual in any land.

Whether you are trying to deepen a friendship or close an important business deal (no elbows on the tables, please), what you say with your face and body language are just as important as what is coming out of your mouth.

FACT

You may notice that people in Japan use their fingers differently for counting. Westerners usually indicate "one" with a single finger pointing up, "two" with two fingers and so on. Japanese people will start with an open hand, however, and bring each finger down, consecutively, starting by bringing the thumb in towards the palm to indicate "one." "Five" is a closed fist, and "six," then, is indicated by a raised pinky finger. This is a convenient way of counting because ten digits can be conveyed on a single hand.

Quizzes and Exercises

1. Make up *katakana* versions of the following words:

   bird   _____
   car   _____
   cooking _____

2. What do people in Japan say when answering the phone?

   _____

3. Which of the following words refers to someone who is not Japanese?
   Gaikotsu, mukoo, gaijin

4. How do you indicate the number six on your fingers if you do it Japanese style?

   _____

Appendix A

Japanese-to-English Glossary

A

abiru: bathe, shower
agaru: step up
ageru: to give
ai: love
aida: between
aimasu (au)
aisatsu: greeting
aisu kuriimu: ice cream
Ajia: Asia
aka: red
akagumi: red team
akemashite omedetoo gozaimasu:
   Happy New Year (after Jan. 1st)
aki: fall, autumn
akishitsu: available room
aku: open
amai: sweet
amari: not very
Amaterasu oomikami: Sun Goddess
ame: rain
Amerika: U.S.A.
anata: you
ane: older sister
ani: older brother
ano: that, the (over there)
anshin: safe
ao(i): blue
araiba: washing area
arau: to wash
are: that, it (over there)
arerugii: allergy
arigatoo: Thank you
aru: to have, to be (inanimate)
aruku: to walk

asa: morning
asa gohan: breakfast
ashi: legs, feet
asobu: to play
asoko: over there
atama: head
atashi: I, me (feminine)
ato: after
atopii: eczema
atsui: hot
atsukan: hot rice liquor
attakai: warm
au: to meet

B

baibai: bye-bye
baiku: bike
ban: platform
banana: banana
basu: bus
basutei: bus stop
basuto: bust
bataa: butter
bejitarian: vegetarian
ben: dialect
benkyoo: study
bideo: video
biiru: beer
bijin: beauty
booifurendo: boyfriend
boku: I, me (masculine)
botan: button
boonenkai: end-of-year party
buchoo: division manager
budoo: grapes

bunka no hi: culture day
bunkasai: culture festival
butsudan: Buddhist altar

C

chaahan: fried rice
chairo: brown
chekku-auto: check-out
chi-chi: father (own)
chiisai (na): small
chikai: near
chikatetsu: subway
chippu: tip
chizu: map
choko: chocolate
choonan: eldest son
chooshi: condition
chooshoku: meal
chotto: a little
chuu: medium, regular
Chuugoku: China

D

dai ni kayoobi: second
   Tuesday of the month
dai suki: favorite
daidokoro: kitchen
daifuku: sticky rice cake
   with red bean jam
daijoobu: okay
daikon: long white radish
dakara: therefore
dake: only
dame: bad

danna-san: husband
danshi: boys, males
dare: who
dashi: broth
datsuiba: changing room
dekoreeshon: decoration
densha: train
deru: to leave, go out
desu: is, are, to be
dochira: which one
doko: where
donna: what kind of
donna fuu: what style of, type of
dono: what, who
doo: how
doo itashimashite: you are welcome
doo iu fuu: which way, type of
doobutsu: animal
doomo: thanks
dooshite: why
doozo: please, go ahead
dore: which

E

ebi: shrimp
echiketto: etiquette
eiga: movie
eigo: English
eikaiwa: English conversation
eki: train station
en: yen
enkai: drinking party
enpitsu: pencil
enryo: polite refusal
eta: "untouchable" caste

F

fianse: fiancé
fooku: fork

fukuro: bag
fun: minute
furai: fry
furaido poteto: French fries
furonto: front desk
furu: to fall (rain, snow, etc.)
furusato: hometown
furuutsu: fruit
futabin: two bottles
futari: two people
futatsu: two items
futomaki: fat sushi roll
futon: futon
futsuka: the second day of the month
fuusui: feng shui
fuyu: winter

G

gaarufurendo: girlfriend
gai: floor (of a building)
gaikokujin: foreigner, alien
gakkoo: school
gasorin sutando: gas station
gatsu: month
gawa: side
genkan: entryway
genki: lively, fine
getsu: month
go: five
gogo: afternoon
gohiki: five small animals
go-kekkon: wedding (honorific)
gomennasai: I'm sorry
gomi: garbage, trash
gooshitsu: room (hotel)
go-shussan: birth, labor (honorific)
gozenchuu: A.M.
gurai: about
guramu: grams

H

haburashi: toothbrush
hachi: eight
hada: skin
hadairo: orange (literally: skin color)
hade (na): flashy
hage: bald
hai: yes, okay, I understand, I see
haiiro: gray
haiku: 5-7-5 syllable poem
hairu: to enter, to go inside
haitta (hairu)
hajimari: the beginning
hajimaru: to begin
hajimemashite: Nice to meet you.
hajimeru: to start
hakaru: to measure
haku: to wear, put on,
    counter for nights
hameru: to wear (gloves)
hamigakiko: toothpaste
han: the half hour
hana: nose, flower
hanasu: to speak
hanbaagaa: hamburger
hane: wing (s)
hanko: signature stamp
happyookai: recital
hare: fine weather, blue sky
hareru: to clear
haru: spring, to stick, affix
hashi: bridge, chopsticks, edge
hashiru: to run
hatachi: twenty years old
hataraku: to work
hayai: fast
hayaku: quickly
hayaoki: waking up early
hazukashii: shy
hebi: snake
heitan: flat

heiwa: peaceful
heya: room
hidari: left
hiita (hiku)
hiitaa: heater
hikooki: airplane
hiku: to catch a cold
hima: free (time)
hinoiri: sunset
hippu: hips
hiroi: spacious
hirugohan: lunch, noon meal
hiruma: daytime
hirumeshi: noon meal
hirune: nap
hiruyasumi: lunch break, recess
hito: person
hitobin: one bottle
hitokoto: one word, a short speech
hitotsu: one thing
hitto: hit
hoeru: howl, bark
hon: book
honno: just
hontoo: really
hoo: direction
hooritsu: law
hoshii: want
hoshita: dried
hoteru: hotel
hotoke-sama: the Buddha
hyaku: hundred

I

ichi: one, market
ichiban: number one
ichidai: one (car, washing machine, etc.)
ichido: one time, once
ie: house
ii: good

iie: no
ikebana: flower arrangement
ikemasen: not allowed
iki: outward journey
ikkan: one piece of sushi
ikko (iku): one of something
iku: to go
ima: now, living area of a home
imasu (iru)
inaka: countryside, rural
inkan: signature stamp
inu: dog
ippai: one (bowlful, cup)
ippon: one (bottle, pencil)
irasshaimase: welcome,
　may I help you?
irasshaimasu: to be, to go,
　to come (honorific)
iru: to need, to be (animate)
issho: together, same
isu: chair
itadaku: to humbly receive
itai: painful
itami: pain
ito: thread
itsu: when
itsuka: someday
itsumo: always
itsutsu: five of something
iu: to say
iyagaru: to dislike, to oppose
izakaya: Japanese pub, bar

J

jaa: well . . .
jaga imo: potato
janken: rock, scissors, paper game
ji: character, hour (time)
jibun: oneself
jikan: time
jikka: family home

jikokuhyoo: schedule
jikoshookai: self-introduction
jimaku: subtitles
jimi: subtle
jinja: shrine
jinkoo: population
jitaku: home (own)
jiyuuseki: nonreserved seat
jizoo: statue of the Buddha
joozu: well done
josei: girls, females
joshi: females, girls
junbi: preparation
juppun: ten minutes
juu: ten
juusho: address
juusu: juice

K

ka: mosquito, question indicator
ka mo shirenai: probably, per-
　haps, most likely
kabuki: Japanese comedy theater
kaburu: to wear (hat)
kachoo: supervisor
kado: corner
kago: basket
kai: floor (in a building), shellfish
kaidan: stairs
kaigan: coast, beach
kaimono: shopping
kairo: disposable hot pad
kaisha: company
kakeru: to put on, to drape
kaki: oysters, persimmon
kakko ii: "cool"
kaku: to write
kamera: camera
kami: god, goddess, paper, hair
kamidana: Shinto altar in the home
kaminoke: hair (on head)

kamisori: razor

kamu: to bite, to chew

kan: suffix for time

kangae: thought

kangaeru: to think

kanji: Chinese characters

kanningu (suru): to cheat

kanojo: her, girlfriend

kanpai: "cheers"

kanten: gelatin dessert

kao: face

kaori: scent

kappa maki: cucumber sushi roll

kara: from

karada: body

karai: spicy

karaoke: singing with taped music

karee raisu: curry rice

karuta: card game

kashikomarimasu: I understand (humble)

kasu: to loan

katahoo: one of a pair (shoes, socks, etc.)

kataippo: the other one of a pair

katakana: syllabary for writing loan words

katakori: tense shoulders

katsudon: fried pork cutlet bowl

kau: to buy

kawaii: cute

kawaru: to change

kaze: wind

kazoedoshi: a way of determining age

kazokuburo: family bath

ke: hair, fur

kedo: but, however

keito: yarn

kekkoo: good, fine

ken: prefecture

kendoo: bamboo sword fighting

kenka: fight

kenkoo: health

kentooshimasu: to consider

kesa: this morning

ketsu: behind, buttocks

ketsuron: conclusion

ki: tree, life-force energy

kiiroi: yellow

kikai: machine

kimi: you (punitive)

kimochi: feeling

kimono: traditional Japanese dress

kingyo: goldfish

kinjo: neighbors

kinyoobi: Friday

kippu: ticket

kirai: hateful

kirei: pretty

kiro: kilogram

kiru: to cut, to wear

kisetsu: season

kita: north

kita (kuru)

kitanai: dirty

ko: child

kodomo: children

koe: voice

koi: carp, deep (color), strong (flavor)

koko: here

kokonoka: the ninth day

kokusai: international

koma mawashi: top spinning

kome: rice

konbanwa: good evening

kondo: next

konnichiwa: hello, good afternoon

kono: this

kono aida: the time before this

kono hen: in this area

konya: this evening

kooen: park

koohai: inferior

koohii: coffee

kopii: copy

kore: this, the

korosu: to kill

kosaji: teaspoon

koshi: lower back

kotatsu: heated table

koto: Japanese harp

koto: thing, matter, incident

kotowaru: to refuse

kowai: scary

kowasu: to break

ku: nine

kuchi: mouth

kudamono: fruit

kudasai: please

kudasaru: to give (honorific)

kun: term of endearment for boy

kura: storehouse for treasures

kuraberu: to compare

kurai: dark

kureru: to give, to be given

kuru: to come

kuruma: car

kurumi: walnut

kusai: stinky, smelly

kushami: sneeze

kushi: comb

kutsu: shoe

kutsushita: socks

kuukoo: airport

kuuraa: cooler, air conditioner

kyoodai: sibling

kyoomi: interest

kyootoo sensei: vice principal

kyuu: nine

kyuu ni: suddenly

M

maamaa: so-so

machi: town, wait

mada: still

made: until
mae: before, in front of
maefuri: smalltalk
maemuki: positive attitude
magaru: to bend, to turn
mai: every
mai: counter for flat things
makiburo: wood-fire heated bath
makura: pillow
man: 10,000
mannenrei: way of determining age
manzoku: satisfied, full
massaaji: massage
massugu: straight
mata: again, once more
mawashi: sumoo uniform
mei: counter for people
meishi: business card
men: noodles
menkyoshoo: driver's license
menyuu: menu
meshi: meal, rice
mezurashii: rare, unusual
michi: road, path
midori: green
migi: right (direction)
mikan: tangerine
mikka: the third day
mimikaki: ear cleaner, pick
minami: south
mina-sama: ladies and gentlemen, everyone
mina-san (mina-sama)
minshuku: Japanese-style guesthouse
miririttoru: milliliters
miru: to see, to watch
mise: store
miseru: to show
miso: soybean paste
mittsu: three items
mizu: water
mizuburo: cold-water bath

mizuumi: lake
mo: too, both
mochi: sticky rice cakes
mochiron: of course
moeru: burnable, to burn
mokuyoobi: Thursday
momijigari: autumn maple leaf "hunting"
mono: thing
mooningu kooru: wake-up call
morau: to receive
moshi-moshi: excuse me, hello? (on the phone)
motsu: to hold, to keep, to carry
motto: more
moo: already, yet, any more
moofu: blanket
mooshikomu: to apply
mooshimasu: to be called (formal)
mooshiwake: apology
mugi: barley
mugicha: barley tea
muika: the sixth day of the month
mukae: to go and meet
mukashi: a long time ago, once upon a time
mukoo: over there
munoo yaku: organic
murasaki: purple
musume: daughter
muzukashii: difficult
myooji: family name

N

nado: such as
nagai: long
naifu: knife
naka: inside
nakigoe: cry
naku: to cry
nama: raw

namazake: raw rice liquor
nan: what, how many
nana: seven
nande: why
nande daroo: I wonder why, good question
nandemo: anything
nani: what
nanoka: the seventh day of the month
naosu: to fix
nara: if it comes to, supposing
naru: to become
naru hodo: as expected, I see
nashi: without
nasubi: eggplant
natsu: summer
nattoo: fermented soybeans
naze: why
nemuru: to sleep
nen: year
neru: to lie down
netsu: fever
nezumi: rat
ni: two, at, to, towards
nichi: day
nigakki: second semester
nihaku: two nights stay
Nihon: Japan
nihongo: Japanese
nihonshu: Japanese rice liquor
nijikai: second party
nikan: two pieces of sushi
niku: meat
nimono: boiled things
nimotsu: luggage, packages
nin: people, person
nioi: smell, odor
nisatsu: two books, bills
nise: fake
nishi: west
niwa: garden
niwatori: chicken

no: possessive particle
nobasu: to stretch out
nomu: to drink
nonbiri: relaxing, taking it easy
noo: traditional Japanese theater
nooyaku: pesticides, fertilizers
noriba: platform
nugu: to remove (shoes, clothing)

O

oagari: help yourself
o-baa-san: grandmother
oban: evening
oba-san: aunt
o-bentoo: boxed lunch
obi: wide belt for kimono
oboeru: to learn, to memorize
o-cha: tea
odoru: to dance
o-furo: bath
o-hagi: sticky rice cake
o-hanami: flower viewing party
o-hayou gozaimasu: good morning
o-hisashiburi: long time, no see
o-hitsu: wooden container for rice
oide: come here (casual)
o-ikura: how much
o-ikutsu: how old, how many
oishii: delicious
o-jama-shimasu: may I come in
ojigi suru: to bow
ojiichan: grandpa
o-kaeri: welcome home, return home
o-kaeri nasai (o-kaeri)
o-kaeshi: return item, change (money)
o-kage-sama: thanks to you
o-kane: money
okashii: funny
okimari: decision (honorific)
okimasu (okiru)
okiru: to awaken

okosu: to wake someone up
okuremasu: to be late
okuru: to send
o-kyaku-sama: customers, guests
omae: you (punitive)
omae: guest entrance
omakaseru: to defer to someone's expertise
o-medeta: celebratory occasion
omedetoo: congratulations
omikoshi: miniature shrine used in festivals
o-miyage: souvenirs, gifts
omoi: heavy
omoshiroi: interesting
omou: to think, to feel, to hope
omuraisu: rice omelet
omutsu: diapers
onaji: same
ondo: temperature
o-nee-san: older sister
onegai: favor
onegai itashimasu: please do this for me (formal)
onegai shimasu: please do this for me
ongakushitsu: music room
onidaiko: demon dancing
onigiri: rice balls
onna: woman
onna-no-ko: girl
onsen: hot springs
ooendan: cheerleader
ooendanchoo: head cheerleader
ookii: big
ookisa: size
oomare: birthplace
oosaji: tablespoon
orenji: orange (color and fruit)
osaki ni: before you, to go first
o-sewa ni nattemasu: to be taken care of
o-shibori: wet handtowel
oshieru: to teach

o-shokuji: meal
o-shoogatsu: the New Year
o-sooji: cleaning
o-sooshiki: funeral
ossu: casual greeting
o-sumai: home (polite)
o-susume: today's special
otaku: home (someone else's)
o-tanjoobi: birthday
o-tera: temple
o-tetsudai: assistance, help
oto: sound
otoko: male, man
otoko-no-ko: boy
otona: adult
o-too-san: father
otooto: younger brother
otoshidama: gift of money for children
otosu: to drop
otsukai: use (polite)
o-tsukare sama deshita: thanks for your hard work
otsumami: appetizer for beer, alcohol
otsuri: change (money)
otsuyu: soup
o-yasumi: good night (casual)
o-yasuminasai: good night, take a rest
oyogu: to swim
o-yome-san: bride, daughter-in-law
o-yu: hot water

P

pan: bread
pasokon: personal computer
pateii: party
piero: clown
pinku: pink
piza: pizza
poteto chippusu: potato chips
pun: minute

R

raamen: Chinese noodles
raishuu: next week
rajio tairoo: radio exercises
rashii: suffix: typical of
renkon: lotus root
rentakaa: rental car
reshiito: receipt
resutoran: restaurant
rimokon: remote control
ringo: apple
rokkaa: locker
roku: six
roomaji: Roman letters
roppon: six bottles, pencils, towers
ryokan: Japanese-style hotel
ryokoo: travel
ryokoo gaisha: travel company
ryookin: fee
ryoori: cooking
ryooshuusho: receipt
ryuu: reason

S

saabisu: free, no charge
sabaku: desert
sadoo: path of tea (ceremony)
sai: age
saifu: wallet
sain: sign, signature
saishokushugisha: vegetarian
saizu: size
sakana: fish
sakanatsuri: fishing
sake: rice liquor
sakkaa: soccer
sakura: cherry blossoms
sama: honorific title
samishii: lonely

samui: cold
samurai: warrior
san: three
san bon: three bottles, pencils, etc.
san butsu: products
san kan: three pieces of sushi
sarada: salad
sashimi: sliced raw fish
satsu: counter for books and bills
sauna: sauna
sawaru: to touch
sayoonara: goodbye
se: height
seito: student
seisoo: formal
seki: seat
sekihan: celebration rice
sen: line
senaka: back
senchi: centimeters
senpai: superior
sensei: teacher
sentoo: public bath
setto: set
shaberu: to speak
shachoo: president, boss
shawaa: shower
shi: city
shichi: seven
shigoto: job
shiiru: seal, sticker
shika: nothing to do but . . .
shima: island
shimaru: to be closed, to be shut
shimeru: to shut, to close
shimoza: worst seat
shindo: scale for measur-
   ing earthquakes
Shinkansen: bullet train
shinsetsu: kind
shinshitsu: sleeping room
shintoo: folk religion of Japan

shirogumi: white team
shiru: to know
shishi: lions used in onidaiko
shiteiseki: reserved seat
shitsurei: rude
shodoo: the path of calligraphy
shooganai: it cannot be helped
shoogi: Japanese chess
shoogo: noon
shooji: paper doors
shoo-shoo: a little
shuppatsu: departure
shushoku: staple food
shusshin: birthplace
shuu: state, week
shuuji: calligraphy
shumi: hobby
shuuzu: shoes
soba: buckwheat noodles
sobo: grandma (own)
sodatsu: to raise (plants, children)
sokkusu: socks
soko: there
soku: counter for shoes
sono: that, it, thing
soo: that way, like that
soomen: skinny wheat noodles
sore: that, it
sorosoro: soon, almost
soshite: and then
soto: outside
sotsugyooshiki: graduation
sudomari: overnight only,
   no meals (hotel)
sugiru: to do something to excess
sugoi: great
sugu: soon
suki: like, enjoy
sukoshi: a little
sumimasen: excuse me, I'm sorry
sumoo: Japanese wrestling
sumu: to live

sunakku: hostess bar, club
supeingo: Spanish
supootsu: sports
supuun: spoon
surippa: slippers
suru: to do
sushi: vinegared rice topped with (often raw) fish
sutando: gas station, market stall
suteeki: steak
suteki: lovely, nice
suu: to smoke, to inhale
suutsu: suit
suwaru: to sit
suzushii: cool

T

tabako: cigarettes
tabemono: food
taberarenai (taberu)
taberu: to eat
tada ima: I'm home (colloquialism)
tadashii: correct
taiikusai: sports festival
taijuu: weight
taiko: drum
takai: tall, expensive
tako: octopus, kite
takusan: a lot
takushii: taxi
tamago: egg
tame: for the sake of
tanoshimi: looking forward to
tantoosha: office worker
tanuki: raccoon dog
taoru: towel
tarai: wooden tub
tasu: to add
tasukarimashita (tasukaru)
tasukaru: to help, to assist

tasuu: majority
tataku: to drum
tatami: rice straw mats
te: hand
teinei: polite
teishoku: set meal or menu
tekitoo: take it easy, in an easy way
tempura: battered, deep-fried vegetables and fish
tenkeiteki (na): typical
tenki: weather
terebi: television
to: and
toire: toilet
tokidoki: sometimes
tokonoma: alcove
tokoro: place
tokubetsu: special
tomaru: to stop
tomo: all, both, of course
tomodachi: friend
tondemonai: terrible
tono koto desu: I think (polite)
tori: bird
torizara: dish, small plate
toru: to take
toshi: year, age
tottemo: very
too: counter for large animals
toofu: tofu
tooka: the tenth day
tsuaa: tour
tsugi: next
tsuitara (tsuku)
tsukaikata: how to use
tsukare: tiredness
tsukau: to use
tsukekata: how to pickle
tsukemasu (tsukeru)
tsukemono: pickled vegetables
tsukeru: to pickle
tsuki: moon

tsukimasu (tsuku)
tsuku: to be included, to be attached
tsukuru: to make
tsumaranai: not satisfying
tsumetai: chilly, cold
tsumori: intention
tsunami: tidal wave
tsutsumu: to wrap
tsuyoi: strong

U

uchi: house, personal reference
uchiawase: meeting
udon: fat, wheat noodles
uesuto: waist
umai: delicious
umaremashita (umareru)
umareru: to be born
umeboshi: pickled Japanese apricot
umi: sea, ocean
undookai: sports festival
unko: bowel movement
unten: driving
urayamashii: jealous
uru: to sell
urusai: noisy, loud
usui: thin (color, taste)
utau: to sing
uuron-cha: Oolong tea

W

wa: ring, counter for birds and rabbits, harmony
wa: subject indicator
wafuku: Japanese clothing
wafuu: Japanese style (anything)
wakaru: to understand
waribashi: disposable chopsticks
warui: bad

washitsu: Japanese room
wasuremono: forgotten item
wasureru: to forget
watashi: I, me

Y

yakiniku: grilled meat
yakisoba: fried noodles
yakuza: Japanese mafia
yakyuu: baseball
yama: mountain
yappari: as expected, nevertheless
yaru: to do (casual)
yasashii: gentle
yasui: cheap
yasumi: rest, vacation
yobu: to call, to invite
yobun: extra
Yoi o-toshi o: Happy New Year (before)
yokatta: I'm glad, it was good
yokka: the fourth day of the month
yoko: next to

yoku: good
yomu: to read
yon: four
yon kan: four pieces of sushi
yopparai: drunken person
yori: than, from
yoroshii: good (polite)
yoroshiku: Please take care of me.
yoru: night
yoru: to drop in, to visit
yotei: schedule, plans
yottsu: four things
yooka: the eighth day of the month
yookan: Japanese sweet
yookoso: welcome
yoyaku: reservation
yukata: cotton, summer kimono
yuki: snow
yukkuri: slowly
yunyuu: import
yurusu: to forgive
yuube: last night
yuugata: evening

yuuhan: evening meal
yuuhi: sunset
yuumei: famous

Z

zabuton: floor cushion
zashiki: formal room for entertaining
zeikin: tax
zen: thousand (three)
zenzen: not at all
zookin gake: floor cleaning race
zubon: pants
zutsu: each
zutto: for a long time

English-to-Japanese Glossary

A

a little: sukoshi, shooshoo
a lot: takusan
A.M.: gozenchuu
abdomen: o-naka
about: gurai
add: tasu
address: juusho
adult: otona
after: ato de
afternoon: gogo
again: mata
age: toshi, sai
airplane: hikooki
airport: kuukoo
all: zenbu
allergy: arerugii
almost: hotondo
already: moo
always: itsumo
and: to
and then: soshite
animal: doobutsu
anything: nandemo
apple: ringo
Asia: Ajia
assistance: o-tetsudai
at: de, ni
aunt: oba-san
autumn: aki
awaken: okiru

B

back: senaka
bad: warui, dame
bag: fukuro
bald: hage
banana: banana
barley tea: mugi-cha
baseball: yakyuu
basket: kago
bath: ofuro
be: iru (animate); aru (inanimate)
become: naru
beer: biiru
before: mae, osaki ni, konoaida
begin: hajimaru, hajimeru
beginning: hajimari
bend: magaru
between: aida
big: ookii
bike: jitensha
bird: tori
birthday: o-tanjoobi
birthplace: furusato, o-umare
bite: kamu
blanket: moofu
blue: ao, aoi
body: karada
book: hon
born: umareru
boss: shachoo
both: ryoohoo, mo, tomo
bow: o-jigi suru
boy: otoko-no-ko
boyfriend: kareshi, booifurendo

bread: pan
break: kowareru
breakfast: asa gohan
bride: o-yome-san
bridge: hashi
brown: chairo
buckwheat noodles: soba
Buddhist altar: butsudan
bullet train: Shinkansen
burn: moeru
bus: basu
bus stop: basutei
business card: meishi
bust: basuto
but: ga, kedo
butter: bataa
button: botan
buy: kau
bye-bye: bai-bai

C

call: yobu, yoru
calligraphy: shuuji, shodoo
camera: kamera
car: kuruma
carry: motsu
catch (a cold): kaze o hiku
centimeters: senchi
chair: isu
change: kawaru
change (money): o-tsuri, o-kaeshi
character (letter): ji
cheap: yasui
cheat: kanningu suru
check-out: chekku-auto

cheers: kapai
cherry blossoms: sakura
chicken: niwa tori
child: kodomo
China: Chuugoku
Chinese characters: kanji
Chinese noodles: raamen
chocolate: choko
chopsticks: o-hashi
cigarettes: tabako
city: toshi, shi
cleaning: o-sooji
clear up (weather): hareru
close: chikai, chikaku
coast: kaigan
coffee: koohii
cold: samui
come: kuru
come here: oide
come with: tsuku
company: kaisha
compare: kuraberu
conclusion: ketsuron
condition: chooshi
congratulations: omedetoo
consider: kentoo suru
cook: ryoori suru
cool: suzushii
cooler (air conditioner): kuuraa
copy: kopii
corner: kado
correct: tadashii, attari
couch: sofa
country: kuni
countryside: inaka
cry: naku
customer: o-kyakusama
cut: kiru
cute: kawaii

D

dance: odoru
dark: kurai
daughter: musume
day: hi, nichi
daytime: o-hiru
decision: kimari
defer: omakasemasu
delicious: oishii, umai
departure: shuppatsu
desert: sabaku
dialect: hougen, ben
diapers: o-mutsu
difficult: muzukashii
direction: hoo
dirty: kitanai
dish: osara
dislike: suki ja nai, iyagaru
disposable chopsticks: waribashi
do: suru, yaru
dog: inu
drape: kakeru
dried: hoshita
drink: nomu
drinking party: enkai
driver's license: menkyoshoo
driving: unten
drop in: yoru
drum: taiko, tataku

E

each: zutsu
eat: taberu
edge: hashi
egg: tamago
eggplant: nasubi
eight: hachi
eighth day: yooka
English: eigo

enter: hairu
entryway: genkan, omae
etiquette: echiketto
evening: oban, yuugata
evening meal: yuhan
every: mai
everyone: mina-san, mina-sama
excuse me: sumimasen, moshi-moshi
expensive: takai
extra: yobun

F

face: kao
fake: nise
fall (precipitation): furu
family: kazoku
family name: myooji
famous: yuumei
fast: hayai
father: o-too-san
father (own): chi-chi
favor: onegai
favorite: dai suki
fee: ryookin
feeling: kimochi
feet: ashi
females: josei, joshi
fever: netsu
fight: kenka
fine: kekko, genki
first: ichiban
fish: sakana
fishing: sakana tsuri
five: go
fix: naosu
flashy: hade
flat: heitan
floor (in a building): kai, gai
floor cushion: zabuton
flower: o-hana
flower arrangement: ikebana

food: tabemono
foreigner: gaikokujin, gaijin
forget: wasureru
forgive: yurusu
fork: fooku
formal (clothing): seisoo
four: yon, shi
fourth day: yokka
free: saabisu, tada
free (time): hima
Friday: kinyoobi
fried: furai
friend: o-tomodachi
from: kara
front: mae
front desk: furonto
fruit: furuutsu, kudamono
full: ippai
funeral: o-sooshiki
funny: okashii
fur: ke

G

garbage: gomi
garden: niwa
gas station: gasorin sutando
gentle: yasashii
gifts: o-miyage
girl: onna-no-ko
girlfriend: gaarufurendo
give: ageru, kureru
go: iku
god, goddess: kami-sama
goldfish: kingyo
good: ii
good (polite): yoku
good afternoon: konnichiwa
good evening: konbanwa
good morning: o-hayou
goodbye: sayoonara
graduation: sotsugyooshiki

grams: guramu
grandfather (own): sofu
grandfather: o-jii-san
grandma (own): sobo
grandmother: o-baa-san
grapes: budoo
gray: haiiro, nezumi-iro
great: sugoi
green: midori
greeting: aisatsu
guest: o-kyaku-san

H

hair: kaminoke
half hour: han
hamburger: hanbaagaa
hand: te
Happy New Year (after):
    Akemashite omedetoo
Happy New Year (before): Yoi o-toshi o
hate: kirai
have: aru, motsu
head: atama
health: kenkoo
heater: hiitaa
heavy: omoi
height: se
hello: konnichiwa
Hello (on the phone): moshi-moshi
help: o-tetsudai, tasukeru
her: kanojo
here: koko
hip: hippu
hit: hitto
hobby: shumi
hold: motsu
home: uchi
home (own): jitaku
home (someone else's): o-taku
hometown: furusato
hot: atsui

hot spring: onsen
hot water: o-yu
hotel: hoteru
hour: ji
house: ie
how: doo
how many: ikutsu
how much: o-ikura
how to (suffix): kata
hundred: hyaku, byaku, pyaku
husband (own): otto
husband (someone else's):
    danna-san, go-shujin

I

I'm sorry: gomennasai
ice cream: aisu kuriimu
import: yunyuu suru
incident: koto
inferior: koohai
inside: naka
intention: tsumori
interest: kyoumi
interesting: omoshiroi
international: kokusai
invite: yobu
is: desu
island: shima
it: kore, sore, are

J

Japan: Nihon
Japanese: nihongo
Japanese chess: shoogi
Japanese clothing: wafuku
Japanese harp: koto
Japanese mafia: yakuza
Japanese pub, bar: izakaya
Japanese religion: shintoo

Japanese rice liquor: o-sake
Japanese room: washitsu
Japanese style (anything): wafuu
Japanese traditional theater: noo
Japanese wrestling: sumoo
Japanese-style guesthouse: minshuku
Japanese-style hotel: ryokan
jealous: urayamashii
job: shigoto
juice: juusu
just: honno

K

kill: korosu
kilogram: kiro
kind: shinsetsu
kitchen: daidokoro
kite: tako
knife: naifu
knot, belt: shimeru
know: shiru

L

ladies and gentlemen: mina-sama, mina-san
lake: mizuumi
late: okureru
law: hooritsu
learn: oboeru
leave: deru
left: hidari
legs: ashi
lie down: neru
life-force energy: ki
like: suki
line: sen
live: sumu
lively: genki
living room: ima
loan: kasu

locker: rokkaa
lonely: samishii
long: nagai
long ago: mukashii
long time no see: o-hisashiburi
long white radish: daikon
look: miru
looking forward to: tanoshimi
lotus root: renkon
loud: urusai
love: ai suru
lovely: suteki
lower back: koshi
luggage: nimotsu
lunch: hiru gohan, ranchi
lunch recess: hiruyasumi

M

machine: kikai
majority: tasuu
make: tsukuru
male: danshi
man: otoko no hito
map: chizu
market: ichi
marriage: kekkon
massage: massaaji
me: jibun, watashi, atashi, boku
meal: gohan, meshi, shokuji
measure: hakaru
meat: niku
medium: chuu
meet: au
meeting: uchiawase
menu: menyuu
milliliters: miririttoru
minute: fun, pun
money: o-kane
month: tsuki, getsu, gatsu
moon: tsuki

more: motto
morning: asa
mosquito: ka
mountain: yama
mouth: kuchi
movie: eiga
music room: ongakushitsu

N

name: namae
nap: o-hirune
near: chikai, chikaku
need: iru
neighbor: kinjo
New Year: o-shoogatsu
next: tsugi
next to: yoko, tonari
next week: raishuu
nice: yasashii, shinsetsu, suteki
Nice to meet you.: hajimemashite
night: yoru
nine: kyuu, ku
ninth day: kokonoka
no: iie
noise: oto
noisy: urusai
nonreserved seat: jiyuuseki
noodles: men
noon: shoogo
noon meal: hiru gohan
normal, regular: futsuu
north: kita
nose: hana
not: ja nai
not allowed: ikemasen
not at all: zenzen
not enough: tsumaranai, tarinai
not very: amari
now: ima

O

ocean: umi
octopus: tako
of course: mochiron
okay: daijoobu
older brother: o-nii-san, ani
older sister: o-nee-san, ane
oldest son: choonan
once more: moo ikkai, moo ichido
one: ichi, hitotsu
oneself: jibun
only: dake
oolong tea: uuron-cha
open: aku
orange (color and fruit): orenji
organic: munoo yaku
outside: soto
over there: mukoo, asoko, soko
oysters: kaki

P

packages: nimotsu
pain: itami
painful: itai
pair: katahoo, soku (shoes counter)
pants: zubon
paper: kami
paper doors: shooji
park: kooen
party: paateii
path: michi
peaceful: heiwa
pencil: enpitsu
people: hito-tachi
perhaps: kamoshirenai
persimmons: kaki
person: nin, jin, hito
personal computer: pasokon
pesticide: nooyaku

pick up: mukae
pickle: tsukeru
pickled Japanese apricot: umeboshi
pickled vegetables: tsukemono
pillow: makura
pink: pinku
pizza: piza
place: tokoro, basho
platform: ban, noriba
play: asobu, asobi
please: kudasai, doozo
polite: teinei
population: jinkoo
potato: jaga imo
potato chips: poteto chippusu
prefecture: ken
preparation: junbi
president: shachoo (company), daitooryoo (country)
pretty: kirei
probably: tabun, ka mo shirenai
public bath: sentoo
purple: murasaki
put on: kiru, tsukeru

Q

quickly: hayaku

R

rain: ame
raise: sodatsu
rare: mezurashii
rat: nezumi
raw: nama
razor: kamisori
read: yomu
really: hontoo (ni)
reason: ryuu
receipt: reshiito, ryooshuusho
receive: morau, itadaku (humble)

recently: kono mae, kono aida, saikin
recital: happyookai
red: aka
refuse: kotowaru
regular: futsuu
relaxing: nonbiri
remote control: rimokon
remove: nugu
rental car: rentakaa
reservation: yoyaku
reserved seat: shiteiseki
rest: yasumi
restaurant: resutoran
restroom: toire, tearai
rice: o-kome
rice liquor: o-sake
right: migi (direction), tadashii (correct)
ring: wa
road: michi, doro
Roman letters: roomaji
room: heya, shitsu
rude: shitsurei
run: hashiru

S

safe: anshin
salad: sarada
same: onaji, issho
satisfied: manzoku
sauna: sauna
say: shaberu, iu, hanasu
scary: kowai
scent: kaori, nioi
schedule: yotei (plans), jikokuhyoo (bus, train)
school: gakkoo
sea: umi
seal: shiiru
season: kisetsu
seat: seki

second day: futsuka
second party: nijikai
second term: nigakki
see: miru
self introduction: jiko shokai
sell: uru
send: okuru
set: setto
set meal/menu: teishoku
seven: nana, shichi
seventh day: nanoka
shellfish: kai
shoes: kutsu, shuuzu
shopping: kaimono (suru)
show: miseru
shower: shawaa
shrimp: ebi
shrine: jinja
shut: shimaru, shimeru
shy: hazukashii
sibling: kyoodai
side: gawa
sign: sain (suru)
signature: sain
signature stamp: hanko, inkan
sing: utau
sit: suwaru
six: roku
sixth day: muika
size: saizu, ookisa
skin: hada, hifu
sleep: neru
slippers: surippa
slowly: yukkuri
small: chiisai
small talk: maefuri
smell: nioi (suru)
smelly: kusai
smoke: kemuri, suu
snake: hebi
snow: yuki
soccer: sakkaa

socks: sokkusu
sometimes: tokidoki
soon: sorosoro, moo sugu
sorry: gomennasai
so-so: maa-maa
sound: oto
soup: otsuyu, shiru
south: minami
souvenirs: o-miyage
soybean paste: miso
spacious: hiroi
Spanish: supeingo
speak: shaberu, iu, hanasu
special: tokubetsu
special of the day: o-susume
spicy: karai
spoon: supuun
sports: supootsu
sports festival: undookai, taiikusai
spring: haru
stairs: kaidan
stamp: kitte
staple food: shushoku
start: sutaato, hajimari
state: shuu
steak: suteeki
step up: agaru
sticker: shiiru
still (ongoing): mada
stinky: kusai
stop: yameru, tomaru
store: mise
straight: massugu
stretch out: nobasu
strong: tsuyoi
student: seito
study: benkyoo (suru)
subtitles: jimaku
subtle: jimi
subway: chikatestu
such as: nado
suddenly: kyuu ni

suit: suutsu
summer: natsu
sunset: hinoiri, yuuhi
superior: senpai
supposing: nara
sweet: amai
swim: oyogu

T

tablespoon: oosaji
take: toru
take it easy: tekitoo (ni)
tall: takai
tangerine: mikan
tax: zeikin
taxi: takushii
tea: o-cha
tea ceremony: sadoo
teach: oshieru
teacher: sensei
teaspoon: kosaji
television: terebi
temperature: ondo
temple: o-tera
ten: juu
ten thousand: man
tenth day: tooka
than: yori
thank you: arigatoo, doomo
that: sore, are, sono, ano
there: soko
therefore: dakara
thin (color, taste): usui
thing: mono
think: kangaeru, omou
think (polite): tono koto desu
third day: mikka
this: kore, kono
this area: kono hen
this morning: kesa
thought: kangae

thousand: sen, zen (three)
thread: ito
three: san
Thursday: mokuyoobi
ticket: kippu
tidal wave: tsunami
tie: shimeru
time: jikan
tip: chippu
tiredness: tsukare
to: ni
tofu: toofu
together: issho (ni)
toilet: toire
tonight: konya
too: mo
too much: sugiru
toothbrush: haburashi
toothpaste: hamigakiko
top: koma
touch: sawaru
tour: tsuaa
towel: taoru
town: machi
train: densha
train station: eki
travel: ryokoo
travel company: ryokoo gaisha
tree: ki
turn: magaru, mawaru
twenty years old: hatachi
two: ni
typical: tenkeiteki (na)

U

U.S.A.: Amerika
understand: wakaru, kashiko-marimasu (humble)
until: made
unusual: mezurashii
use: tsukau

V

vacation: yasumi
vegetarian: bejitarian
very: tottemo
vice principal: kyootoo-sensei
video: bideo
visit: yoru, asobi ni iku/kuru
voice: koe

W

waist: uesuto
wait: matsu, o-machi (polite)
wake up: okiru
wake up (someone): okosu
wake-up call: mooningu kooru
wake up early: hayaoki
walk: aruku
wallet: saifu
walnut: kurumi
want: hoshii
warm: attakai
warrior: samurai
wash: arau
washing area: araiba
water: mizu
wear: kiru, haku, suru, hameru, shimeru
weather: tenki
week: shuu
weight: taijuu
welcome: irasshaimase, yookoso
welcome home: o-kaeri
well done: joozu
well . . . : jaa
west: nishi
what: nani, nan, doo
what (kind of): dono, donna
what (style, type of): doo iu fuu, donna fuu

when: itsu
whenever: itsudemo
where: doko
which: dotchi, dono
who: dare
why: naze, dooshite
wind: kaze
wing: hane
winter: fuyu
without: nashi
woman: onna no hito
work: hataraku
wrap: tsutsumu
write: kaku

Y

yarn: keito
year: toshi, nen
yellow: kiiro
yen: en
yes: hai
you: anata, kimi (informal, puni-tive), omae (punitive)
you are welcome: doo itashimashite
younger brother: otooto
younger sister: imooto

Appendix C

Answer Key

Chapter 4

1. Answers will vary.
2. kan
3. Ringo o tabemasu ka.
4. mikka kan—three days, shichi—seven, ippaku—one night, yekka—the 4th, futari—two people, go-haku—five nights
5. Sumimasen, juusho o misete kudasai.
6. –te, –imasu, –tai-n, –te

Chapter 5

1. oyogu—oyoide, oshieru—oshiete, kaku—kaite, naru—natte, mieru—mite
2. O-namae o go-hon ni kaite kudasai.
3. san-ji han; juu-ji yon-juu go fun; juu-ni-ji, ni-juu san pun
4. toothpaste
5. What time is dinner?

Chapter 6

1. Turn right. Go straight, turn left at the corner. (It's) on your left.
2. Asoko de migi ni magarimasu.
3. itte, magatte, arimasu
4. Shinkansen no kippu o san mai kudasai.
5. 4:10, platform five
6. neru—netara, nomu—nondara, yomu—yondara, miru—mitara, taberu—tabetara

Chapter 7

1. yon-juu go en, roku-juu kyuu en, hyaku ni-juu hachi en, san byaku nana-juu en, go hyaku
2. height
3. esu, emu, eru
4. Kutsu wa o-ikura desu ka.
5. ookii—big, hade—flashy, jimi—subtle, chiisai—small, kiiro—yellow
6. Issho ni tabemasen ka.

Chapter 8

1. Ringo juusu o futatsu kudasai.
2. Niku
3. yomenai/yomemasen, dekinai/dekimasen, ikenai/ikemasen
4. ni, o
5. before and after you eat

Chapter 9

1. jump, mix, drive
2. 4, 2, 1, 3
3. Amerika no shusshin desu ka.
4. m, o, m, m, o, o
5. Kore wa boku no kanojo desu.
6. mura—village, shi—city, ken—prefecture, machi—town, shima—island

Chapter 10

1. konnichiwa—hello; o-hayou gozaimasu—good morning; doomo, itsumo o-sewa ni natte imasu—thanks for always taking care of me; o-ban desu—good evening; o-yasuminasai—good night
2. doozo
3. Ashita no asa o-jama shite mo ii desu ka.
4. See you tomorrow.
5. nenasai, ikinasai
6. nemukunatta

Chapter 11

1. dekiru
2. home
3. Sore wa nan desu ka.
4. Japanese
5. O-sushi wa suki desu ka.
6. Pinku wa suki ja nai desu.

Chapter 12

1. Koko de hataraku no wa tanoshii desu.
2. tanoshikatta
3. suru—dekiru, nemuru—nemureru, taberu—taberareru, nomu—nomeru, yomu—yomeru
4. yotei
5. Nani mo nai to omoimasu
6. kyoo, raigetsu, kotoshi, senshuu

Chapter 13

1. keredo mo
2. kimochi ga ii
3. daidokoro, toire, genkan
4. These slippers feel good because they are warm.
5. Ashi o nobashite mo ii desu yo.
6. Moo o-naka ippai desu.

Chapter 14

1. pesky neighbor
2. dashikata, tsukaikata, tabekata, nomikata
3. Do you understand the term "o-sake"?
4. Tuesday and Thursday
5. Buy that person some o-miyage.
6. *tsukeru* and *mono*

Chapter 15

1. a formal self-introduction and just a quick word
2. Yuhan no tame ni kaimono o shite imasu.
3. nandemo
4. a meeting
5. The music room is on the third floor.
6. *Undookai* is a sports festival. *Bunkasai* is a culture festival.
7. Say *O-saki ni shitsurei shimasu* and back out of the door.

Chapter 16

1. from ten to six
2. how to drink, how to wash, how to make
3. Sono koto wa yatte o ikemasen.
4. scarf—suru, shoes—haku, sweater—kiru, underwear—haku, belt—shimeru, gloves—hameru
5. nuide
6. Kimochi ga ii.

Chapter 17

1. Iya da.
2. Hai, tabeta koto arimasu. Iie, tabeta koto nai desu.
3. itsumo—never, dareka—someone, nandemo—anything, dokomo—anywhere, nanika—something
4. Mata
5. naze, nande, dooshite
6. Nande hashi o tsukawanai no.
7. kimi, omae

Chapter 18

1. Mada heta desu.
2. If your legs hurt, please rest.
3. ni
4. help yourself to the food
5. suru
6. gura-gura; pera-pera; guru-guru; pasa-pasa; chika-chika
7. one horse—ittoo, eight rabbits—hachi wa, six dogs—roppiki, five books—go satsu, two bottles—futabin, three bowlfuls—san bai

Chapter 19

1. small talk; before getting down to business talk
2. no deal; things look good
3. irasshaimasu
4. Kochira wa uchi no shachoo desu.
5. yarisugiru
6. Naruhodo osshatteiru koto wa yoku wakarimasu ga shikashi watashitomo wa koo kangaete orimasu.

Chapter 20

1. baado, burudo; kaa, karu; kukkingu (answers may vary)
2. moshi-moshi
3. gaijin
4. hold up the pinky finger on one hand

Index

THE EVERYTHING SERIES!

BUSINESS

Everything® Business Planning Book
Everything® Coaching and Mentoring Book
Everything® Fundraising Book
Everything® Home-Based Business Book
Everything® Landlording Book
Everything® Leadership Book
Everything® Managing People Book
Everything® Negotiating Book
Everything® Online Business Book
Everything® Project Management Book
Everything® Robert's Rules Book, $7.95
Everything® Selling Book
Everything® Start Your Own Business Book
Everything® Time Management Book

COMPUTERS

Everything® Computer Book

COOKBOOKS

Everything® Barbecue Cookbook
Everything® Bartender's Book, $9.95
Everything® Chinese Cookbook
Everything® Chocolate Cookbook
Everything® Cookbook
Everything® Dessert Cookbook
Everything® Diabetes Cookbook
Everything® Fondue Cookbook
Everything® Grilling Cookbook
Everything® Holiday Cookbook
Everything® Indian Cookbook
Everything® Low-Carb Cookbook
Everything® Low-Fat High-Flavor Cookbook
Everything® Low-Salt Cookbook
Everything® Mediterranean Cookbook
Everything® Mexican Cookbook
Everything® One-Pot Cookbook
Everything® Pasta Cookbook
Everything® Quick Meals Cookbook
Everything® Slow Cooker Cookbook
Everything® Soup Cookbook

Everything® Thai Cookbook
Everything® Vegetarian Cookbook
Everything® Wine Book

HEALTH

Everything® Alzheimer's Book
Everything® Anti-Aging Book
Everything® Diabetes Book
Everything® Dieting Book
Everything® Hypnosis Book
Everything® Low Cholesterol Book
Everything® Massage Book
Everything® Menopause Book
Everything® Nutrition Book
Everything® Reflexology Book
Everything® Reiki Book
Everything® Stress Management Book
Everything® Vitamins, Minerals, and
    Nutritional Supplements Book

HISTORY

Everything® American Government Book
Everything® American History Book
Everything® Civil War Book
Everything® Irish History & Heritage Book
Everything® Mafia Book
Everything® Middle East Book

HOBBIES & GAMES

Everything® Bridge Book
Everything® Candlemaking Book
Everything® Card Games Book
Everything® Cartooning Book
Everything® Casino Gambling Book, 2nd Ed.
Everything® Chess Basics Book
Everything® Crossword and Puzzle Book
Everything® Crossword Challenge Book
Everything® Drawing Book
Everything® Digital Photography Book
Everything® Easy Crosswords Book
Everything® Family Tree Book

Everything® Games Book
Everything® Knitting Book
Everything® Magic Book
Everything® Motorcycle Book
Everything® Online Genealogy Book
Everything® Photography Book
Everything® Poker Strategy Book
Everything® Pool & Billiards Book
Everything® Quilting Book
Everything® Scrapbooking Book
Everything® Sewing Book
Everything® Soapmaking Book

HOME IMPROVEMENT

Everything® Feng Shui Book
Everything® Feng Shui Decluttering Book, $9.95
Everything® Fix-It Book
Everything® Homebuilding Book
Everything® Home Decorating Book
Everything® Landscaping Book
Everything® Lawn Care Book
Everything® Organize Your Home Book

EVERYTHING® KIDS' BOOKS

All titles are $6.95

Everything® Kids' Baseball Book, 3rd Ed.
Everything® Kids' Bible Trivia Book
Everything® Kids' Bugs Book
Everything® Kids' Christmas Puzzle
    & Activity Book
Everything® Kids' Cookbook
Everything® Kids' Halloween Puzzle
    & Activity Book
Everything® Kids' Hidden Pictures Book
    Everything® Kids' Joke Book
Everything® Kids' Knock Knock Book
Everything® Kids' Math Puzzles Book
Everything® Kids' Mazes Book
Everything® Kids' Money Book

All Everything® books are priced at $12.95 or $14.95, unless otherwise stated. Prices subject to change without notice.

Everything® Kids' Monsters Book
Everything® Kids' Nature Book
Everything® Kids' Puzzle Book
Everything® Kids' Riddles & Brain Teasers Book
Everything® Kids' Science Experiments Book
Everything® Kids' Soccer Book
Everything® Kids' Travel Activity Book

KIDS' STORY BOOKS

Everything® Bedtime Story Book
Everything® Bible Stories Book
Everything® Fairy Tales Book

LANGUAGE

Everything® Conversational Japanese Book
    (with CD), $19.95
Everything® Inglés Book
Everything® French Phrase Book, $9.95
Everything® Learning French Book
Everything® Learning German Book
Everything® Learning Italian Book
Everything® Learning Latin Book
Everything® Learning Spanish Book
Everything® Sign Language Book
Everything® Spanish Phrase Book, $9.95
Everything® Spanish Verb Book, $9.95

MUSIC

Everything® Drums Book (with CD), $19.95
Everything® Guitar Book
Everything® Home Recording Book
Everything® Playing Piano and Keyboards Book
Everything® Rock & Blues Guitar Book
    (with CD), $19.95
Everything® Songwriting Book

NEW AGE

Everything® Astrology Book
Everything® Dreams Book
Everything® Ghost Book
Everything® Love Signs Book, $9.95
Everything® Meditation Book
Everything® Numerology Book
Everything® Paganism Book
Everything® Palmistry Book
Everything® Psychic Book
Everything® Spells & Charms Book
Everything® Tarot Book
Everything® Wicca and Witchcraft Book

PARENTING

Everything® Baby Names Book
Everything® Baby Shower Book
Everything® Baby's First Food Book
Everything® Baby's First Year Book
Everything® Birthing Book
Everything® Breastfeeding Book
Everything® Father-to-Be Book
Everything® Get Ready for Baby Book
Everything® Getting Pregnant Book
Everything® Homeschooling Book
Everything® Parent's Guide to Children
    with Asperger's Syndrome
Everything® Parent's Guide to Children
    with Autism
Everything® Parent's Guide to Children
    with Dyslexia
Everything® Parent's Guide to Positive Discipline
Everything® Parent's Guide to Raising a
    Successful Child
Everything® Parenting a Teenager Book
Everything® Potty Training Book, $9.95
Everything® Pregnancy Book, 2nd Ed.
Everything® Pregnancy Fitness Book
Everything® Pregnancy Nutrition Book
Everything® Pregnancy Organizer, $15.00
Everything® Toddler Book
Everything® Tween Book

PERSONAL FINANCE

Everything® Budgeting Book
Everything® Get Out of Debt Book
Everything® Homebuying Book, 2nd Ed.
Everything® Homeselling Book
Everything® Investing Book
Everything® Online Business Book
Everything® Personal Finance Book
Everything® Personal Finance in Your
    20s & 30s Book
Everything® Real Estate Investing Book
Everything® Wills & Estate Planning Book

PETS

Everything® Cat Book
Everything® Dog Book
Everything® Dog Training and Tricks Book
Everything® Golden Retriever Book
Everything® Horse Book
Everything® Labrador Retriever Book
Everything® Poodle Book

Everything® Puppy Book
Everything® Rottweiler Book
Everything® Tropical Fish Book

REFERENCE

Everything® Car Care Book
Everything® Classical Mythology Book
Everything® Einstein Book
Everything® Etiquette Book
Everything® Great Thinkers Book
Everything® Philosophy Book
Everything® Psychology Book
Everything® Shakespeare Book
Everything® Toasts Book

RELIGION

Everything® Angels Book
Everything® Bible Book
Everything® Buddhism Book
Everything® Catholicism Book
Everything® Christianity Book
Everything® Jewish History & Heritage Book
Everything® Judaism Book
Everything® Koran Book
Everything® Prayer Book
Everything® Saints Book
Everything® Understanding Islam Book
Everything® World's Religions Book
Everything® Zen Book

SCHOOL & CAREERS

Everything® After College Book
Everything® Alternative Careers Book
Everything® College Survival Book
Everything® Cover Letter Book
Everything® Get-a-Job Book
Everything® Job Interview Book
Everything® New Teacher Book
Everything® Online Job Search Book
Everything® Personal Finance Book
Everything® Practice Interview Book
Everything® Resume Book, 2nd Ed.
Everything® Study Book

SELF-HELP/ RELATIONSHIPS

Everything® Dating Book
Everything® Divorce Book
Everything® Great Sex Book

All Everything® books are priced at $12.95 or $14.95, unless otherwise stated. Prices subject to change without notice.

Everything® Kama Sutra Book
Everything® Self-Esteem Book

SPORTS & FITNESS

Everything® Body Shaping Book
Everything® Fishing Book
Everything® Fly-Fishing Book
Everything® Golf Book
Everything® Golf Instruction Book
Everything® Knots Book
Everything® Pilates Book
Everything® Running Book
Everything® T'ai Chi and QiGong Book
Everything® Total Fitness Book
Everything® Weight Training Book
Everything® Yoga Book

TRAVEL

Everything® Family Guide to Hawaii
Everything® Family Guide to New York City, 2nd Ed.
Everything® Family Guide to Washington D.C., 2nd Ed.
Everything® Family Guide to the Walt Disney World Resort®, Universal Studios®, and Greater Orlando, 4th Ed.
Everything® Guide to Las Vegas
Everything® Guide to New England
Everything® Travel Guide to the Disneyland Resort®, California Adventure®, Universal Studios®, and the Anaheim Area

WEDDINGS

Everything® Bachelorette Party Book, $9.95
Everything® Bridesmaid Book, $9.95
Everything® Creative Wedding Ideas Book
Everything® Elopement Book, $9.95
Everything® Father of the Bride Book, $9.95
Everything® Groom Book, $9.95
Everything® Jewish Wedding Book
Everything® Mother of the Bride Book, $9.95
Everything® Wedding Book, 3rd Ed.
Everything® Wedding Checklist, $7.95
Everything® Wedding Etiquette Book, $7.95
Everything® Wedding Organizer, $15.00
Everything® Wedding Shower Book, $7.95
Everything® Wedding Vows Book, $7.95
Everything® Weddings on a Budget Book, $9.95

WRITING

Everything® Creative Writing Book
Everything® Get Published Book
Everything® Grammar and Style Book
Everything® Grant Writing Book
Everything® Guide to Writing a Novel
Everything® Guide to Writing Children's Books
Everything® Screenwriting Book
Everything® Writing Well Book

Introducing an exceptional new line of beginner craft books from the *Everything*® series!

EVERYTHING C·R·A·F·T·S®

All titles are $14.95.

Everything® Crafts—Create Your Own Greeting Cards
1-59337-226-4
Everything® Crafts—Polymer Clay for Beginners
1-59337-230-2

Everything® Crafts—Rubberstamping Made Easy
1-59337-229-9
Everything® Crafts—Wedding Decorations and Keepsakes
1-59337-227-2

Available wherever books are sold!
To order, call 800-872-5627, or visit us at *www.everything.com*
Everything® and everything.com® are registered trademarks of F+W Publications, Inc.